Northwestern University
STUDIES IN *Phenomenology &*
Existential Philosophy

Obstacle and Value

René Le Senne

Translated, with an Introduction, by

Obstacle
and Value

BERNARD P. DAUENHAUER

NORTHWESTERN UNIVERSITY PRESS

EVANSTON 1972

Originally published in French under the title
Obstacle et Valeur, 1934,
by Aubier Editions Montaigne

Bernard P. Dauenhauer is
assistant professor
of philosophy at the University
of Georgia.

Contents

Translator's Introduction

RENÉ LE SENNE (1882–1954) is not widely known in English-speaking philosophical circles. His thought, however, has been deeply influential in France and has received substantial notice in Italy and Spain. This notice is not misplaced. His work deserves attention because of the profundity and originality with which it develops the Cartesian tradition and because of its affinities with or anticipations of prominent themes in the thought of Sartre, Merleau-Ponty, and Marcel.

Le Senne was educated in the grand tradition of French academic philosophy. He successively studied under Lachelier, Delbos, Brunschvicg, Hamelin, and Rauh. From 1910 to 1931 he taught at various *lycées,* and from 1931 to 1946 he taught at the Ecole Normale Supérieure de Sèvres. In 1942 he was appointed to the faculty of the Sorbonne, where he held the chair of pedagogical psychology until 1949. In that year he was awarded the chair of ethics, which he held until his retirement in 1952.

He was elected to honorary membership in the Society for Philosophical Studies founded at Marseilles, to membership in the French National Academy of Ethical and Political Sciences, to corresponding membership in the Academy of Sciences of Turin, to associate foreign membership in the National Academy Dei Lincei of Rome, to honorary membership in the General Society for Philosophy in Germany, and to corresponding membership in the Academy of Ethical and Political Sciences of Madrid.

In 1934 Le Senne, with Louis Lavelle, founded the Philosophie de l'Esprit movement. This movement was not a school with doctrines and adherents, but rather a shared outlook, an orientation. Le Senne explained that the movement was based on the two central theses of Cartesianism: (1) The *cogito*. The primary truth is not an axiom but is "an experience or, rather, *the* experience, whose peculiar property is that it is to be found in *every* experience: the experience of thought in thinking."[1] (2) The human mind, in making an inventory of its contents, discovers God as the source and guarantee of our knowledge.[2]

Negatively, on the basis of these two theses, the Philosophie de l'Esprit rejects all attempts to reduce the uniqueness of the mind to something other than mind. Positively, it explores all the implications of the bivalent term *esprit*. On the one hand, esprit taken as having empirical and psychological connotations is *mind*. On the other hand, taken as having metaphysical and even religious connotations, it is *spirit*. The Philosophie de l'Esprit seeks out the relations and distinctions between man and man and between God and man. In its treatment of the human spirit, the Philosophie de l'Esprit investigates all the relationships which unite a man to the world, to other men, and to the ideal. It studies the intellectual dialectics and processes which go into science, art, ethics, and religion. Further, it studies the dialectics and processes whereby a man recognizes and appreciates both his own uniqueness and the communality and universality of the truths his mind comes to know. These investigations lead one to a belief in the Absolute as the guarantee of man's aspirations toward value. This belief, with all the antecedent and accompanying dialectics and processes, yields a metaphysics which both directs man's efforts toward values and helps to unify these efforts by turning them to the unity of all values. Thus the Philosophie de l'Esprit calls for both a complete description of the human mind and a meditation on the metaphysical principle of other things and other selves.[3] The Philosophie de l'Esprit as Le Senne understands it is not a mere neo-Cartesianism. It is a thought rooted in a Cartesianism unmistakably modified both by the Hegelian idealism of Octave Hamelin and by the insights of Maine de

1. René Le Senne, "La Philosophie de l'esprit," in *Philosophic Thought in France and the United States*, 2d ed., ed. Marvin Farber (Albany, N.Y.: State University of New York Press, 1968), p. 103.
2. *Ibid.*, pp. 104–5.
3. *Ibid.*, pp. 111–18.

Biran and Henri Bergson. But it flowers as a new and fundamentally original enterprise.

All of Le Senne's thought moves within this general framework. In *Obstacle and Value,* the most important of his books, he offers a systematic overview of his entire thought. *Obstacle and Value* is the work of a mature philosopher. Its themes are those he continues to deal with for the remainder of his career. These themes are: (*a*) the nature and role of philosophy; (*b*) the unity of consciousness, the *I;* (*c*) determination and value; (*d*) the double *cogito,* and the self and God; and (*e*) characterology. Though these themes appear in somewhat earlier works, e.g., *Le Devoir* (1930), they are most systematically worked out in *Obstacle and Value* (1934).

Le Senne sees his philosophy as a concrete philosophy of salvation:

> My philosophy has three centers: duty, the self, and God, the divine subject; *all three should come together in happiness.* Philosophy should start from and come back to concrete reality. A point of departure has to be such that one cannot start from any other point. That which requires us to start from it and from nothing else, that which unquestionably thrusts itself upon us, is suffering. Suffering is thus the concrete point of departure. And, on the contrary, that which is such that we ask for nothing else is happiness. Happiness is the concrete point of arrival. All thought is enclosed between the concrete poles of suffering and happiness.[4]

In *Le Devoir,* Le Senne develops the theme that all suffering involves a contradiction and every contradiction is a source of suffering. The experience of suffering, he argues, is the experience of not being able to maintain a harmonious relation among the givens of our experience. We are confronted with incompatible givens and we are in pain until we can resolve

4. "Ma philosophie a trois centres: le devoir, le moi et Dieu, sujet divin; *tous trois doivent venir concourir dans le bonheur.* La philosphie doit partir de l'actualité et revenir à l'actualité. Pour avoir un point de départ, il faut qu'il y ait un point tel qu'on ne puisse partir d'un autre. Ce qui nous arrache à tout autre chose pour nous contraindre d'en partir, ce qui nous impose indiscutable sa nature, c'est la souffrance: la souffrance est donc l'actualité de départ. Ce qui est tel au contraire que nous ne demandons pas autre chose, c'est le bonheur. Le bonheur est l'actualité d'arrivée. Toute pensée s'enferme entre la souffrance et le bonheur" (René Le Senne, *La Découverte de Dieu* [Paris: Aubier, 1955], pp. 21–22).

the incompatibility. Contradiction, then, is not merely a logical category. Contradictions can occur in any realm of our experience. Wherever they occur they are experienced as suffering. We experience every contradiction, like every suffering, as something to be resolved, to be integrated into a harmony. For Le Senne, contradiction and suffering give rise to duty, basically the duty to resolve that which instigates duty. In concrete experience duty, contradiction, and suffering are always intertwined. There is no definitive resolution of contradiction or suffering. But neither is there a definitive triumph of contradiction or suffering. Duty is always required and it is always in some measure discharged. Thus not only is all thought enclosed between the concrete poles of suffering and happiness, but all human existence is the exercise of duty as it ranges between these poles.

Because Le Senne's philosophy is to start and end in the concrete, it is fundamentally descriptive. And because all thought lies between the poles of suffering and happiness, philosophy is primarily the description of consciousness. Le Senne offers four theses to explicate his insight. These four theses, he says, are crucial to his *Le Devoir*, and thereafter continue to play a major role in his thought:

1. Philosophy is the description of consciousness, and as such has no method. Such a philosophy is opposed both to empiricism and to pure intuitionism as well as to rationalistic idealism.

2. The essential act of consciousness consists in the *I* distinguishing and opposing within itself two "selves," the particular self and the universal self. Consciousness, he says, is the relation between the *I* and determinations.

3. Science, which develops to resolve interior contradictions and to move on to a new unity, is animated by morality. Le Senne understands morality, as distinct from ethics, to include all conscious response to whatever is not what it ought to be.

4. Morality involves both liberty and some absolute.[5]

In the first thesis, Le Senne is expressing a fundamental insight. But at the same time he is reflecting and trying to harmonize the thought of his great professors, Lachelier, Rauh,

5. René Le Senne, "Le Devoir comme principe de toute valeur," *Bulletin de la société française de philosophie*, XXXII (1932), 6–14. These four theses, of course, are not intended to be an adequate précis of *Le Devoir*.

and Hamelin. And in a broader sense this thesis flows from a sympathetic but critical meditation on Maine de Biran and Bergson on the one hand, and Hume and Kant on the other. It is with a development of this thesis that Le Senne begins *Obstacle and Value*. The suffering engendered by the attempts to subject philosophy to a method or to root it in something other than experience, as well as by the insufficiency of both empiricism and intuitionism, imposes itself on him as his necessary point of departure. What he offers in place of these unsatisfactory attempts is a "noology of dialectics and intimate processes." [6] Thus his philosophy is knowledge of knowledge. But that is not all it is. It should be a bearer of salvation. Le Senne therefore offers what can be called an axiological metaphysics. "There is . . . place beyond the doctrinal metaphysics for an existential metaphysics whose object is to put at man's disposal the dialectics favorable to the success of his movement toward the Absolute." [7]

Unlike Sartre and Merleau-Ponty, Le Senne does not give existence priority over thought. Nor does he assign knowledge to a restricted range of concrete experience. Every dimension of concrete experience can be brought into the scope of knowledge. But no concrete experience is exhaustively or adequately dealt with simply by knowing it. Le Senne's position has important similarities to Marcel's position on first and second reflection. We will return to this point later.

Le Senne argues that if philosophy is to be the description of consciousness and its experience, then it can have no method. Every method is simply one element of the conscious experience which is to be described. Nevertheless, Le Senne cannot simply discourse haphazardly. His thought moves in a kind of spiral. There is both a dialectical turning back on itself from another aspect and a steady, general progression from lower to higher limits. He generally moves from a low-grade unity or homogeneity to plurality to a high-grade unity or synthesis. What-

6. *Obstacle and Value*, p. 44. I have translated *démarche* throughout as process. This odd translation is used to convey the relative opposition between *dialectique,* which connotes discreteness of steps, and *démarche,* which connotes continuity.

7. "Il y a . . . place, au-dessus des métaphysiques doctrinales, pour une métaphysique existentielle, dont l'objet soit de mettre à la disposition de l'homme les dialectiques favorables au succes de son mouvement vers l'Absolu" (Le Senne, *La Découverte de Dieu,* p. 163).

ever his topic, Le Senne usually deals with it in this fairly regular, "methodical" way. He would argue, though, that he does not impose a method on the concrete givens of experience. Rather, he is simply describing our complex experience of the givens. Our experience of the givens contains these moments within itself.

These three moments correspond to the three principal phases of human experience discussed by Le Senne in Chapter 7 of this volume. The description of homogeneity is tied to the experience of compulsion. This is the experience of being borne along by a reality from which consciousness is scarcely differentiated and within which a multiplicity of objects is scarcely discernible. The description of plurality corresponds to what Le Senne calls *cold knowledge*. Cold knowledge is simply what is usually designated as *objective knowledge*. The knower is detached from the known. And within the known, objects are distinguished from one another. The description of synthesis is tied to the experience of inspiration. Inspiration is the re-apprehension of the fundamental unity binding together the several objects discoverable in the world and the concomitant reapprehension of the unity obtaining between consciousness and the world. All three of these phases are essential components of human experience. But there is a progression. Inspiration is the apex of human experience. It is only achieved, however, through the mediation of cold knowledge. We will return to these three phases later.

Le Senne's account of experience in *Obstacle and Value* begins with his description of the *I*, the unity of experience. First, he asks us to consider the universe. Everything in it is connected with or in opposition to something else. The universe itself is the relation of these particular relations to one another. Experience shows the omnipresence of relations. A closer examination of the experience of relation, and relation is involved in all experience, reveals three universal aspects of experience: multiplicity, unity, and non-being. A philosophy which seeks to avoid reductionism must deal with each of these aspects and not attempt to reduce one of them to another.

Having these three universal aspects, experience itself is a unity. But it too is a relational unity, a unity of distinguishable terms. It is not an undifferentiated, "massive" unity. Experience is not merely a normative or ideal relation. Experience is not confined to the rational or the intelligible. Experience is also existential. The unity of experience then is *ideo-existential*. It involves both existence and structures and thus can be called *relation-soul*. It is this multifaceted unity of experience which Le Senne calls the *I*.[8]

Among other things, Le Senne refuses to call the unity of experience the world, or God, or Being, because none of these terms in their usual sense is able to encompass the three aspects of experience. The term *I* has the advantage of connoting both some content and an active center which grasps this content.[9]

It is of the very nature of the *I* that it itself cannot be the object of an experience. Yet the unity of experience is given in experience. We experience this unity in those moments when the distinction between the experiencer and the content of experience is practically unnoticed.

In one sense the pure *I* is experience at its most passive level. But this passivity is merely the lowest level of the *I*. The *I*, as the unity of experience, is coextensive with the entirety of experience. As such it is both universal and sublime. From one aspect the oneness of experience is a closed, systematic whole. As such, it functions in our experience as a kind of norm. It is all-embracing in the sense that it is regarded as the unified field in which all particular experiences arise and within which they find their sense. By reason of this aspect the *I* is properly called universal.

The universality of the *I*, however, is an abstract universality, an intellectualized universality within which concrete existence, with its surprises and tragedies, has no place. But surprise and tragedy are experienced realities. And they are experienced realities which lie within the scope of the unity of experience. Thus the *I* is seen to have a second aspect. This second aspect of the unity of experience is the open unity of an unbounded continuum. By reason of this second aspect, the *I* grasps existence in its unanalyzed complexity. Le Senne calls this second aspect the sublimity of the *I*.

Le Senne observes then that consciousness is the gap between what is and what ought to be. It holds in tension knowledge strictly so-called and its own existential goal. Knowledge is fixed, stable, in some sense past. It is what Le Senne calls ideal.

8. See Jules Pirlot, *Destinée et valeur: La Philosophie de René Le Senne* (Paris: Vrin, 1953), pp. 31–33.
9. *Ibid.*, p. 33.

Existence is abstracted from it. On the other hand, the goal of knowing is always in the future, always that which does not yet exist, always in some way indeterminate. Consciousness thus embraces both the ideal and the existential. It is the ideo-existential relation. And the ideo-existential relation is what Le Senne calls spirit. Thus the name, La Philosophie de l'Esprit.[10]

Consciousness then is both Cartesian and Bergsonian. It is Cartesian inasmuch as it is ideal and universal. It is Bergsonian inasmuch as it is existential and sublime. The description of experience does not authorize us to choose between these two. Rather, it obliges us to acknowledge both and to recognize that the unity of these two aspects, the ideo-existential relation, is the center from which the entirety of experience can be derived.[11]

The lower level of the *I*, the level of almost exclusive passivity in which the experiencer scarcely distinguishes himself from the experienced, is certainly not a complete description of experience. Experience is likewise regularly given as uniquely mine. I am regularly conscious of the uniqueness of my own experience. This facet of experience must likewise be accounted for.

Le Senne here makes a crucial move. He calls attention to the fact that in my experience the objects of experience show themselves as in some measure impervious to my own existential thrust. They are over against me. They are obstacles. Confronted with an obstacle, I discover in one multifaceted intuition matter, self, God, and other. The solidity of the obstacle, maintaining as it does a negative pressure on the spirit, is recognized as matter. The *I* finds limitations imposed on itself. And by this very discovery it comes to realize that it is a situated, limited self. Faced with the obstacle, one experiences an aspiration to go beyond it. This aspiration is a presentiment of or a source of hope for a divine spirit. Further, by an imaginative effort the self comes to an empathic foretaste of the possibility of, and indeed the need for, another limited self like itself.[12] Thus, as a consequence of having encountered an obstacle which impedes its spontaneous existential thrust, the *I* is seen to be not an undifferentiated unity but a uniplurality.

10. See Le Senne, *La Découverte de Dieu*, pp. 54–55.
11. *Ibid.*, p. 51.
12. *Ibid.*, pp. 80 ff.

From the description of how the experience of obstacle diffracts the *I*, two central themes emerge. One of these themes is the relation between determination and value. Determinations are whatever is not consciousness. They are whatever consciousness can be conscious of. Thus ideas, memories, physical things, and at times other persons and even myself are determinations for me. These determinations interrupt the free movement of consciousness and introduce discreteness into experience. In a quite real sense, determinations force us to acknowledge that experience embraces non-being and negativity. Le Senne does not attempt to give a causal explanation of where determinations initially come from. Wherever they come from, they are found in experience and they have these characteristics: (*a*) they exclude as far as possible the unitary flux of reality; (*b*) they make possible temporal and spatial discreteness; (*c*) they introduce the experience of discreteness into the individual consciousness' awareness of itself; and (*d*) they are public, available for anyone.

In our consciousness of these determinations, however, we are not definitively overcome by them. We seek to go beyond them. In fact, we try to convert them into means with which to pursue our own existential thrust. That is, we attempt to suffuse them with value. Le Senne argues that it is in seeking to overcome the diffraction of the *I* that we allow value to arise in the world. The diffraction of the *I*, we just saw, gives one a source of hope that there is a divine spirit and shows the need for another limited self like oneself. In seeking to further the dynamic unity of the universal spirit or the I-as-universal, we are seeking value. The value we seek, then, is the unity of the relation between an infinite source of liberality, an inexhaustible multiplicity of benefits, and a plurality of finite selves. As Le Senne says, "Value is the interexistential relation *which unites* not terms *but persons.*" [13] Thus, in converting determinations into means, we bring absolute value into time and space. In doing so we humanize it and introduce originality into our experience. Thus, though we are not the ultimate source of value, we are sources of limited values. We aspire toward absolute value, but we are conscious of it only through the mediation of the limited, humanized values we actualize in time and space. Value, then, has the following characteristics: (*a*) No value is

13. *Obstacle and Value*, p. 164.

a thing, but every value is a concrete experience involving the spirit; (*b*) by particular values the spirit is directed toward hope; (*c*) value is the radiance illuminating objects or determinations as things capable of being brought into the service of the spirit; and (*d*) value is existence delighting in its own dignity and freedom from the negativity of determinations.

In concrete human experience there is no value which is completely indeterminate. Nor is there any determination which is impervious to human effort seeking to modify it and thus to convert it into a means serving one's own free movement. Determination and value abide in tension both in the individual consciousness and in the uniplurality of the universal *I*.

> All finite consciousnesses throughout space and time unquestionably do not form either a systematic whole or a mere heap. Rather, they form a teeming living ensemble, half ensnared in things and half sovereign over them, always in danger of being crushed by things and by other men, always pushing on . . . toward the values appropriate to each and toward the value whence these values all spring.[14]

The second theme which emerges from the description of the diffraction of the *I* by obstacle is that of the double *cogito*. We were led to make a distinction in the content of experience between determination and value. Similarly, within the unity of consciousness we are led to distinguish between the individual self and God. It must be remembered, though, that God does not become an object for the self, nor does the self become an object for God. Nevertheless there is something about both the self and God that allows us to regard them as objects. In the case of God, regarding him as an object is a mistake which comes about by reifying him, by attempting to situate him in some framework, e.g., the framework of physics or the framework of logic. In the case of man, who is a situated consciousness, we can treat him as an object by emphasizing his situatedness at the expense of his consciousness. Indeed, we can treat ourselves in this fashion. The very activity of cognition makes

14. "Toutes les consciences finies, au travers de l'espace et du temps, forment, non certes un tout systematique, ni un archipel de rocs, mais un tumulte de vivants, à demi intriqués dans les choses, à demi souvrains d'elles, à chaque instante menacés d'être ecrasés . . . par elles et les outres, à chaque instant faisant effort . . . vers les valeurs qui leur conviennent et la valeur d'ou celles—ci jaillissent toutes" (*La Découverte de Dieu*, p. 76).

us tend to objectify everything. Since cognition is ideational and intellectual it progresses precisely by fixing its terms and holding them in stable positions. In other words, it progresses by objectifying the experience with which it deals. Thus when Le Senne speaks of the double *cogito* as the bifurcation of consciousness into a limited self, which is passive, psychophysical, and evaluated, and a universal self, which is infinite, spiritual, active, and evaluating,[15] he is both describing the situation of the limited self and, by negating the situation, pointing toward the universal.

But a philosophy which intends to describe concrete experience and its unity cannot be satisfied with simply using limit concepts. The limited self's situatedness is not all there is to the self. In *Obstacle and Value,* Le Senne distinguishes between the public self and the intimate self. The public self is that aspect of the self which focuses on determinations and details and to some extent is absorbed in them. The intimate self is that aspect of the self which is independent of determinations and is free to go beyond them. Every human self has both aspects. In any given man one or the other aspect may predominate but cannot become exclusive.

Similarly, God is not simply the absolutely Other-than-man. There is no God-without-us. God is always both God-for-us and God-with-us. Insofar as he is God he is infinite, but insofar as he is for-us and with-us he is finite. God is thus both finite and infinite. He is both transcendent to man and immanent in man. Man, as God's existential correlate, likewise has two aspects. Insofar as he is an intimate self, man is, in Le Senne's terminology, divinized. Insofar as he is a public self, man is simply human. It must be stressed here, though, that this simply human aspect, this aspect of the public self, has no intrinsic pejorative connotations. The public self is not worse than the intimate self. It is simply a necessary aspect of every man. Nevertheless it is true that the public self can become blameworthy should it repress the intimate self.

In speaking of the uniplural *I*, then, one must recognize a double *cogito:* the *cogito*-as-God and the *cogito*-as-man. Having come to the double *cogito,* Le Senne finds neither a theoretical nor an experiential foundation for introducing a transcendental subject. Given the double *cogito* and the universality of the *I*

15. Le Senne, "Le Devoir comme principe de toute valeur," p. 1.

there is no danger of psychologism. Le Senne therefore finds no reason for positing either a Kantian or a Husserlian transcendental ego.[16]

Le Senne claims that the double *cogito* was implicitly recognized by both Descartes and Malebranche. In Cartesian doctrine the "natural light" is that which allows man to reach beyond the confusion of sensible appearance to the true. It is also the necessary condition for our idea of God. And without the idea of God, the self could never get any certitude beyond itself. The natural light, then, is the common point between man and God. It transcends their duality and establishes their unity. "After having theoretically distinguished the terms, Descartes reconciles them in the unity of intelligence. In turn, Malebranche had conceived Paradise as an inundation of light." [17] Thus the self and God, the twofold *cogito,* are radically unified in intelligence and truth.

Le Senne sees the Cartesian doctrine of the natural light as a doctrine of contemplation, a doctrine expressing the best tradition of classical intellectualism. This doctrine, however, is insufficient. It does not express the unity of action and existence between God and man, a unity which Le Senne discovers in the course of describing experience. The Cartesian doctrine expresses the ideational side of the unity of the *I,* but leaves the existential side unexplored.

Though Le Senne does not explicitly mention it, the Cartesian system is under severe strain when it attempts to account for the stability of the created in conjunction with God's radical independence. When he attempts to get beyond experience and to explain God's existential independence, Descartes is forced to relinquish his intellectualism in favor of a divine volitionalism by virtue of which God freely decides what is going to be true, and decides it freely at each and every instant. At best, man contemplates God's activity. Man and God do not existentially interact. But if they do not existentially

16. Though Le Senne refers to Husserl in his later writing, it is always in connection with the question of the transcendental ego. To say that Le Senne made a careful study of Husserl's thought apparently would be an exaggeration. For a typical offhand comment, see Le Senne's remarks in Gaston Berger, *Phénoménologie du temps et prospective* (Paris: Presses Universitaires de France, 1964), pp. 143–45.

17. *Obstacle and Value,* p. 271.

interact, then how is even the unity of intelligence, the ideational unity of the *I*, maintained? This same problem, in a more roundabout way, appears if one attempts to apply Descartes's definition of substance rigorously to both God and man.

Le Senne will not attempt to account for the existential aspect of the unity of the *I* by forsaking the realm of experience for some theoretical construct. Consequently, there is no basis for talking about divine activity apart from man. If there were such activity we would neither know it, deny it, nor doubt it. In brief, there is no God-without-us. Whatever the existence of God involves lies within the range of the unity of experience. God's whole existence is to be for-us and with-us. In comparable fashion, man's whole existence also lies within the unity of the *I*. He too exists only insofar as he is for-others and with-others. The concrete experience of the unity of action and existence between man and man and between man and God is the experience of that which is unfinished. Not even its paths are fully marked out. A philosophy which is faithful to experience, then, can never be a finished doctrine.

In Le Senne's view, Descartes and, to a lesser extent, Malebranche purchased a closed system at the price of leaving the description of experience and going into fiction. Le Senne himself is willing to pay for remaining faithful to the description of experience by recognizing that his "system" is incurably incomplete. This incompleteness is not a consequence of defective description or of inadequate "method." It flows directly from man's historical, ongoing character and from the character of experience itself.

In the Cartesian scheme of things the human *cogito* recognizes itself as the initial Archimedean point. Then by virtue of the natural light it recognizes God as the ultimate Archimedean point of both formal and objective reality, the creator of entities and the guarantor of knowledge. Human consciousness, fortified by the awareness of God, can then proceed to a *mathesis universalis* embracing all the objects of consciousness.

Le Senne's description is much more fluid. There is no Archimedean point in the sense of an axiom from which theorems can be deduced. When the free flight of consciousness is interrupted by an obstacle, by determination, then both the human self and the divine self are recognized. Each *cogito* is clarified and experienced in conjunction with the other. The entire process, of course, takes place from what might be called the human standpoint, but the sense of the human arises in tension with that of the divine. The interaction between the human self and the divine self extends to the whole field of experience, e.g., love, ambition, fear, etc. It is not confined to knowledge. Likewise, this interaction, in its entirety as a relation and simultaneously in the distinctness of its terms, is dialectically intertwined with the entire field of determination as well as with specific determinations in that field. This dialectical intertwining embraces not merely the physical but the entire scope of the determined.

Le Senne, however, could hardly hold both that he was describing concrete experience and that man constantly experienced himself as mutually implicated with God. Man obviously does experience himself as one who is "on his own." How can this aspect of experience be related to the doctrine of the double *cogito* and the unity of experience, the *I*? Le Senne responds to this issue in the last three chapters of *Obstacle and Value*. These chapters sketch the outline of a philosophical anthropology. Le Senne filled out this sketch in *Traité de caracterologie* (1945), *La Destinée personelle* (1951), and two unpublished manuscripts, "Les Puissances de l'esprit" and "Précis d'idiologie." [18]

At the very outset of the discussion of man's separation from God, Le Senne reaffirms that both the union and the separation of God and the self are not states but operations.[19] The meaning of separation is absolute, though there may be degrees of it. The absoluteness of separation refers to the directional thrust of the self away from God. The relativeness of separation refers to how far this operation has gone.

Separation occurs when man focuses on things as ultimates instead of seeing them as revelations of the absolute. In effect, separation occurs when one immerses himself in determinations, loses his awareness of his personal uniqueness in the "objective" massiveness of what is non-self, and gives up the pursuit of his goal, the pursuit of value. Separation occurs by virtue of man's activity. It cannot be blamed either on God or on things. All philosophical efforts to exonerate man from re-

18. See André-A. Devaux, "Bibliographie des travaux de et sur René Le Senne," *Giornale di metafisica*, XXIII, nos. 2–3 (1968), 259–82.

19. *Obstacle and Value*, p. 230.

sponsibility for this separation eventually naturalize man. That is, they end up denying the uniqueness of the human spirit.

But man's concrete experience of separation, of being "on his own," contains within itself the experience of being distinct from what is other than himself. He stands apart from God but he is not merged into determinations. He is neither God nor determination. Dialectically, then, through the experience of separation we come to recognize the validity of and the necessity for the Cartesian emphasis on the irreducibility of the human *cogito*. There cannot be a Spinozistic reduction of the self to God. Nor can the self be reduced to matter. But the human self is not an Archimedean point, if one understands such a point to be radically discrete. As Descartes hinted and as Pascal stressed, man is a mid-point. He is a subject subjected to matter and a person separated from the absolute.[20] Indeed, he is not united to the absolute. But he experiences his separation from the absolute as a suffering, as something to be overcome. This mid-point existence is the source of both his dignity and his danger. And the experience of his perilous dignity gives rise to the recognition of his freedom.

Thus, though obstacle engenders a dialectic which brings about the separation of man from God, obstacle cannot absorb and naturalize man. Obstacle, by reason of the multiplicity of its determinations, gives rise to a multitude of dialectical movements. Each determination in its insufficiency calls for other determinations. Each dialectical movement calls for other dialectical movements. These determinations and dialectical movements when taken singly are movements of separation. But when taken together or when taken in their insufficiency they lay a foundation for man's search for value.

Le Senne gives further expression to man's mid-point character in his discussion of the three principal phases of human experience mentioned above: compulsion, cold knowledge, and inspiration. Again, we must not be betrayed by metaphors such as "mid-point" into forgetting that we are speaking of operations, not of states. Compulsion is the prevalence of determination over existence; inspiration is the prevalence of existence over determination. Both compulsion and inspiration are existential

20. *La Découverte de Dieu*, p. 39. Le Senne's work has with reason been called a vast commentary on Pascal. See André-A. Devaux, *Le Senne: Ou le combat pour la spiritualisation* (Paris: Seghers, 1968), p. 50.

phases. Compulsion is the lower extreme of the *I* in which consciousness is not distinguished from the object of consciousness. Inspiration is the upper extreme in which consciousness synthesizes the energy coming from compulsion with the control coming from cold knowledge. Cold knowledge mediates between compulsion and inspiration by converting compulsion into determination pitted over against the particular self. Cold knowledge is the ideal phase of the *I*. Human experience is constantly marked by these three phases. The phases interact in each man throughout his life. Man is never a total stranger to any of them. Every man is in the phase of inspiration with reference to some determinations, cold knowledge with reference to others, and compulsion with reference to still others. Human development consists in the expansion of the sphere of inspiration with the consequent shrinking of the sphere of compulsion. These phases, however, never become immobile. Human development is never such as to preclude the possibility of human degeneration.

An important consequence of the doctrine of the three interacting phases of human experience is that there is no "absolute evil." No man is totally estranged from God. Determination can never so completely absorb man that he can no longer extricate himself. On the other hand, though man never is absorbed into God, there is nonetheless an "absolute good" which is value. Le Senne constantly addresses himself to describing value. Value, he sees, is not reducible to a mirage, to fact, to desire, to a mode of intentionality, or to a determination of being. Value, he says, is never a determination. Each particular value arises when a particular consciousness refers a determination to absolute value.

Absolute value, though, is not a determinate entity which is exclusively transcendent to particular consciousness. Absolute value is correlatively immanent in and transcendent to determined values. Value is both ultimate and intrinsically intersubjective. An Absolute-without-man would be of no value. Man-without-God would be valueless. He would be lost in the multiplicity of determinations. In Le Senne's philosophy, Being is not ultimate. Value is ultimate. His metaphysics is an axiology. Le Senne's doctrine, then, has an ultimate, but this ultimate is not an "independent" ultimate. It is not a Plotinian One. Le Senne's ultimate is an "implicated" ultimate, a related and mediated ultimate. Because the ultimate is always a relational ultimate, man is in no danger of being absorbed into a massive "divine" unity. Relatedness implies opposition. Man is therefore irreducible.[21]

Le Senne holds that the interacting phases of human experience which he has identified are common to every man. But the uniqueness of each self's experience with reference to that of other selves is not adequately described by merely "quantifying" the several phases and then "adding up" the totals. To be satisfied with so mechanical a procedure would make one guilty of blatant reductionism. Le Senne early saw that a more subtle description would be required. For instance, he recognized that men concretely experience reality in a way different from women. Thus in 1925 he published his translation of G. Heymans, *The Psychology of Women*. But still further refinement was necessary. The description of consciousness must be pushed both in the direction of the uniquely specific and in the direction of the universal. *Obstacle and Value* concludes with an outline of a program for describing consciousness.

In some sense then, Le Senne has come back to his starting point. Philosophy, he announced at the outset, has as its task and glory the description of consciousness. At the end of *Obstacle and Value* he offers a program to be used in accomplishing this task. The description of consciousness must move on several levels. There is need for a transcendental description, which will give an account of the universal ideal characteristics belonging to any subject considered abstractly, that is, without reference either to existence or to whatever distinguishes one subject from another. There is need for a characterological description, which will take into account the diverse types of character and disposition to be found among men and the special dialectics by which each of these types can increase either their passivity or their activity. There is need for an "idiological" description, which will study the alternation of dialectics and processes by which each person deals with determinations of various sorts, sometimes undergoing a deforming impact from them and sometimes exploiting them for his own development. Le Senne selected the term *idiologie*

21. It is impossible to give a fully satisfactory and precisely nuanced account of Le Senne's theory of values in the space available. Le Senne's own account in Chapter 4 of this work sketches his general position, but it would be rash to claim that Le Senne ever believed that he had definitively refined his view.

(from the Greek *idios*) to denote the study of the individual person and the uniqueness of his character structure. Finally, there is need for an axiological description, which will focus on the description of the modes of value and thus, mediately, on value itself. Le Senne devoted substantial efforts to all these kinds of description except transcendental description. Apparently he felt that transcendental description was getting an excessive share of attention from philosophers anyway. His task was to expand the philosopher's vision and field.

Obstacle and Value stands, then, as a thoroughgoing investigation of concrete experience and its implications. Acknowledging and indeed glorying in its Cartesian origins, Le Senne's thought, as expressed in *Obstacle and Value* and foreshadowed or developed in his other works, extends in a highly sophisticated and original way the French Cartesian tradition into the present. He confronts much of modern and contemporary Western philosophy with a stimulating contemporary Cartesianism which will brook no naturalistic reduction of the uniqueness of the spirit. Nor will it yield to any philosophy which becomes so infatuated with existence that it despises the world of matter or regards matter as man's implacable enemy.

II

LE SENNE'S RELATION TO his younger but more famous contemporaries such as Sartre and Merleau-Ponty is not easily specified in detail. The notorious French habit of sparse footnoting makes detective work here a highly uncertain enterprise. Matters are further complicated by the obviousness of the influence of Husserl and Marx on a Sartre or a Merleau-Ponty. Nevertheless it can be shown that in Le Senne's handling of the Cartesian tradition he dealt with issues and themes which play a prominent role in French phenomenological thought.

I do not, then, claim to be able to prove that Le Senne "influenced" Sartre or Merleau-Ponty. To my knowledge, they do not acknowledge his existence. Rather, I will point out how some of the prominent themes in the works of his better-known contemporaries have affinities with and anticipations in Le Senne's studies. Their conclusions, though different, have interesting structural similarities. I surely do not deny any of the originality of a Sartre or of a Merleau-Ponty. I am, however, asserting that they have deep roots in the Cartesian tradition and that these roots become apparent when one notes the thematic similarities between them and the explicitly Cartesian Le Senne.

I also claim that Le Senne is not merely another "representative" of Cartesianism. His work has an originality which gives it intrinsic interest. His conclusions deserve to be considered in their own right as legitimate alternatives to those reached by his more well-known colleagues. In an Introduction one could hardly give a thorough justification for these claims, but a rough outline can be sketched.

Further, it should be noted that Le Senne saw in Max Scheler a kindred spirit. To be sure, Le Senne and Scheler disagreed completely about the legitimacy of speaking about a hierarchy of values. This is no minor point for either of them. But Scheler's clear recognition that no exclusively "intellectual," ideational description of man was adequate, that the sympathetic, existential dimension of man could not be reduced to the ideational and thus had to be taken into account in its own right, meshed nicely with Le Senne's guiding insight that the *I* is the ideo-existential relation. It is no accident that the French translation of six of Scheler's books appeared in the Philosophie de l'Esprit collection. Thus Le Senne was by no means uninterested in or unaffected by the German phenomenological thought which influenced his younger French contemporaries.

Before indicating links between Le Senne and some of the more prominent contemporary French thinkers, I should like to call attention to two major notions employed by Le Senne. These two notions provide a useful frame within which specific connections can be indicated. These notions are "absence" and "infection." They are important in their own right and they have structural analogues in contexts in which they do not explicitly appear. Absence is related to non-being, contradiction, and diffraction. Infection is related to oscillation, process, atmosphere, etc.

Le Senne argues against what he calls "the partiality in favor of being." Correlative to every experience of presence, of being, there is the experience of absence, of non-being. A philosophy of description may neither deny nor cancel out absence. "Absence is . . . the first product of time. . . . By canceling simultaneity, time introduces absence into our lives, and introduces it not accidentally, but essentially, necessarily." [22] Absence, then, has two forms. First, we can recognize the collection of things, individuals, and determinations which are "absent." Thus a forgotten tune, a lost ball, a missed friend are absent. Further, we can recognize the realm of the indeterminate non-present. This realm extends over both the pastness of the past and the futurality of the future. Thus in experience we are neither given presences from which we infer the absent nor vice versa. The present and the absent are given together.

In an attempt to be faithful to this ambiguity of concrete experience, the ambiguous intermingling of presence and absence, Le Senne will not accept the primacy of metaphysics. Metaphysics as he understands it leads to giving priority to the systematic, objective, "massive" oneness at the expense of the relative, the novel, the erratic diversity. What he calls the "objective one" or the "metaphysician's one" is simply an ideal unity treated in isolation from existence. If he is constrained to speak metaphysically, he will speak of an "axiological metaphysics" which deals with the perpetual tension between what-is and what-ought-to-be. This tension involves the oscillation between the presence-absence of these two poles.

The experience of absence, then, is not the experience of absolute nothingness. Nor is absence wholly negative. But the experience of absence is the experience of non-being. Without absence, the present would be undifferentiated, unknowable. Indeed, without absence there would be no presence. The converse also holds: without presence, no absence. Without silence, no sound; without sound, no silence. Without absence, no time; without time, no absence.

The second notion is that of "infection" (*contaminer*). Whether Le Senne borrowed this term from Scheler, whom he so admired, is unclear. At any rate they both employ this odd term in strikingly similar ways. As Le Senne uses it, *contaminer* does not have pejorative connotations. It refers to the most intimate and pervasive penetration of one element by another. For example, in any experience that we have, determination

22. "L'absence est . . . le premier produit du temps. . . . En niant la simultanéité, le temps doit introduire l'absence dans notre vie, et l'introduire, non accidentellement, mais essentiellement, nécessairement" (*La Découverte de Dieu*, p. 174).

infects indeterminateness, and vice versa. If I focus on a tree, then that tree becomes the center of my field of vision and the remainder of the field is peripheral to it. But in realizing that the tree has a periphery, and that the tree's centrality is not immutable, and that there are an indefinite number of links which this tree might have, could have, or should have with other things, I recognize the indeterminateness infecting the determinateness of the centrality of the tree and indeed of the tree itself. The notion of infection does, however, generally emphasize the introduction of a destabilizing element. It connotes movement and a certain fluidity. But this has to be understood in such a way that if one were to try to absolutize and "define the structure of" the flux, then a faithful description would have to report that determination did infect and "destabilize" the flux. Bergsonism, Le Senne thinks, needs complementation just as surely as does Spinozism.

This notion of infection, however, must not bemuse us into being satisfied with a Hegelian kind of intellectual synthesis such as that proposed by Hamelin. Infection is a relation-with-terms. However intimate the relation, the terms are existentially distant from one another, and that distance, too, has to be recognized. In other words, the existential intimacy of infection cannot legitimately be reduced to an idealized structure in which the elements would lose their existential uniqueness.

Parenthetically, Le Senne's criticism of Hamelin on this score brings to mind Sartre's criticism of orthodox communism's version of Marxism. Other points of contact between these two will be noted shortly, after a few remarks about Le Senne and Gabriel Marcel.

Le Senne, like Marcel, moved away from the French idealism of his early years. They both came to recognize the importance of the concrete existential experience and the responsibility of philosophy never to subordinate its descriptive tasks to abstract demands for systematization. Marcel agrees with the emphasis Le Senne places on the necessity for obstacle in the development of human values. Man is incarnate, and human value can develop only through an appropriate response to our embodiment. He who claims that man can escape his body is not entering a realm of non-corporal value. Rather, he precludes the possibility of attaining value. Obstacle and value, I and my body, are in dynamic tension. To disregard either is to falsify experience.

Secondly, Marcel's celebrated distinction between mystery and problem has an analogue in Le Senne's refusal to give primacy to conceptual knowledge. For Le Senne, knowledge or science pertains to that which is somehow "past," to the settled. But concrete experience is by no means confined to the settled. An adequate description of experience must therefore take into account both the unsettled and the self in its entanglement with the unsettled. For Marcel, when one reaches mystery through second reflection he overcomes the subject-object dichotomy which is required for conceptual knowledge. Second reflection, necessarily presupposing first reflection, enables man to acquire the awareness that he is not radically over against the totality of the world but that he participates in it. For Le Senne, the particular value realized when consciousness converts an obstacle into an object of knowledge is itself oriented to absolute value, in which all particular values participate. Knowledge of objects, then, mediates man's quest for absolute value.

While these are by no means the only points of contact between Le Senne and Marcel, space requires that we now turn to Sartre and Merleau-Ponty. Since a number of the themes of Sartre and Merleau-Ponty are related to Marcelian themes, as Richard Zaner has shown in *The Problem of Embodiment*, the connections between Le Senne and both Sartre and Merleau-Ponty will frequently, with appropriate adjustments, apply to Marcel as well.

It would obviously be ridiculous to claim that Sartre is somehow really in the same camp as Le Senne. But Sartre's insistence, even within his Marxism, on the radical irreducibility of the individual man to anything other than himself is enough to keep him within the Cartesian tradition. It also is enough to require him to deal thematically with irreducible man.

In 1945, Le Senne denounced Sartre's doctrine that all values were illusions forged in our imagination and that our search for value is destined to stalemate after stalemate until death, the final stalemate. Le Senne used an argument from Lachelier: "Error cannot be by itself in our experience. It is united in an indestructible solidarity to truth." [23] If all values are false, then that truth must be a valuable acquisition. Or,

23. "L'erreur ne peut être seule dans notre expérience: elle est unié par une solidarité indestructible à la verité" (Le Senne, "Qu'est-ce que la valeur?," *Bulletin de la société française de philosophie*, XL [1947], 96).

from a different perspective, disvalues, e.g., illusions, cannot exist by themselves. They are indissolubly linked to positive value. But of greater interest here is the fact that Sartre's account of concrete values, like that of Le Senne's, demands human activity in their coming to be. Whether they are illusions or not, concrete values are humanized values. The realm of values is not reducible to the realm of things. It is not detached from things but neither is it identical with them.

Similarly, whether Sartre's *pour-soi* introduces nothingness into being or whether Le Senne's spirit transforms obstacles into means for achieving value, in either case consciousness is irreducible to determinate being. Further, determinate being is not simply a given. It is a given-for-consciousness. The relation between consciousness and determinate being is not a sheerly extrinsic relation. Whether the activity of consciousness is absurd or meaningful, it is an activity whereby man transcends the given toward the non-given.

From a somewhat different angle, Le Senne holds that consciousness is the gap between what is and what ought to be, whereas Sartre claims that what ought to be is an absurdity which man introduces into what is. Yet both are in agreement that what ought to be does not have an absolute priority over what is. To give such a primacy to what ought to be is to fall into the trap of classical rationalism. Ideas and their consistency are elevated over existence. Such an approach, both hold, simply does not do justice to our experience either of what is outside us or of our own intimate existence.

An even more striking structural similarity shows up in their respective accounts of the stages in the emergence of the individual's self-awareness. For Le Senne, consciousness is initially in a state of naive spontaneity. In naive spontaneity it does not distinguish itself in any way from its environs. Then the undifferentiated thrust of naive spontaneity is ruptured by an obstacle, by that which consciousness cannot immediately absorb. Through the mediation of the rupture introduced by the obstacle, the self emerges as this particular consciousness. Corresponding to these three moments—spontaneity, rupture, self-awareness—are the three Sartrean moments of prereflexive consciousness, fissure, and presence-to-oneself. Prereflexive consciousness has no immediate awareness of itself. But in its intentional activity it distances itself from itself by intending an object. This distancing is the fissure consciousness introduces into itself by its essential mode of activity. By virtue of this fissure consciousness grasps itself across its intended object and thus comes to presence-to-itself, to initial self-awareness. The difference between Le Senne's interpretation of this movement and Sartre's are, of course, of capital importance. But that fact in no way detracts from the importance of the structural similarities.

These are only a few of the striking structural similarities between Sartre's *en-soi* and *pour-soi* and Le Senne's obstacle and *I*. Each of these terms, of course, has its proper content. But when they are taken as correlates, then it becomes clear just how similar the role played in Sartre's thought by the *pour-soi*'s encounter with the *en-soi* is to the role in Le Senne's thought played by the *I*'s encounter with obstacle.

Again, Sartre's rejection of Husserlian egology stems in part from the experience of discontinuity.[24] Like Le Senne, he finds no adequate experiential base for positing the transcendental ego. However systematically satisfying something like the transcendental ego might be, a philosophy which faithfully describes experience may not posit that which concrete experience does not warrant. Le Senne and Sartre unquestionably come to different assessments of consciousness and the self, but they agree about the grounds on which their assessments stand or fall. Here, as elsewhere, their conclusions are incompatible, but they share a number of central concerns. This is not a mere coincidence. It is a consequence of the tradition they both inherited and stand within.

More clearly than in the case of Sartre, however, crucial themes and notions in the work of Merleau-Ponty are anticipated by Le Senne. Again, the claim is not being made that Le Senne originated these notions. The point here, rather, is that Merleau-Ponty and Le Senne, like Sartre and Marcel, shared a common heritage, extending from Descartes, Pascal, and Spinoza through Maine de Biran and Bergson. The heavily idealistic side of this tradition, given modern expression by influential thinkers like Hamelin and Brunschvicg, had not proved to be finally satisfying. The men we are discussing here, and others like Lavelle and Jean Nabert, were all engaged in rethinking this tradition. All of them gained important new insights. But

24. See Sartre, *The Transcendence of the Ego,* trans. Forrest Williams and Robert Kirkpatrick (New York: Noonday Press, 1957).

these insights all arise within the scope of their common heritage.[25]

But now let us concentrate briefly on Le Senne and Merleau-Ponty. We will examine two major convergences, which will serve as indicators of a far more extensive similarity. First, both stress the inherent ambiguity of any philosophy which is faithful to experience. For Le Senne, there is an essential ambiguity infecting both the object of consciousness and consciousness itself. The object of consciousness is always experienced both as something given and fixed and as an indicator of an ideal to be achieved. The object is, as it were, translucent. There is enough opacity there to force a recognition of its particular determinateness but not so much that consciousness can be satisfied with having reached this determinateness. Similarly, the realm of objects is encountered as having something of an established structure. But at the same time this realm is seen as amenable to further structuring by consciousness. The established structures of objects are never all that they might become.

Consciousness itself is ambiguous. This ambiguity shows up most clearly when consciousness reflects upon itself. When I am aware of myself and of what is mine, what is it of which I am aware? Is it not a specification, a determined entity, a fixed and located object or relation? But consciousness is neither an object nor a determinate relation. This ambiguity is indeed incurable, but it is not an absurdity. Consciousness can be recognized only when it is objectified. But it is recognized as that which always and necessarily resists objectification, as that which makes objectification meaningful and therefore possible.

Le Senne's account of the inherent ambiguity of consciousness bears evident resemblances to Merleau-Ponty's account of the ambiguity of embodied existence. For Merleau-Ponty the body is both *être-au-monde*, i.e., a lived project, and a sedi-

---

25. Unquestionably, these thinkers were also influenced by the German tradition. Kant, Hegel, Marx, and Fichte, in particular, had a strong impact. But my point is that the German influence was received through the mediation of the French tradition. It was the French tradition which primarily shaped the problematic. At bottom, the respective problematics of Le Senne, Sartre, and Merleau-Ponty, and to a lesser extent Marcel, have more in common with one another than any of them have with a Marx or a Husserl.

mented corporeal scheme firmly embedded in the world. Its whole reality is to be both of these at the same time, not consecutively. Only because my body is embedded can it be recognized as distinctive. But it is always recognized as a lived project toward the world, as that peculiar kind of reality which is *au-monde*. The ambiguity of the body extends to its activity. Its engagement in the world is both free and necessary. And each act of engagement is both the affirmation and the restriction of a freedom. Likewise, the body's perceiving is done anonymously and not personally. What is perceived is not given immediately to the *I* who chooses and thinks but to a body fully incorporated in the world. Thus the body, my lived body, mediates between the conscious *I* and the world. It can perform this mediation because of its essential ambiguity.

Both Le Senne and Merleau-Ponty recognize the important consequences flowing from this central ambiguity. For example, the entire "human world," with its institutions and its sciences, will always be permeated by ambiguity. Le Senne and Merleau-Ponty differ in emphasis and perspective, but their fundamental insights and modes of development are in more than fortuitous harmony. It is no mere accident that as Le Senne was led to emphasize the relative superiority of process over dialectic, an emphasis which stresses continuity rather than discontinuity, so Merleau-Ponty is led in his later writings to emphasize the interpenetration of the body and the world rather than the dialectical tension between more or less discrete terms.

The second major convergence in some sense follows from the first, but its importance is such that it deserves to be singled out. Neither Le Senne nor Merleau-Ponty admits that conceptual knowing is either the most basic or the supreme mode of human activity. Le Senne does not admit that all values are known in any meaningful sense of "knowing." Thus all values cannot be reduced to cognitive values. For example, love and sympathy, though they admit of some cognitive dimension, are not primarily experienced as activities of knowing. Knowledge is not, therefore, coextensive with consciousness. On the one hand, not everything of which I am conscious is knowledge. Further, knowledge is not the highest modality of consciousness. It is simply one of four intertwined modes, none of which is absolutely primary. Knowledge is indeed a cardinal value, but it is not Absolute Value. It can only exist by virtue of determination. On the other hand, metaphysics and science are the formulations of the conscious resolutions of antecedently encountered contradictions and stalemates. Knowledge is not definitive. It always has fringes calling for development and completion. Likewise, its fringes call for it to be referred to other basic modes of experience, e.g., conduct. For Le Senne, the highest mode of human activity is what he calls "communion" with other selves. Communion, unlike mere communication, is an interpenetration of the entire texture of thought, feeling, willing, etc., of at least two selves. It is not restricted to a mere intellectual exchange.

Merleau-Ponty, too, refuses to give primacy to conceptual knowledge. Man exists as a consciousness-*engagée*. He is not beside the world. He is with it. Perception of the world is not either a passive reception of impressions or a cameralike snapping of "views." It is, rather, a "communion" with the world. As Merleau-Ponty says, "sensation is literally a communion."

It is this perceived world which is the base for all knowledge. All our ideas find not only their origin but also their legitimacy in this precognitive experience of communion. The communion with the world, then, is no confusion to be dispelled by clear thought. It is the matrix within which thought can make sense.

Both Le Senne and Merleau-Ponty change the Cartesian emphasis on the "I think." For Le Senne, it becomes the "I ought." For Merleau-Ponty, as for Sartre and Husserl, it is the "I can." Both changes abandon the rationalist insistence on the supremacy of the idea and thought. But neither change abandons the Cartesian insistence on the irreducibility of the human spirit to anything else. In fact, both Le Senne and Merleau-Ponty expand the scope of the self. Thus the irreducible human spirit stands out more clearly as a fullness rather than as an impoverished residue.

This common refusal to give preeminence to the idea and thought leads them both to conclude that philosophy is essentially uncompletable. Le Senne regards philosophy as the description of experience. And since experience in general is an indefinitely open field and each experience is ambiguous, no philosophy can be definitive. Merleau-Ponty also takes note of the ambiguity in our experiences. In fact, an essential part of the philosopher's equipment is a "feeling for ambiguity." Philosophy, according to Merleau-Ponty, is primarily the expression of experience. Both thinkers are in complete accord that philosophy cannot transcend experience in the sense of detaching itself from experience. Philosophy makes sense only by reason of experience and it can be no more definitive than experience itself is.

Noting these and other thematic similarities between Le Senne and Sartre, Marcel, and Merleau-Ponty enables one to gain a better perspective on the context of contemporary thought and to see more clearly the alternative lines of inquiry and doctrinal development that can take place within the Cartesian tradition. But the pertinence of Le Senne's thought does not spring exclusively from the fact that it is a modern revamping of Cartesianism or from its connections with better-known contemporary French thinkers. Le Senne has proposed his own trenchant and original interpretation of experience. For him, man's existence is originarily an "I ought," which strives to embrace absolute value.

III

LE SENNE EMPLOYS SOME TERMINOLOGY which is far from standard for an English-speaking audience. It is a terminology that has been molded both by the tradition out of which he worked and by the exigencies of his own thought. Negatively, he reacts against an exclusively rationalistic thought, without however dismissing rationalism in a radically empiricist manner. Positively, he wants to hold in tension aspects of experience that have often been treated in isolation from one another. His terminological peculiarities are always in the service of his fundamental insight, namely, that there is a unity of experience which is not a unity of sameness but a unity which synthesizes disparate elements without destroying their disparateness. The unity of experience, he holds, is a unipluarity. In addition, Le Senne does not hesitate to infuse a dramatic note into his vocabulary. This is not introduced for rhetorical effect. Rather, experience manifests itself with its several tensions as inherently dramatic. Some examples of Le Senne's peculiar usages will illustrate the point and also reduce the discomfort English-speaking readers will experience on first encountering this mode of expression. I have called attention to some of these terms already, but it may not be amiss to repeat them in this context.

A key image for Le Senne is that of two poles in relation to each other. Neither pole is reducible to the other, but each is a pole only by virtue of the other pole and its relation to that other pole. Experience regularly occurs in this form. To describe this complex experience, Le Senne argues that one must describe it both analytically and synthetically. Analysis focuses on the distinctness of each pole of the relation and the distinctness of the relation from the two poles. Synthesis focuses on the unity between poles and relation which constitutes them a totality, a totality, however, which is grasped as a totality-in-tension. Analysis deals with experience by moving from discreteness to discreteness. This is the kind of operation in which an intellectualist excels. When consciousness approaches experience in this fashion Le Senne says that it is involved in a dialectic (*dialectique*). On the other hand, when consciousness approaches experience synthetically, and this involves not only a synthesis of objectified elements but a further synthesis between these elements and consciousness, then consciousness is engaged in a process (*démarche*). Le Senne regularly juxtaposes *dialectique* and *démarche* as two alternative ways in which consciousness is involved with objects. Movement (*mouvement*) is a general term for conscious activity.

Other terminological peculiarities are linked with these. For example, "determination" and the particular consciousness are polar opposites. Thus whatever is not consciousness is determination. Determination is used both generically and for particulars. Determination calls for consciousness to bring both dialectics and processes to bear upon it. On the other hand, consciousness, confronted by determination's appeal, recognizes that its experience is not exhaustively confined to the determinations it encounters. In other words, determinations do not exhaustively determine consciousness. The encounter between consciousness and determination is open to value. Value, however, is not localized in either of these poles; rather, it is the atmosphere within which the operations of a consciousness confronted by determination takes place. Le Senne calls value atmospheric (*atmosphérique*) because it has no parts and because it pervades every determinate reality in such a way that no determinate reality is definitively isolable from the unity of experience. The concept of atmosphere is related to that of infection, which usually occurs in its verbal form *contaminer*. Infection is used only with reference to processes, not to dialectics. It emphasizes the mutual dependence and indeed the existential interpenetration of poles, an interpenetration which does not, however, annihilate the tension between the poles.

Le Senne also uses in a specialized way the terms experience (*expérience*), concrete experience (*épreuve*), and sentiment (*sentiment*). Experience is a general term which refers to whatever we can become aware of. Experience admits of no restriction. Feelings, concepts, things, logical connections, theories—all are contained within experience. Concrete experience, on the other hand, is what might be called a "first order," or unmediated encounter. When I existentially encounter any kind of object of experience, prior to actually undertaking some *specific* dialectic or process to deal with it, I have a concrete experience of it. Concrete experience, it should be noted, is not confined to the encounter with physical objects. I can have concrete experience of a theory as well as of a door. My concrete experience is not an occurrence which is discrete from my engaging in a specific dialectic or process to deal with it. Rather, my concrete experience calls upon me to deal with the object, but it does not call for me to do so in one and only one fashion. A theory can call for me to admire it as well as to confirm it. Le Senne calls my immediate felt response to a concrete experience *sentiment*. Sentiment is as such unspecified, but it calls for me to specify it by engaging in some specific dialectic or process which will lead to cognition or aesthetic transformation or moral appraisal or religious reverence. Again, sentiment can be subsequently specified in more than one fashion even with reference to one and the same concrete experience. In fact, it is usually the case that we deal with objects of concrete experience in more than one way.

Relation, relation-norm, and relation-soul (*relation-âme*) make up another important set of terms for Le Senne. He takes the term *relation* from Hamelin. In his lengthy discussion of Hamelin's thought in his *Introduction to Philosophy*, Le Senne says of relation that it is the fundamental fact. Terms, and thus things, presuppose connections, and not vice versa. Otherwise terms would be in principle unintelligible. These multiple connections again presuppose a primary relation. This relation engenders connections and ultimately things, which are, as Hume indicated, simply complexes of connections.[26] Le Senne holds that Hamelin has interpreted relation in too intellectualist a fashion. It becomes, in Hamelin's hands, relation-norm, fundamentally deterministic and impersonal. Le Senne himself holds that the unity of experience is constituted by relation-soul. Thus Le Senne is able to convey, as Hamelin had not succeeded in conveying, that relation lives. The relation-soul is "the unity of the relation-norm and existence, the ideo-existential unity." [27] This ideo-existential unity is what Le Senne calls the *I*.

There are a few other unusual terms that might well be mentioned here. Le Senne mentions "dialectics of deliverance." These are simply any movements of the spirit which reject the subordination of subject to object. When he speaks of "emotional movements," he is referring to Bergson. Emotional movements, for Bergson, are the fundamental ground of experience on which intellectual activity rests. Le Senne occasionally uses the terms "mobile" (*mobile*) and "mobilize" (*mobiliser*). Sometimes he gives these words a dramatic, military sense. More often he uses them simply to indicate that the "center of gravity" of something or some relation shifts about. Finally, an important term for Le Senne is "fiction-limit." A notion which is a terminus arrived at by a logical or dialectical procedure but which is in principle devoid of all existence is a fiction-limit. For example, the Kantian pure-thing-in-itself is in Le Senne's terminology a fiction-limit. It is that limit which understanding can neither grasp as having existential reality nor go beyond. Other difficulties in Le Senne's usage should be clarified by the context.

IV

LE SENNE WROTE EIGHT BOOKS and some forty-one articles, in addition to numerous communications to professional meetings and congresses. His books are as follows:

26. See René Le Senne, *Introduction à la philosophie*, 5th ed., rev. (Paris: Presses Universitaires de France, 1970), pp. 143–50.
27. *Obstacle and Value*, p. 73.

Introduction à la philosophie. 1925. 5th ed., revised and edited by Edouard Morot-Sir. Paris: Presses Universitaires de France, 1970.

Le Devoir. Paris: Alcan, 1930.

Le Mensonge et le caractère. Paris: Alcan, 1930.

Obstacle et valeur. Paris: Aubier, 1934.

Traité de morale générale. Paris: Presses Universitaires de France, 1942.

Traité de caracterologie. Paris: Presses Universitaires de France, 1945.

La Destinée personelle. Paris: Flammarion, 1951.

La Découverte de Dieu. Paris: Aubier, 1955.

A complete bibliography of Le Senne's works, together with a bibliography of publications on Le Senne through 1967, has appeared in the *Giornale di metafisica.*[28]

V

WITH DEEP GRATITUDE I acknowledge the assistance of M. Edouard Morot-Sir in preparing this translation. Somehow he found time for my multitudinous questions about both content and language. I am also indebted to Mrs. Raymonde Britt for reading the entire manuscript and for straightening out any number of crooked passages. This work was supported by a grant from the Memphis State University Faculty Research Fund.

28. See André-A. Devaux, "Bibliographie des travaux de et sur René Le Senne," *Giornale di metafisica,* XXIII, nos. 2–3 (1968), 259–82.

Obstacle and Value

Analysis

PHILOSOPHY IS the description of experience. To enter into the study of experience, one must recognize that experience admits of multiplicities, unities, and absences. Further, one must recognize that philosophy is possible only if there are not only unities in experience but also a unity of experience. This unity of experience is the *I*, and the omnipresence of the *I* is expressed in its universality and sublimity.

When most impoverished, the *I* is merely a unity devoid of apperception. Insofar as it contains and conveys the content of experience, the *I* constitutes *naive spontaneity*, the essence of which is undividedness, almost perfect undividedness. Experience gives a foreshadowing of, and ultimately permits the comprehension of, the fact that naive spontaneity must eventually burn itself out. Thus one must not confuse spontaneity with the glory of the Spirit.

The emergence of an obstacle ruptures the I. With the emergence of an obstacle, both discontinuity in experience and the bisecting essential for consciousness appear. Objectively, the content of experience is subdivided into *determination* and *value*. Subjectively, the content of experience is divided into the *I* of determination, or the *self*, and the *I* of value, or *God*. Every determination is localized, relatively opaque and relatively clear, and always insufficient. Not only does it *call* for other determinations, but it influences the existence through which the self, within the limits defined by its situation and structure, participates in value. Value, on the other hand, is atmospheric.

[3]

Either gently or violently, it introduces the infinite into the depths of souls. Value is sufficient and goes beyond all the negativity in determination.

Though the *I* makes possible the distinction between value and obstacle, its unity prevents this distinction from becoming radical. And thus determinations and value necessarily infect one another. Their solidarity is to be found precisely within the self. The self is itself always the ideo-existential relation between a *detail*—which is a furnishing of clear consciousness and which permits communication between men—and an *intimacy*, which gives the self the absolute sentiment of existence.

This relation is nothing other than a particularized expression of the double *cogito*, which indissolubly unites the self and God, though it does not make them identical. The seriousness of life consists in that secret and complete intimate choice, a choice transcending nature and society, independent of time and always in need of being renewed, by which the self either abandons itself to determination or opens itself through the love of value to happiness and beneficence. By this intimate choice the self either naturalizes itself or spiritualizes itself.

If the self chooses to natualize itself, the double *cogito* is oriented to exteriority. The self becomes more and more impassioned energy and material inertia. The self becomes an object for God. God withdraws from a state of intimacy with the self and retires unnoticed into the solitude of God-without-us. In this process the lengthening shadow of his absence beclouds experience. If the self chooses to spiritualize itself, determination intervenes only to mediate the communion between God-with-us and the self in value. The will makes us worthy of this union by setting aside the dialectics of separation, which necessarily engender a competition among egoistic ambitions and a contempt of man for himself.

Description confirms these analyses by recognizing this dialectic in the three phases of human experience: (1) *compulsion*, in which determination plays against us; (2) *cold knowledge*, whose value is only that of an abstract mediation; and (3) *inspiration*, in which peace, i.e., the convergence of all determinations, is united with ardor, i.e., the infusion or irruption of value in us.

With these givens as a starting point, the ever more precise description of both ideational and emotional consciousness must be undertaken. The program for this inquiry can be sketched here. From the outset it will institute a transcendental description, the object of which is to recognize the processes through which the primordial relation of determination and intimacy is specified.

1 / Experience and Philosophy

[I] KNOWLEDGE IS ENCLOSED WITHIN EXPERIENCE

1. *Philosophy can have no method*

IT IS IMPOSSIBLE to restrict the philosopher's investigations to the application of a method. Even though the dialectics of deliverance, which prevent philosophy from letting itself be confined to any objects or procedures already known to it, are insufficient to constitute philosophy, because the goal of philosophy is not exclusively negative, they do open a path for philosophy. To be convinced of the philosophical inadequacy of every method, the spirit has only to turn back to that milieu of experiences into which a method is introduced. First, the philosopher has to experience the more or less cruel embarrassment of being pressed into a situation brought about by relatively contradictory actions. Only then does there arise a demand for a solution, a demand which may suggest to him the idea of a mediation that will help him to handle the situation. He then has to undertake a more or less laborious search. And even when the success of his search has brought him relief, he realizes with a shudder that without this mediation he would have been trapped in the situation and might have perished there. At that moment, profiting from the leisure which his success has gained for him, he tries to extract for use in other contexts a mediating formula which is more or less fundamentally independent of certain historical and contingent details of the initial situation. And thus he establishes a method.

[6]

Can one develop a *universal* method for philosophy in this fashion? To do so would reduce philosophy to a technique just as specialized as the technique itself. The purification whereby the spirit leaves aside something of the historicity of the initial situation cannot be complete. One has passed from a concrete factual situation to an abstract conceptual situation, but *the latter is still determined* and therefore is opposed to other situations. This determination limits the field of application of the method. Intellectual experience confirms that a method, when stretched too far, loses its efficacy and wears out. Failure forces the spirit back upon itself. And philosophy, which is discredited while the method is succeeding, regains vigor and confidence. Too often the dialectics of deliverance are merely tools of polemical rhetoric whereby one denigrates all intellectual or affective methods except one, the one which the polemics serve. When a method which is inordinately relied on reveals its inadequacy, the cancellation of its preeminence restores to the spirit its proper liberty.

Indeed, liberty is already present in the act by which the spirit converted the difficult situation into a method. The spirit could do so only by rising above the situation. To know is always to go from one condition, in which the spirit is a man who is entrapped in a situation because the source of the totality of which he is only a part is unfavorable to him, to another condition, in which he is divinized inasmuch as he himself becomes the source of a whole which is created of parts. Instead of being one who is integrated, he becomes the integrator. Philosophy, then, can only advance by successively breaking through the limits which any situation whatsoever imposes on it. And, consequently, philosophy must break clear of every method issuing from situations. It must always do so by an original action. If the spirit is to live, then it is necessary that methods be embodied as procedures, machines, and things. They move away from the spirit's intimacy and become fossilized in some corner of experience.

2. *There is nothing to seek or to postulate beyond what is experienced or what might be experienced*

The whole of experience, open before our eyes! To justify the conviction that by enclosing philosophy in experience one is not placing restrictions on it, we must show that the first and last truth is that knowledge can never refer to anything other than experience. Knowledge either grasps an experience and brings it to light or it suggests an experience by some allusion. Knowledge picks and chooses between experiences, distinguishing those which are solid and fertile from those which are frail and deceiving. It stays attached to a given or manifests its insufficiency. It apprehends relatively perfect experiences or, on the contrary, it evokes experiences whose value consists in what they still lack. In these and in all other cases, experience supplies whatever content there is and whatever hope is added to the content. A spirit enters into the realm of philosophy when it realizes that everything knowable is essentially given to it in its own experience. This may happen at any time or any place. The actualized and the actualizable are simply aspects or parts of an eternal actuality. Experience can always give a man the capacity to recover or to produce some experience. But no experience has to teach a man what experience is, for the very act by which he would deny experience is still experience. Experience is abstract and concrete universality. Every time sentiment brings us back to experience, its immensity seems to swamp each limited interest. A particular object has scarcely more importance for us than a shell on the seashore.

3. *Intuitive knowledge*

That knowledge cannot get away from experience is evident first of all in those cases in which knowledge is intuitively confused with the givens which it is meant to apprehend. Whatever the process—analysis, elaboration, or emanation—by which knowledge arrives at "green" or "sugar," at bewilderment or at the sentiment of inability-to-conclude-other-than-one-has-concluded, these givens, taking this term in as broad a sense as possible, can only be what they are insofar as they are seen or sensed. Whatever might be said about them has no value except in reference to their concretely experienced content. An intellectualism like that of Hamelin claims in vain that the spirit can give a complete or at least a sufficient account of itself by means of relations. It could only do so if it first ceased to be blind.

This first observation has an unlimited scope. Mediations are not only what they are by reason of an intuition, a sensed unity of identity, or an accidental conjunction to which they lead, but they display themselves as mediations only if they are suffered or endured. It is dialectically evident that mediation and immediacy are possible only by virtue of their liaison with each other. Pure immediacy would be lost in the indiscernibility of the two within the one. A mediation which is nothing but a mediation would make the mean and the extremes things which mutually exclude one another. The *cogito* cannot be either merely reasoning or merely intuition. The *cogito* is an existential passage through an itinerary of ideas among which there is no intellectual continuity except by reason of a concretely experienced continuity which surpasses the intellectual continuity. All discourse, and generally every mode of expression, is at one and the same time an experience, an allusion to another experience, and a fragment of the total experience which embraces the previous two. Even when I simply speak to myself, I turn by means of an intermediary experience from a previously discovered experience to one I seek. And these experiences are distinguished from and united to one another in experience. At each instant of my life I possess myself and I flee myself, I seek myself and I find myself.

It is likewise clear that both species of mediation involve intuition. Sometimes I pass from one concrete experience to another by means of a perception or a thought. This is what happens in purchasing something, or in the calculation which makes the purchase possible. The experience of a desire is replaced, because of some mediate thing, by an experience of satisfaction. At other times, on the contrary, an intimacy, which cannot be circumscribed but which is surely recognized, is indispensable for the passage from an object of desire to an object of satisfaction. This is what happens in invention. The very meaning of invention always supposes that between the discriminative knowledge of means and the emergence of the invented newness there is interwoven a phase of gestation within which one cannot distinguish among the antecedent givens, the results, and the parts. Mediation, then, can be *objective* or *existential*. But it can be called either one or the other only because it is always, in differing degrees, both one and the other. For example, one would suppress the activity of enumeration if he were to tear it away from its intuitive center, without which it would fall apart like a broken rosary. Likewise, one

would suppress the activity of enumeration if he were to dissolve it by depriving numbers of their distinctness from one
another.

4. *The a priori*

It evidently does not follow from the fact that philosophy
can do no more than apprehend experiences that it must therefore judge them to be equivalent. For every given there is an
attached sentiment, half retrospective, half prospective, which
grasps the given as unified or inconsistent, profound or superficial, real or illusory. Often the cohesion which we attribute to
a given seems to work against us. The perceived seems more
real to us than the imagined, but it isolates us from itself and
it can lead to our becoming depressed. We tend to think that
we can grasp only the surface appearance of the given. On the
contrary, let us consider those intellectual forms or, following
Scheler, those material values to which the name *a priori* is attached. Whether the self judges them to be transcendental or
ontological, it always expects some efficacy, either limitless or
limited, from them. This expectation prevents the self from regarding their appropriation as trivial.

Does this make the self depart from experience? By no
means. Philosophy has to start from experience in order even to
recognize the a priori. It is within experience that knowledge
eventually becomes aware of either the impetus that the
spirit receives from the a priori or the obstructions that the
spirit suffers from it. It is within experience that the spirit
authenticates its activities. Experience infects both givens and
theories. The a priori is a theory relative to certain givens. If
one believes a theory to be true, it is necessary to seek the
proof of its truth in experience. Experience must be both open
and closed; it must be bounded in certain directions, for there
are things, and unbounded in other directions, for things can
only be known if they are opposed to everything which they are
not. Thus, the a priori sometimes barricades the way and sometimes breaks it open. How could one consider the a priori without referring it to this sensed or experienced alternative? The a
priori has circumstances. It is defined or named in the context
of perspectives and operations. And these latter are the things
which give it its significance. The a priori must be studied
within experience as, for example, must be the French constitu-

tion of 1875. The constitution, like the a priori, is prior to the applications deducible from it. The a priori is an iterative occurrence, like a triangle, a qualm [*scrupule*], or a novel. Thus to know such things as triangles is to proceed from experiencing them to experiencing the scope of their applicability.

5. *Mediate knowledge*

Let us now pass from those cognitions which present themselves as intuitions to *those which grasp only signs of intuitions*. These latter do not force us to abandon experience; they only force us to elaborate it. Green is an experience. The word *green* or a symbol of green or the connection between green and its sign are other experiences. Signification is a network of operations whose complexity extends to infinity but within which one can make whatever divisions one wishes. What a word or an idea actually signifies within the spirit is merely an aspect of what it could signify for the spirit. But only experience can teach us what it can signify. For example, we know that at the completion of a sketch or in the articulation of a sign we may be either satisfied or frustrated depending on whether the signified comes to fulfill or does not come to fulfill the expectation awakened by the sign. This presence or this absence can exist only if it is concretely experienced.

What is true of the relation between the sign and the signified is true of the relation between the abstract and concrete thought. An "empty" dialectic, a sheerly mental dialectic which is only a game of the abstract intellect, is nonetheless experienced. The spirit which engenders the dialectic discovers it to the degree that it produces it. This is an impoverished experience. One distinguishes it from a "full" dialectic, a dialectic of the heart charged with qualitative or emotional matter, because the latter is a rich experience. But the first kind of dialectic does not keep us away from experience on the grounds that it is unreal, nor does the second kind carry us beyond experience on the grounds that its reality has a value superior to that of every possible experience.

6. *Value*

It must be asked whether the restriction of philosophy to experience does not lead to the suppression of the value of knowledge and of everything else. What we mean by knowledge or by reality is not only the presentation of a given. Knowledge without truth is only an illusion of knowledge, a reality without resonance beyond what is called real, a false appearance. An unrelenting exigency inspires the effort to know. It moves from objects which have less reality to those which contain more. The sentiment of the real admits of an indefinite number of modes, but all knowledge and all investigation must satisfy this sentiment. Does it not follow that experience cannot suffice for philosophy and that philosophy involves, somehow, a meta-empirical pretension?

Let us first observe that the sentiment of reality is only a special case of the sentiment of value. Reality is the value peculiar to theoretical knowledge. Theoretical knowledge presupposes a disengagement from the passion which orients us to the future. Thus knowledge achieves as reality only that which is already realized. It is impossible to restrict value to this aspect since the already realized can be found to be disappointing or useful, harmful or base.

Let us see, then, whether value, considered without restriction, can be exiled from experience. How could something be perceived or experienced in such a way that value is universally absent, or, better, simply nothing? *A value without efficacy and influence in experience would be without value.* No doubt value, like relation, does not consist exclusively of a specifiable set of terms. The law of successors [1] posits 2, but it is not exhausted in the positing of 2. This law opens up an unlimited perspective. The exchange value of a currency is merchandise and it presupposes the value of usage, which is its utility. But, ultimately, utility is of value only if it reinforces the power and generosity of the soul and inspires a search which goes on to infinity. As is true of knowledge, then, value too requires for its verification that there be both terms and something more than terms. But the soul can consider neither what it has nor what it is if there is no experience present in either value or knowledge. The finite must be given if there is to be determination; the infinite must be given if there is to be presentiment. Otherwise neither the determined and limited positivity of knowledge nor the open and limitless positivity of

---

1. This refers to the formation of each integer by adding 1 to its predecessor.—Trans.

value could be identified. Thus the artist, even when beauty delights him, still knows what he perceives and what he experiences. The colors come into existence because of the light they disturb, but the light also comes into existence because of the colors which reflect it.

It is noteworthy that the philosopher who has felt most strongly a concern with preventing the contamination and restriction of the Absolute by any appearance, F. H. Bradley, encloses his philosophy between the "whole of feeling" and "absolute experience." One can argue about the possible meaning of this latter expression, and can especially take care not to let it signify an experience absolutely other than the experience with which we are involved. Nonetheless, it is the case that even for Bradley philosophy is enclosed within experience.

7. *The allegation of transcendence*

It does not at all follow from the foregoing that one must renounce the allegation of any and all transcendence. Transcendence is a relation between the transcending and the transcended and is opposed to immanence only in being identifiable as its correlative. For one term to be transcendent to or immanent in another, it is necessary that, from two points of view, the one be exterior to the other. It was necessary for Spinoza to distinguish God from *natura naturata,* and this cannot be done without alternately threatening either the unity of the divine or the multiplicity of modes. The spirit is needed to organize and mobilize the system. It is impossible, therefore, to replace an immanence which is opposed to transcendence with an exclusive immanence. Likewise, it is impossible to retain only transcendence, since that would presuppose an absolute exteriority of the transcendent vis-à-vis the transcended. Such a supposition would prevent not only an encounter between them but even their juxtaposition. That which makes possible an opposition between immanence and transcendence can only be *the manner in which one of their terms introduces itself into the other*. Their distinction will derive whatever meaning it has from sensible, intellectual, or affective experience.

If, then, one cannot have transcendence through contact with total and infinite experience, one will have to have some transcendence as well as some immanence *within the confines* of experience. Thus we have nothing to eliminate. If the first part of this conclusion seems to exclude the thing-in-itself, all that is excluded is the pure thing-in-itself, which rules itself out as a fiction-limit[2] occurring when the exteriority of the apparent and the real is pushed to the extreme and which negates, one with the other, both nothingness and the thing. The pure thing-in-itself negates the thing by emptying it of all content, and it negates nothingness by filling it with existence. Since in some felt or thought way the thing-in-itself would be sensible or thinkable and one with experience, the thing-in-itself would be a possible and already initiated experience. Thus it would no longer be closed within itself. Even simple juxtaposition supposes the unity of one space, a space which encloses the juxtaposed in experience. The contradiction between the thing-in-itself and experience is an absolute contradiction.

But it is not the same in the case of the thought thing-in-itself, or the allegation of the thing-in-itself, or, generally, the allegation of transcendence. It is necessary to grasp, on the one hand, how some spirits have been led to such allegations and thoughts and, on the other hand, what aspect of experience allowed them to make such allegations. Between absolute skepticism and Eleaticism the domain of all dialectics is unfolded. *To expand philosophy to the dimensions of experience is not only to protect it against that which would discredit it but also to oblige oneself to discover as far as possible all its modes.* The field of experience yields, as a given, the allegation of transcendence. One may not dismiss it out of hand on the pretext that there is no transcendence. The truth of transcendence is the value of the allegation of transcendence. But this is not the occasion to begin such a study. Manifestly, the self who alleges transcendence supposes thereby his own limitation, and undoubtedly his own lowliness. Thus experience must first present the self to us so that we can recognize the situations and purposes leading the self to allege transcendence.

We simply note here that even if the thing-in-itself, as soon as it is thought by the self, casts its shadow over the whole of

2. See Introduction, p. xli. Fiction-limit designates a logical terminus which cannot correspond to any specific thing but which nevertheless is not an absurdity. It too comes to light in experience.— Trans.

experience in such a way that the self gives itself over to distress, the existential mediation of the *cogito,* here as everywhere else, opens the way to recuperation. Since the self recognizes that the transcendence from which he suffers finds expression only through the allegation that he makes about it, the idea of the thing-in-itself replaces for him the thing-in-itself. *The myth of the pure thing-in-itself dissipates in the face of the actuality of the thought thing-in-itself.* One could object that the transcendent cannot be reduced to the reality of the allegation of transcendence. But in conceiving that the other-than-self is not the idea of the other-than-self, the self merely makes an intellectual duplication, and this process is in principle indefinitely repeatable. The allegation of transcendence, then, leads the self first to activate itself in casting its glance upon an indefinitely open perspective, and then to recognize at the source of this dynamism a strictly infinite power which will free it from distress. The thing-in-itself will no longer appear to it as anything but the objectively supported but arbitrarily reified shadow of an Infinity immanent in experience itself. Experience is animated by that which tries to destroy it. To deny experience is not to suppress it but to add to it. Thus, where are all those dialectical games which direct emotional movements? They are within experience itself.

In itself, the allegation of the transcendent serves equally to open experience and to close it, and closing it simply breaks it open in another sense. This thought thing-in-itself is no more than a polemicist's argument. It indiscriminately permits one to cast discredit on metaphysical knowledge, to the advantage of that negativism called scientific positivism, and permits one to be enticed into ontological investigation. The thought thing-in-itself can just as easily permit a condemnation of the individual consciousness as it can allow a tying of individual consciousness to the absolute. In all these cases it is experience which manifests the effects of the allegation-of-transcendence. It must be so, for if one posits the transcendent apart from experience, then he would think that he was pointing to the most elevated reality that it is possible to conceive. But he would come to the frustrating conclusion that the most exalted reality is also the most impoverished reality. Experience would then be set in the inexhaustible richness of its content only in order to be destroyed. The One which rules over everything would be volatilized for the sake of the One which is devoid of everything. In place of the full positivity of experience there would be instead the nothingness of a suppressive oneness.

What can we conclude from the foregoing except that we are faced with a movement of experience,[3] which is turned against part or all of the rest of experience? One might free oneself by a desperate movement of the imagination. But such a movement is destined to collapse on itself by reason of its lack of content. Such a movement would require an effort of total negation. But its value would lie in its connection with the experience which surrounds it. To pass judgment on this movement of the imagination, one must first locate it in experience. Barrier or perspective: The barrier inspires disappointment, the perspective engenders vertigo. Even where the thought thing-in-itself putatively serves to annul experience, experience remains, for *only that which occurs can be thought to be null and nonexistent.*

8. *Nothingness*

This last observation answers every effort which tries to drive nothingness out of experience. The position of non-being, to express a paradoxical idea paradoxically, cannot lead us beyond experience. Nothingness can be whatever it may be only within experience. And, on the contrary, the limitless variety of negative judgments and sentiments is first of all given to us empirically. It is within experience that we find the gaps, slits, and obstructions which are the occasions for specifying nothingness. Without them, how could there be so many theories about it? Even if nothingness merely frees the spirit of the philosopher from fascination by the object, what experience could be more important than that? There is nothing of importance which does not have the double determination of mattering in its own right and of having some consequences. If nothingness is necessary for the circumscription of every determination, it is so in so many ways as there are categories and determinations. And if the list of these determinations cannot

3. A movement of experience is a directional thrust or a line of development considered as an ongoing operation which tends to organize experience around itself. It itself, as Le Senne stresses, is experienced.—Trans.

be exhaustive, then nothingness enriches being into infinity. Every absence is added to former presence, and this is another presence. Obscurity is seen, silence enlarges and startles consciousness, anguish stuns us, and the dead haunt us. And each time we know it. Negation and the consequences of negation do not efface experience. They multiply it, dramatize it, and render it passionate.

It is useless, therefore, to claim that one goes beyond experience when one alleges the existence of objects of which there is no possible experience. If one speaks of such objects, it is first of all because one now grasps some effects of these objects. Among these effects are the words used for such objects. Subsequently one begins to imagine and thus to perceive, think, or feel another experience whose possible occurrence one discounts or denies. If this state of affairs proves anything, it is that experience is capable of bringing newness to itself indefinitely. It does not prove that experience can escape knowledge or that knowledge goes beyond experience. The other side of the moon is the incomplete imagination of a possible perception. William Tell is one of Schiller's characters. The Sirens have been described and painted. Again, here are full absences.

9. *The other-self-than-self*

If the thing-other-than-self and nothingness do not give us the means to go beyond experience, neither will we find the means in an "other-self-than-self." The very words used to designate this hypothesis imply that every "other self," whether it be vis-à-vis the self as "yourself" or whether it serve as the "himself" of existential mediation between myself and yourself, is nevertheless simply one with the self as self. The self-insofar-as-self must be the same in every self since, when considering the self independently of every specification, one recognizes a universal value in it. Consequently, it has the power of access to any representation whatsoever. Experience of the other self is thus in principle accessible to me. If in gaining access to it I alter it, the alteration will amplify experience. But the alteration is only possible by reason of experience. How would we know that experience has been altered if we cannot compare what there is after the alteration with what there was before?

The distinction between the other's experience and my experience can only be a distinction within experience. Experience devoid of all subjective specification is what we here propose that philosophy respect and study. Almost all his life Maine de Biran was condemned by an unfortunate philosophy to be confined within an experience restricted to the psychological self. When he finally rose to the sentiment that the life of man was not necessarily an exclusively human life, it was too late for him to create the convergence of reasons and tendencies which are woven together in a conviction capable of giving happiness.

10. *The subject*

One might claim that experience presupposes a subject to receive it and accept it, that the essence of this subject is its incapability of being an object and, consequently, that the subject itself is outside of experience. Hume looked for the subject, but he did not find it because he was looking for the permanent identity of a given in which to install the person, much as one might seat a child on a chair. His search had to run aground, for a subject is not something which can be localized through discrimination.

Does it therefore follow that experience gives us nothing with which we can connect the idea and name of *subject?* How could one believe that? If nothing in experience corresponds to *subject, self, someone, such a one,* etc., how could the words ever have been formed and used? When Hume looked for Hume, he did so because he knew him. He ended up by making causality, objectively reduced to constant conjunction, the matter of a subjective belief. But a belief even more imperiously presupposes a subject, for it is much more contingent. The very act of binding, whereby the unity of a determination is constituted, presupposes an existence in which the binding takes place. When, on the contrary, discrimination separates two determinations from each other and when the process of comparing them allows one to objectify the existential unity of the comparing self in the ideal and objective unity of a relation between determinations, then the subject opposes itself to the object, now isolated by perception and intelligence, as a concretely experienced existence opposes itself to a definite term.

The only reason for such an opposition is that mediation, whose mark is found in the object, can be separated from the immediacy which is enclosed in the self's limited existence. What could a mediation be which did not receive its intellectual continuity and its distinctiveness from an existential continuity? And what could an immediacy be if exteriority were so completely eliminated that knowledge would vanish for lack of a knower and a known?

Without further concerning ourselves with the examination of the content which experience gives to the idea and term *subject,* it suffices for us to recall that if the subject were only an illusion, as all the philosophers of impersonalism affirm, an illusion nonetheless exists in experience. Even if the subject is merely an object, a skeleton, a dead thing, it is one of those dead things which it is necessary to kill. Many such dead things are hard to kill. Even if we ourselves are illusory, in the sense of being foredoomed to die, we still resist death as best we can. It remains to be asked whether this aspect of degeneration exhausts the meaning of subjectivity. This question can only be answered through an analysis of experience, within which all philosophies are situated as dialectics. Experience undergirds every answer. Even if the subject were only a nothingness, what has been said about nothingness shows that it is a positivity.

Similar dialectics apropos other notions would also lead us to respect experience. As a matter of fact, knowledge has never historically originated with a *tabula rasa.* How could it ever get beyond such a state? This metaphor is only a symbol of a universal negation. The purpose of such a negation is not to suppress everything but to prevent any one thing or set of things from assuming tyrannical primacy to the detriment of other things. This metaphor points much more to the affirmation of something than to the negation of everything. By means of this metaphor, the entire range of experience, both the realized and the possible, in its fullness as well as in its emptiness, is presented in a jumbled manner. One does not know at first whether everything is rejected or ratified. Consciousness infects both the indifference which comes from weariness with everything and the indifference which joyously expresses sympathy with everything. Over and above the details of experience, the spirit experiences the happiness of the traveler who from the top of the hill is intoxicated with liberty and infinity

when he sees spread out before him the plains and the sea
which the horizon limits without, however, impeding his imagination.

[II] EXPERIENCE AND EMPIRICISM

WE DEFEND THE POSITION that philosophy has the
whole of experience and nothing but experience for its subject
matter, though there are reasons why one might consider experience as limited from some perspective or other. But we
clearly do not intend to hold either the doctrine of empiricism
or the doctrine of extra-intellectual intuitionism. Each of these
doctrines limits the consideration of experience. The former
limits the consideration of experience to discrete, determined,
already consolidated givens, while the latter limits it to the intuition of a continuity of felt interpenetration.

The classical empiricist and the Bergsonian intuitionist
both hold to the common sentiment of the irreducibility of existence as such to essence. The empiricist satisfies this sentiment
by replacing every relation with its separated and concretized
terms. He attributes to these terms the objectivized existence
which a perception adds to the idea expressing its essence,
and then is satisfied to treat these parcels of determined
existence either as phenomena or as fragments of matter. The
memory of the perception always weighs on his spirit. The intuitionist, on the contrary, instead of descending below the relation in concrete practice, rises above it. Even when taken dy-
namically, the relation in synthetic intellectualism is never more
than a thought unity. The relation is a trajectory more than an
operation and it is conspicuous in the spirit. Bergsonism is
promptly led to what one might call the existential relation
which entails and grounds its terms in its own history. Bergsonism succeeds in avoiding the flaw of abstract intellectualism,
which consists in replacing reality with a seriously impoverished
expression of it.

Unfortunately, one is still abstracting, whether one abstracts perception or abstracts the continuity of intimate existence, from the ideas and dialectics which manifest intelligence.
The abstracting is analytic when intelligence isolates these elements, and is synthetic when it links them together. *Respect
for experience requires first of all that nothing be given pri-*

macy by postulate. Continuity and discontinuity, existence and intellectual determination, are both opposed and composed in experience. One has to start by taking experience whole and entire. Over and above both the intellectual, with its well-circumscribed and sharply etched clarity and distinctness, and the continuous and expansive existential, there is their relation. The cognitive connection is only one expression of this relation. Each element, taken alone, denies the other. Experience therefore must contain both of them. Let us suppose for the moment that the perpetual conflict between a mysticism directed toward pure existence and an intellectualism devoid of content unless it involves some determination should be resolved. Before this conflict is resolved by a value judgment which would treat one of them as an illusion to be dissolved and the other as the revelation of reality, philosophy should first consider the terms and experiences which allow them to be opposed to each other. In other words, idealism itself leads to the consideration of existence. Contingency can exist only as that which is absent. For if the intellectual relation can be shattered, as Hamelin supposes when he admits the notion of an "appeal," even if it is shattered only provisionally so that the act of liaison can be distinguished from the reason for making the liaison, this is because *for one moment the divorced terms float in the unity of an existence* which embraces them separately before merging them into a unity. On the other hand, how could philosophy, which can be expressed only if it is determinate, even be possible if experience can admit nothing but an indiscernible without dimensions, an indiscernible which could neither endure nor be expressed?

11. *The insufficiency of empiricism*

First, empiricism is insufficient because no specific philosophy is sufficient. Philosophies are no more than publications of philosophy. Universally conceived, philosophy is the ever exploring description of experience. The description of perception is not set forth in order to restrict perception to what has been described. Even if one wanted to reduce empiricism to the description of perception, one would be unfair to it, for empiricism is the result of a point of view which defines empiricism only in order to go beyond it. A doctrine is never anything other than the countenance through which a way of living and thinking, like love in a glance, tries to reveal itself. History would indeed be ill-advised if, under the inspiration of science, which can neglect the soul of man because it is a function of the impersonal, it did not look beyond objective manifestations for intimate experience. To follow science would be to throw away the grain to preserve the husk. Philosophy must revivify the doctrinal past by suffusing it with the sentiment of value. The immediate effect of this kind of revivification is that everything it touches is animated, as a child gives living actuality and spiritual efficacy to the glories of the past when he admires them. To understand empiricism, then, one must go beyond the expressions which constitute its essence or modes and rediscover in experience both those situations which called for it and that value whose eruption it mediates.

There is a risk of being deceived by empiricism, because empiricism is the result of a "detotalization." We use this term to designate a frequent operation which consists in *passing from the consideration of a whole,* in the largest sense of that word, *to a consideration of the whole now deprived of one of its parts, without ceasing to attribute to the truncated whole both the name and the properties of the original whole.* A banknote can have its corners torn off and still preserve its exchange value if the serial numbers are left intact. An abstraction can take an idea out of the system in which it was embedded and regard it as being identical to what was in the system. A battalion does not lose its military individuality because it has lost a slight part of its effectiveness. Similar cases abound everywhere. Evidently, detotalization is not a logical operation, in the sense that no logical operation is valid unless it moves from the identical to the identical. But logical thought itself is a systematic alteration of real thought; otherwise the passage from the identical to the identical would not be a movement, but rather would be immobility. It is idle for the logician to admit detotalization on condition that it suppress no essential element of the truncated whole. As the distinction between the essential and the accidental presupposes a pure invariability of essences, which is again nothing more than a limit of intellectual experience, so real thought will have successfully or unsuccessfully utilized detotalization before the logician has authorized it and will do so to a degree that he would never wittingly authorize.

The detotalization by which the empiricist has replaced experience with a certain family of experiences is not always the same. Empiricism has generally depended on modes of rationalism, for the function of empiricism consisted in circumscribing rationalism, in drawing attention back to aspects of experience which rationalism slights. Rationalism tends to make the idea a unity of connection. Empiricism reinstates the consideration of a discrete multiplicity by breaking experience down to atomic facts. Again, whereas rationalism presents the idea as a necessary norm, empiricism reintroduces the sentiment of contingence and turns away from the error of mistaking reason for usage. In opposition to those who would make the idea an objective eternity, empiricism has made clear the intrinsic unforeseeableness of the future. In opposition to those who would discredit quality [4] by calling it confusion, empiricism has reacted by calling attention to the formality of the idea and by preventing the idea from being turned into an idol. Until its conversion to intuitionism, empiricism was more negative than positive and only served liberty indirectly, by stressing contingency. But this service did more than simply break the fascination which logical necessity held for the spirit.

Is it necessary then to be an empiricist? One can only answer this value question, and all such problems are initially value problems, after studying the experience in which the dialectic of the empiricists is located. As a mere introduction to this study, we should notice that the solution of this debate presupposes a distinction between men with restricted vision and men with broad vision. The former are tied at every point to some determination which occupies the center of their attention. They go from one determination to another, like a calculator whose intellectual movements resemble a captive looking for the way out of a labyrinth. Thus certain logicians, who have consciously or otherwise crystallized certain principles and fixed certain concepts immutably, try to solve problems which result from the relative contradictoriness of the accepted conditions. They are like checker players who obey the rules of the game. Similarly, the physicist is one who looks for solutions to problems which arise from the relative contradictoriness of his perceptions.

On the contrary, flexible and large spirits find their happiness in the ease with which they disengage themselves from

4. Le Senne is here referring to Bergson's meaning of quality.— Trans.

all situations. They become like acrobats who reach such a point of plasticity that any bodily movement whatsoever seems to be possible for them. There are no more obstacles; everything is a means for them. And the means are grounded in the continuity of the action in which they are caught up. By virtuosity, one juggles whatever determinate rigidity persists. Virtuosity is achieved by a plastification of experience. Rigidity appears merely as the wake of objects which are in the process of being liquefied.

Since empiricism has suggested itself both to men of restricted vision and to men of large vision, it has functioned in opposing ways. In brute form it has drawn nearer to perception and has become materialistic. In a supple and dynamic form it has made itself intimate. From perceptive empiricism to eidetic empiricism, from formal eideticism to material eideticism, from material eideticism to continuist intuitionism— such is the nuanced spectrum of empiricism's possibilities. But this very expansion allows one to go beyond whatever partialness there is in each of these forms. This very expansion permits one to decide in favor of a description of experience which will study all of them as matters of preference and intimate methods, methods and matters which are sometimes passionate and often delicate.

Thus it is especially expedient to turn *away from the partialness of a scientific empiricism,* which subordinates respect for experience to its own demands for schematization and measurement. Such a partialness ends up by restricting experience to that which can be found in laboratories by means of some apparatus and which is expressed in a mathematical formalism. This is not the place to point out the value and the insufficiency of these transformations. One need only indicate the partialness both of the adopted attitude and of the favored experiences to prevent the restricting of experience to this interpretation and to this utilization of only certain experiences. Comparatively few things happen in a laboratory or over a table at the French Academy. The aurora borealis, the discovery of America, Waterloo, the devotedness of a savior, and the assault on Mount Everest are facts, and they take place somewhere else. Notably, if one tries to understand man only through objective psychology, one is condemned to exclude thought, love, hate, and everything else which gives each man a sense of life. What psychological reality a manual of psychology contains is miserably slight when compared to what is contained in the fables of La Fontaine. To want to limit oneself to scientific experience is to end up, in the name of experience, eliminating from knowledge almost all experience. Philosophy, then, must be the regular protest of the spirit against positivism.

We acknowledge, then, that the spirit cannot "go beyond experience." When one uses the expression "to go beyond experience" one usually means that the spirit abandons some experience which it is appropriate and interesting to consider for some special purpose and moves on to some other experience when it need not do so. The scientist accuses the metaphysician of deserting experience, because science has perception for its domain. When he himself moves from perception to the intellectual, modified imagination of a hypothesis, he claims that he too is going beyond experience. But in reality, like the metaphysician, he simply goes from a sensible experience to an intellectual one. Every man whom the philosopher does not protect from specialization defines for himself a reality which is located at the point of the convergence of needs arising from his impotency and of actions manifesting his power. For the athlete, the game is reality because he wants to play and knows how to play. For the psychiatrist, whose task is to heal men with defects in perceptual and social life, and who sometimes succeeds, perceptual and motor experience, which assures only a minimum of communication between men, contains the totality of the real. Thus Freud treats religion and art as vain sublimations. And so forth. At the same time, each man has his own experience. But no one, not even a specialist, can legitimately reduce experience to *his* experience, for he can oppose what is his to what is not his only within experience.

One must, then, begin with *experience without specification*. When one does specify, he must keep in mind that he has done so. In essence, experience is neither external nor internal, neither affective nor intellectual, neither determinate nor vague, neither static nor dynamic. It can be one of these only if it is also otherwise, only if it is indeed the opposite. Every epithet which is imposed on it both limits and manifests the fecundity of experience. But no designation can embrace its fullness. This is true also of scientific experience. Scientific experience is highly artificial in the conditions which it presupposes and in the goal which it proposes. Experience reduced to scientific experience is harshly mutilated experience. And this mutilation would be even more serious if, after having been undertaken for professional reasons, it were engaged in at the most personal level. Humanity, and it could die from this, would ultimately lose all the aptitudes which such a selective approach would discredit. One might as well claim that experience is exclusively ordained to bring about the science of heraldry, or begging at a race track. Poetry, the system of Spinoza, the dialectic of the ontological argument, a sunset, anger, the life of St. John of the Cross, and taking a stroll are just as indisputably experiences as is a measurement by a cathetometer.

[III] EXPERIENCE AND INTUITIONISM

IN GOING BEYOND EMPIRICISM, which is simply one event and one process within experience, experience also surpasses the boundaries of Bergsonian intuitionism. But surpassing requires a prior integrating. It is therefore necessary not only to receive Bergsonian philosophy kindly but to admire it. Without Bergsonian philosophy neither the recent efforts to bring into consideration the totality of experience nor the phenomenological examination of *Erlebnisse* (experience), nor Scheler's theory of emotional intentionality, nor Heidegger's existential analysis, would have been possible. If philosophy's perennial vocation is to lead the spirit away from enslavement to perceived or conceptual determinations and back to its own unity and infinity, then Bergsonism has indeed been faithful. Particularly at a time when the works of science have reinforced the pressure of the object upon the spirit, Bergsonism has contributed an eminent force to prevent consciousness either from constricting itself in determinations which are consolidated into structures or from dissipating itself among determinations scattered across space or time. In showing the singularity of every intuition, it has opened up innumerable perspectives for describing experience.

12. *The insufficiency of intuitionism*

Nonetheless the following is true:

(1) Bergson himself has been able to use only some of the possibilities that he offered. In his work, intuition often almost

amounts to an idea. He considers intuition in its constant common characteristics as the knowledge of dynamic continuity. This intuitionism is unique more in principle than it is in fact. *It is more concerned with recommending intuition than with multiplying intuitions.* Using texts which underscore the tension in his thought, one can obviously spread out a fanlike continuous series from the more contemplative than active cognition of the *Essay* [5] to the divine irruption of the third chapter of *Morality and Religion*.[6] But this is because continuity is always given preeminence over discontinuity. Between the sadness of lost continuity and the joy of rediscovered continuity, one can recognize and follow steps, movements, and modes of research which are always difficult but which permit the passage from discontinuity to continuity. The movement from exteriority to interiority is almost reduced to its terms, just as in *Morality and Religion* the opposition between "duty" and "aspiration" makes it desirable to study all those experiences in which they either are opposed or flow together.

The movement by which Bergson sought to cancel whatever negativity there is in the isolated or the separated is so strong that he returns in one stroke to communion with duration. In reading him, it rather often seems that one need simply break away from analytic thought, as one might remove clothes from a body, for this movement to show itself to us in its naked purity. This position presupposes that we receive everything in intuitive knowledge by illumination. It is as if the intellectual and moral efforts by which we address ourselves to the content of the intuition contribute nothing to it. All study of the intellectual or existential mediations which reunite an intuition received prior to the spirit's fall with the superior intuition pointed out by Bergsonian philosophy is practically eliminated. Too often intellectualism leaps from the minimum content of a concept to its maximum, jumping from the poorest to the richest. Simply by substituting the dynamic unity of a radiating infinity for that static unity of perfect order which is the ideal of objectivism, intuitionism cannot re-

5. Le Senne is referring to Bergson's *Essai sur les données immédiates de la conscience* (Paris: Alcan, 1889).—Trans.

6. This refers to Bergson's *Les Deux Sources de la morale et de la religion* (1932), English translation by R. Ashley Audra and Cloudesley Brereton, with W. Horsfall Carter, *The Two Sources of Morality and Religion* (New York: Holt, 1935).—Trans.

lease us from the duty to study and describe the details of events and modes of participation which constitute the goals of our investigation.

(2) *There must therefore be no partiality shown to the immediate.* Every philosophy is born from the womb of succession and is oriented to the eternity which animates it. The circumstances of a philosophy's birth hardly explain its originality and value, but these circumstances do limit it by the restrictions which they impose. Consequently, philosophy is always made of an appropriate attitude toward polemic and a vision of salvation. In reaction to the coarse realism propounded by Taine and Spencer, the essence of which is to treat determinations as things, Bergson victoriously struck out in the direction of indeterminateness in order to reveal the primary positivity of existence. But in order to refuse to grant that determination is an absolute reality, one has to reduce it to the status of a mediation. And if this is done, then the immediate must be given the metaphysically primary position from which determination has been dispossessed.

Giving the immediate this primary position accorded well-deserved recognition to a misconstrued aspect of experience. Intellectual analysis has too often served to depreciate quality and consciousness by discrediting them as confusions. The objective and abstract interiority of a conceptual relation is made to appear as something other than the special, localized expression of the spirit's existential interiority to all givens. Intellectualism has too often confused the ideal of intelligibility with the poor possessions of human intelligence and has forgotten that our truths necessarily express our limitations even while they manifest infinite thought. Finally, objectivism has too often obliterated the self from some of the terms which on occasion impede and on occasion facilitate its union with the rest of experience: for example, matter, ideas, or the thought-thing-in-itself. But it does not follow from the foregoing that respect for whatever positivity is eventually found in indeterminateness or, if one prefers, in superdetermination *must entail the misapprehension of determination.*

There are three important reasons why this need not happen. First, determinations, whether bound together or scattered, *present themselves everywhere within experience.* From wherever one starts, either from consolidation or from pulverization, determinations are present and are more or less anticipated. Consciousness is always both discrete and continuous; immediacy presupposes the very mediation it cancels. The *cogito* is articulated in a chain of reasoning which must bathe in existence lest the chain be shattered. To exist is to feel oneself while thinking; it is not to think oneself while feeling. It would be paradoxical if from Plato, or before, down to Bergsonism, philosophy had applied its best efforts to all the determined aspects of experience, and then all of a sudden all determinations have to be considered as mere waste. We both live to think and think to live. And human diversity itself shows that even if the source in which we participate has to be unitary, its infinity nevertheless requires that the modes by which this participation takes place are always new. Intellectual love of God consists in finding in this third kind of knowledge the infinite singularity of the Idea at the root of every idea. The existential love of God consists in uniting oneself to the super-abundance of the creative Infinity by means of the thrust of generosity. Each love derives its value from what the self allows it to do and its insufficiency from what the self restricts it from doing. In such love definite determination and limited existence are surpassed. But they have been of service along the way.

If determination is taken in any way other than as a terminus—a terminus which is accessible but not exhaustively so—then determination and indeterminateness are not only juxtaposed but united. *Howsoever we underestimate, depreciate, or deny determination, we do so from aspects of experience which are tied up with it.* To underline the changing character of the givens of experience so as to prevent their assimilation into one another, Bergson has been forced to give a preeminent status to time. Within time the originality of each instant cancels the other instants. As a consequence, Bergson has presented the continuity without parts in which all determinations are grounded as a becoming. How would this dynamic specification of the undetermined, which of itself is unqualifiable, come to be made if intelligence had not first distinguished the terms and then oriented the relation between space and time toward the primacy of time? In Bergsonism the intellectualist can always and everywhere rediscover intellectual dialectics within emotional movements. Is the union of determination and intensive continuity not verified within experience itself? In fact, Bergsonism would dissolve under the impact of those critics who have denounced the unconsciousness of intuition unless the indeterminateness of intuition's fluid matter receives at each instant reflections mixed with the shadow of determination. From the standpoint of knowledge, the absolutely undetermined would be indistinguishable from nothingness.

Finally, *in pushing Bergsonism to pure intuition, one would give it a value foreign to it,* just as if one pushed objectivism to the absolute solidity of necessity. The value of what is judged is in what is felt. Without feeling, thought would be a fantasy. And the value of what is felt is in what is judged. Otherwise the feeling would be a dream. Every man must *concretely experience* either the contradiction or the convergence of representations coming from the judgment. Otherwise truth would be a closed garden which he could not enter. Every man must *judge* his sentiments, for they can be either illusory, like a betrayed confidence, or true, like a sincere and shared love. The Cartesian intuition guarantees certitude because it makes identical, in an atomized trinity, the self reduced to its center, a simple nature, and their undivided connection. Bergsonian intuition promises living beatitude in the intermingling of a broad, continuous, and supple self with the creative duration. But then there can no longer be knowledge of the terms *self* and *duration.* In reality, the breathing of the spirit is constituted by a movement which is at once disjunctive and conjunctive. Within this movement there is both intellectual mediation, which through a thought oneness permits the passage from one phase of existence to another, and existential mediation, which through a spiritual oneness permits the passage from one determination to another. Therefore if there are such things as erroneous perceptions and concepts, then value must be beyond determination. And if there are such things as illusory sentiments, then value must be beyond intuition. Existential intuition, like intellectual intuition, would exclude even the possibility of error if it were perfect. In such a case, one would never go beyond intuition. No one more completely evades the opposition between the psychological and the metaphysical than the man who destroys truth and value by making all representations of them mere modifications of our particular spirit, unless it is he who so forgets the limits caused by the human subject that he treats his cognitions as pure metaphysical revelations. Determination renders value intelligible; intuition renders it lovable. But both determination and intuition depend on that which gives them their worth. Therefore only value can be that which is absolute.

(3) Though Bergsonism rises to the very perfection of intuition, *it has not escaped the temptation confronting every philosophy. Every philosophy, if one can speak thus, is tempted to replace the earth with the heavens.* No philosophy would be attractive if, in the midst of the difficulties of experience, it did not offer both a presentiment of and a method for attaining salvation. Likewise, philosophy imperceptibly passes from the attitude of knowing or reflection, which is scarcely passionate, to the attitude of morality or prospection, which is exhortative. And then if the philosophy is intellectualist it takes on the attitude of theology. On the other hand, if the philosophy is intuitive it takes on the attitude of mysticism. Consequently, the descriptions made within a particular philosophy are progressively limited to those dealing with the most exquisite experiences. Everything in our experience which would belie the eudaemonism of consciousness is washed away. A transfiguration, comparable to an artistic transfiguration, and one which, like art, risks being merely an aesthetic transfiguration, proposes to man an experience which is putatively more than human. Thus objectivism attains its perfection in a system in which incoherences have been eliminated. And intuitionism attains its perfection in imagining a duration which overwhelms us without ever being ruptured by crises or failures. When either of these positions is carried to its limit, the self becomes one with the infinite. Objectivism conceives this unity statically, whereas intuitionism makes dynamism be concretely experienced.

If the description of experience is to help make fruitful and to magnify certain favorable movements of life, it has to acknowledge life. Even if the philosophical life, like the religious life, is oriented to an Ascension which gravity can do no more than moderate, it does not follow that either philosophy or religion comes before life. What would be the difference between rapture and annihilation if all connection with experience is broken? A beatitude which would definitively take away a man's sympathy for the torments of those he leaves behind would be the triumph of egotism. Likewise, a self cannot break all the bonds uniting him to others without losing all its own content. Not only can this ultimate and

fictitious terminus not be attained, but the philosopher himself has no way to make his philosophy influential unless he
avoids alienating himself from the experience with which
others are familiar. When a dialectic is unable to embrace
affectivity, it shows itself to be merely a soulless virtuoso
performance. A rapture which is too elevated is no longer
a rapture. Therefore, without disavowing the adoration due
to value, whose every description and proposed instantiation
is justifiable, description is not exempted from examining the
inquiries, struggles, and operations which simultaneously both
prepare for and retard redemption. No moral or affective preoccupation can be allowed to intervene antecedently in such
a way that it would cast a cloak of uniformity over experience.

(4) When one goes back to the most turbulent parts of
experience, he comes to *the consideration of the particular
self*. In philosophy, the particular self has been treated like
the child of poor and disreputable parents. The objectivists
incessantly hold that it is irrelevant to the object. The ag-
nostics are forced to by-pass and discredit it. And the
empiricists and skeptics do not bother to hunt for it except
to accord both it and philosophy the same scorn.

The slighting of the particular self is not without its price.
First, this slighting exposes metaphysics to an ignorance of
the ever surpassed but just as ceaselessly rediscovered limitations which the self always carries with it in its knowing, its
action, and its free imagination. In other words, not only
does one leave the study of our life to an anthropology for
which man is merely an animal, or, rather, merely a thing,
but even more one forgets to consider the connections between man and man. Or else, and this amounts to the same
thing, one substitutes for these connections the impersonal
objectivity of a society conceived on the model of nature. At
one extreme, there is the stance of the scientist, the viewer
of an independent spectacle, who regards himself as the one
set opposite to things. At the other extreme, there is the
stance of the mystic, who regards himself as the one set opposite to God and who allows God to be substituted in him
for himself. Between these extremes there are the mobile
connections of persons who would not let themselves be reduced to being merely the one set opposite to nature by becoming purely theoretical objects for one another. The progress
of philosophy is not a unilateral development in one direction;

it is an expansion scarred and renewed by failures. The consideration of neglected aspects of experience poses problems. And the examination and solution of these problems affects the results of previous philosophy. The study of the modes of communication and the influence of communion among men must become one of the principal tasks of description.

(5) The explicit consideration of the particular self, which Bergsonian philosophy regards as merely an "effluent" of duration that is sometimes distinguished within duration by a fragile structure, leads back to *esteem for the concept and esteem for the will,* which is the self acting on the basis of the concept. Conceptual determination, as compared to undivided intuition, is something negative. Thus the will can be nothing but a negation of a negation. But such a position brings disrepute either to deduction, which is the determination of one concept by others, or to dialectic, which is sometimes the gestation of a concept and sometimes a movement channeled or guided by concepts. It is essential, of course, to note that duration is a totality with respect to what it can yield. But it is no less essential to recognize the operations which are at work in continuous experience. Thought has not only its forms, objects, and states, but also its movements, and the philosopher is interested in describing them. Even when consciousness proceeds by means of neat categories, it surpasses the categories like so many animated sketches which can equally well be suggested to intelligence by description and to sensibility by intuition.

This is so because the negative function of the will is inseparable from its positive function. Pure religion is abandon, non-willing, infinite docility of the heart. But experience spills over and complicates everything which is proposed as being pure. Even the ideal of quietism can only be defined in opposition to those more severe modes of religious life, such as Jansenism or pietism, which presuppose the intervention of the will. Can the will be nothing but an inhibiting element? To prevent presupposes some power of doing. Censure and inhibition present themselves in experience only in relation to a creation and construction in which the will intervenes with its power of mediation and stimulation. We would indeed be deceived if grace were given only to those who do nothing to obtain it and without anyone doing anything on their behalf. But merit and generosity do have a meaning.

These observations are not repugnant to the spirit of Bergsonism. What is true of all philosophies holds for Bergsonism too. To be faithful to a philosophy, one must go beyond it. *No thought can escape the necessity that the act by which it posits a totality of being or of knowledge is itself a part of that totality.* It was inevitable that, in proposing that the whole of experience is intuition, one would exclude the analysis of the content offered to intuition. But this analysis is itself an experience, and the results of analysis are likewise experiences. But to make such remarks is to be Bergsonian rather than to expand the thrust of Bergsonism beyond the limits imposed on it by the circumstances surrounding its formation. Descartes had helped to liberate the intellectual, discrete consciousness by purifying thought of every kind of tropism which a confused biology had mixed in it. Against this kind of partialness Bergson has followed the opposite process and thus has kept in full view the sentiment that consciousness is also an emotional unity. Experience is sufficiently broad to provide a place for and to encompass the value of both of these dialectics. Why should man have to choose between his intelligence and his heart?

[IV] PHILOSOPHY IS THE DESCRIPTION OF CONSCIOUSNESS

13. *The dynamic range of descriptions*

DEFINING PHILOSOPHY AS THE *description of experience* is adequate only if it is clearly understood that one must refuse to bestow the title of philosophy on any epithets which limit the scope of description by specifying it or on any meanings which restrict description. We do not, therefore, understand *description* in the sense given it by Josiah Royce. Royce opposes it to *appreciation.* For him, the proper expression of description is science. By virtue of the identities of description which it permits, science assures men of the means of encountering each other in objectivity. There is no reason to reproach Royce for this definition of description, because he has avoided the reduction of philosophy to scientific positivism, shown its inadequacy from many angles, and supplied the notion of appreciation which leads to the intimate and the personal.

But this definition calls for two observations.

(1) The very act of describing and the modes of description extend beyond the case in which description projects, as on a screen, both an order of perceptions and an order of intellectual signs, in order to check them and to show that they correspond term for term. This schematization, which simultaneously intellectualizes matter and materializes intelligence, is the result of an operation. But the act which has produced the schematization is neglected in favor of the formal identity between what is described and what describes. The chemist wants to get a correspondence between the serialized list of simple bodies and the patterns of bodies which he gets from perceptual experience. He is concerned neither with the mental labor which propels him, nor with the postulates implied by these objects, nor with the interpretation to which these bodies are susceptible. The empiricist makes the intellectual scheme the copy of the perceptual order; the rationalist makes the scheme the model of the perceived. The opposition between the empiricist and the intellectualist in no way changes the postulate which permits the correspondence by positing the formal identity of the described, i.e., perception, and of the describing, i.e., the theory.

Philosophy cannot confine itself to this result and this type of description, for there are other results and types, and, further, the descriptive operation is no less interesting to analyze than its results are to enumerate. Philosophy must accommodate every mode of description, beginning with those of art as well as those of science. And it must bring these modes together. In effect, whether one wishes it or not, every description is partial with reference to other possible modes because of the manner in which a description modifies and orients the described. Therefore, in order to respect the diversity of experience, it is necessary to broaden the scope of the modes of description instead of fixing on one of them, even if that one were the most "useful."

Like every connection, description oscillates between the interiority and the exteriority of its terms in order to find both the described and what describes it, what one would call the "describing" as one speaks of the defining. The more the distinction between the described and the describing is effaced, the more they approach pure identification and the more description deserves to be called a copy. On the other hand, at the moment when the heterogeneity of the describing and the described is at the point of making them practically strangers to each other, the describing is no more than an index which orients one to the described. Between these extremes, every description is to some extent *a sketch* and to some extent *an allusion*. Every sign, from diverse points of view, is both signaling and signal.

Let us consider the first case for a moment. The thrust toward absolute interiority can almost be achieved when the described and the describing pass through formal identity and approach a real identity which would no longer allow for even an arithmetic duality. To the degree to which the principle of indiscernibles is very near to the truth, the resemblance between the two terms is a mere repetition, either a periodicity of place or a propagation. The only thing separating resemblance from the fusion of terms, or one-to-one correspondence from identity, is an evanescent obstacle at the instant of its evanescence. The connection of the described to its double, the reproducing consciousness, ends by being confused with materiality.

In the second case, in which the description does not duplicate the given as a map duplicates a town or a portrait duplicates the subject, the description does little more than simply designate what it describes. A wink of the eye or a word from the heart does not at all resemble what it indicates. Between such "descriptions" and the given to which they refer there is no connection but that of an identity of expression. Both of these descriptions manifest one and the same sentiment, but when they are understood it is only *because a definite given is designated by each of them without ambiguity.* One could say that they mediate an intuition. But to avoid the speculative connotations of this term we will say that they mediate a *concrete experience.* This latter term has the advantage of being appropriate for a perception whose components are explicitly distinguished, as when a photographer numbers and shows proofs, and for an experiment, as when one tests a piece of steel, a bridge or a machine, and also for the most intimate of spiritual movements, as when one reserves the term *concrete experiences* for those events which most vehemently affect us. *Concrete experience* has the twofold advantage of sometimes uniting the encounters and what is encountered so intimately that it becomes impossible to distinguish them, while on other occasions this term allows one to distinguish between them because it can have both an objective and a subjective sense. Finally, *concrete experience* can be used appropriately both for an intellectual operation and for an emotional movement. One can concretely experience an argumentation as well as a fear.

Thus, by making the idea of description flexible, we go considerably beyond the use which Royce made of it. In general, if one wants to make philosophy mobile in order to permit it to express the endless diversity of mental operations, *one should give every notion its fullest scope.* Every concept is the mobile relation of a unity and a multiplicity. Its *significance* is more supple than it itself is. By stressing the concept's unity, one tends to constrict it. One could then speak of "striking" a concept as one "strikes a coin." By emphasizing its indefinitely rich multiplicity, one finds the way toward an infinite perspective. In this latter case, the concept is opened up. Every mental process, depending on the senses in which it is taken, either ends up in *impasses* or discovers *real passageways*. At one extreme, the conception attaches to a thing, a solid identity, a token which can be passed from hand to hand. This happens, for example, when a man becomes a signature, a birth certificate, an identification card. At the other extreme, the conception becomes a specification of the infinite. Royce's sense of description is at the lower pole, at the minimum level of philosophical description, at the point where philosophical description becomes scientific description.

(2) Not only does Royce's definition petrify description but it also inappropriately excludes description from everything which he attributes to appreciation. Every description, in the universal sense we give it, is both *a knowledge* and *something which involves a preference.* By *preference* we understand the twofold act which consists, on the one hand, of eliminating or expelling what one does not prefer and in returning the non-preferred to the realm of possibility or even to the realms of oblivion and desuetude, and, on the other, of *accentuating*, manifesting, imposing, copying that which one prefers.

Unquestionably, the identity of the description and the described, as we have now brought back into view, is the ideal of theoretic knowledge. It is only a limit, or, better, an aspect, of the relation between them. Inversely, preference is to a greater or lesser extent conditioned and thus limited by knowledge. These very observations simply remind us of the obligation not to betray the lived experience of relations by replacing them with pure notions incapable of being encountered in their pure state. These observations establish that *every description puts us at the crossroads of a given and a vector of value.*

One can indeed consider these two elements apart from each other. Such a consideration will initially find its objectivity in those cases in which the given presses against the vector, eventually reaching the point of subordinating the vector to itself. It will specify the vector and bridle the thrust to which the vector points. This is the case in speculative and theoretic knowledge. We shall call those descriptions which manifest this kind of knowledge *statements-of-fact.* On the contrary, when the thrust of value subordinates every given to itself, as happens when the consciousness becomes normative and passionate, we speak of *evaluations or appreciations.* To evaluate or to appreciate is to begin to pass from an object to its value by means of a presentiment which strives to press beyond determinations. But it does not follow from this distinction that scientific research does not involve some intention. Nor does it follow that heroism and love either should be or are indifferent to the conditions of their triumph.

Description is equivalent to act-of-consciousness. Since description essentially has to link what it describes to what it uses to describe, and since this relation tends to either identity or duality, and since this relation presupposes either the described as prior to the describing (as a copy or a reference) or the describing as prior to the described (as a scale model or a project), the idea of description is equivalent to the idea of *act-of-consciousness,* provided that one leaves open the question whether these acts-of-consciousness are or are not foreign to one another. The essence of an act-of-consciousness is not only to oppose one intellectual term to another, for example, the concepts involved in a judgment, but generally to oppose one given to another. It is an act of consciousness which posits 4 as twice 2. But it is also an act of consciousness which symbolizes sadness with a funeral march.

We can therefore call description the *description-of-consciousness*. This usage has the advantage of avoiding the reduction of description to a theoretic description in which consciousness simply duplicates the given. If a complete and definitive classification of modes of consciousness were possible, then one would have transcendental philosophy. But the openness of experience precludes the possibility of such an achievement. Philosophy can do no more than begin to pursue its task. It will distinguish the various endeavors of consciousness and then define them as types of description without ever claiming to have finished the enumeration.

The description of consciousness is encountered everywhere. The description of consciousness is encountered in the relation between addition or integration and the givens to which the relation is applied, in the correspondence between the values of a function and the points of a curve, in the development of the Roman Empire and its history, in the dancers and washerwomen of Paris and the paintings of Degas, in Phaedra and Eugénie Grandet, in Adam or the man-who-is-only-man and Jesus or God-in-man, in the music of Haydn expressing in one of his "seasons" the languor of the Midi in summer, or in that of Handel suggesting the disarray of the peoples who lack the Messiah. Such are the descriptions which one has to study carefully to see why and how they orient and alter the given. The descriptions keep us within experience because the description and the described and the environs of their relation together constitute a whole. This whole or more-than-whole is experience itself.

Philosophy is an uncivilized child. It is impatient with any restriction. Only if the description-of-consciousness is free from limitations can we be sure that no operations affecting experience will remain unknown. War, will, the novel, assigning a given to the past, searching for a cause, identification and differentiation, the creation of contradictories and their construction, and so on indefinitely are just so many operations of consciousness. They are all both passive and active, but unequally so. When idealism gives the spirit the hope of comprehending everything because everything expresses spirit,

spirit must deny itself to itself by going beyond what it has, i.e., the partialness of abstract doctrine. It must undertake to describe all the *occurrences* which the operations of experience uncover before acting to impede, modify, or renovate them. This task opens up a limitless future for philosophy.

Intentionality and description. Must one set up between description and its object or between the sign and its signification a relationship of idea to content such that the idea is a relative void which the content fills? Such a requirement is inspired by one of the most profound tendencies of contemporary thought. The theory of *meaning* in Royce, the phenomenological notion of "intentionality," Hamelin's progression from the void of the thesis to the fullness of the synthesis, and the notion of *Aufgabe* (task) which has been given importance in psychology by the school of Würzburg all show the effort to maintain a meaning for truth without forgetting the influences of time, action, and investigation. We can say this without misrepresenting either the differences or the similarities among these theories. When rationalism is forced to recognize that the identity of the real and the rational must be constructed with contingency, that is, with obstacle and stalemate, time is presented as a maturation which gives rise to what it accomplishes by purifying itself of all irrationality. The rationalist claims that though reason does not exist it is very near to existing; we are on the threshold. One must admit that this description, like objectivism itself, fits well with certain particularly important aspects of experience. Every description is justified all the more strongly the more frequently it is suggested by experience. And we have recognized, contrary to Bergsonian preferences, the obligation to appreciate intellectualist descriptions.

It is no less true that one must always avoid starting off by limiting experience. The philosopher who uses the postulate of intentionality uses a presupposition which reveals a latent finalism when it is cast in theoretic form. Generally every effort directed toward knowing implies that either being, truth, reason, order, affirmation, or life and creation are primary with reference to their opposites. Such an effort further implies that one understands this anteriority as originally, eternally, and finally primary. Such a postulate discredits in advance all negative judgments by attributing to positivity, on the basis of this principle, a value which has no contrary. The only astonishing thing about this position is that it has not triumphed without combat. But let us set aside this presupposition, however worthy of esteem it may be. He who wants to accept from the outset experience as it is given to him, randomly, or at least to approach it as best he can by moving away from the lower limit of "purely theoretic" knowledge, must necessarily allow experience its Protean indeterminateness. What is there which assures us that value is reducible to positivity and that it will assuredly triumph? Could experience not augment irrationality and war instead of developing order and love? Experience might be a thrust en route to exhausting itself, an organization en route to decomposing. This is what metaphysicians who follow the principle of the degradation of energy have claimed.

There must be some unity to experience. But there is an inexhaustible variety of paralogisms which come about by sliding from the undetermined idea of unity to one of its senses. This is especially so if one takes the sense of identity, which is the unity of sames, or the sense of harmony, which is the unity of a whole. The unity which is indispensable to experience and to description is found just as surely in the conflict of two relative contradictories, which men can make into instruments for war, as in the solidarity of the parts of an ensemble, whether this be in the functional unity of a world or the union of souls in love. Nothing prevents experience from being infernal. One should presuppose neither the order of an ensemble nor even the order of some specifiable part, nor should one presuppose a movement toward an end as if the movement were animated, traversed, and directed by at least a nonvoluntary intentionality. Description must impartially preserve both directed or merely oriented experiences and fragmented experiences. It must embrace inquiries, daydreams, or idle moments as well as disorders and agonies, whether they are independent of the psychological life or whether they constitute that life.

Dialectics and processes. We see that every description is an act of consciousness. Further, every act of consciousness is a bifurcation provided one always understands this to mean both a duality and a placing of the elements in relation to each other. Let us avoid, after what has been said, the exclusive consideration of the case in which description neglects, to the advantage of a duplication of terms taken as objectively connected, the act which has discerned and united these terms. Nevertheless it is true that, from another viewpoint, the bisecting itself, considered as experience, readily allows for modes and degrees. One could rank them between two poles. One pole would be the purely intellectual as it is in a mathematical relation or as it would be if the mathematician never mixed any of his sensibility into the operation. The other pole would be purely emotional, for example, in the restlessness in the face of the unknown, if this restlessness could exist without any reflection.

The bifurcation tends toward the intellectual pole both when it opposes one term to another, e.g., a face to its portrait or one collection of terms to another, as a museum to its catalogue, and when it unites one operation to another, e.g., an algorithmic development to a deduction or an account to a historical episode. On the other hand, the bifurcation tends toward the intuitive pole when it opposes one felt concrete experience to another, e.g., in music when a melodic phrase is connected to either a tranquil or an agitated current of sensibility. *The impossibility of pushing to the ultimate limit either of these two meanings of bifurcation maintains bifurcation as a relationship between intuitive, spontaneous, and affective consciousness and intellectual, reflective, analytic consciousness.* This discrimination of the thought and the perceived from the concrete experience of the felt makes up the diversity of experience.

By abstraction, therefore, one can distinguish two kinds of *operations*, depending on whether experience shows more localized and defined demarcations or whether it points to evolutions, each of which practically vanishes in effective continuity. We call the first kind of operation *dialectics*. Of course, this word must be freed from the derogatory connotations it has in [Kant's] Transcendental Dialectic. A dialectic can be illusory if its fecundity is practically nil, or it can snatch up whole regions of experience like a tornado. The same dialectic can be, depending on the situation, personal or general, of considerable worth or misplaced. The value of a dialectic is something other than its trajectory. It can only be evaluated once it has been recognized. In its explicit form it may appear superficial and empty, the discourse of a theoretician or virtuoso acrobatics. In its implicit form it is energized by a matter which will add its own mass to the activity.

On the other hand, when the richness of the dynamic content seems to submerge the dialectic which sketches its movement, we speak of *emotional process*. This process is not reducible to a dialectic. In this case one simply makes use of a dialectic to *suggest* the concrete movement, which can be investigated provided that one has concretely experienced it in such a way as to recognize it. This is what happens in the case of fear or hope. Since dialectics and processes infect each other in experience, what we have just said is simply the application of the previous observation concerning the solidarity between reflexive and affective consciousness.

Free dialectic. By placing oneself at the point of confluence of dialectic and process in such a way that one can proceed in either of the two opposed senses, one situates himself at an equal distance from both Hamelian dialectic and Bergsonian intuition. If the latter has the advantage of avoiding the dangers of analysis, it correlatively has the disadvantage of discrediting every dialectical description of the intimate and concrete movements of experience. One no longer knows the meaning of tension and activity in all those experiences whose parts or moments are indiscernible. In binding together dialectics and processes by means of the solidarity of the intellectual and the intuitive consciousness, one not only makes description easier for oneself and more diverse in itself, but also avoids all partiality whether for or against intelligence.

But whether one makes a dialectic an allusive expression of an affective process or whether one discovers there the very operation of experience, the dialectic will still be no more than one movement among other possible ones. The inventory of dialectics has as special cases canonized dialectics such as the stylized and systematized dialectics of a table of categories. But other dialectics will elude such systematizations. Regulated dialectics are only one form of dialectical liberty. Hamelin does not describe the life of consciousness with its disputes and wanderings. Rather, he describes an extract of dynamic models, welded firmly at the base and expanding at the top, which inspires the rational operations of the spirit. The table of categories is a ceremonial of thought, an intellectual procession, an ethic of research substituting itself for the spirit. One could say that Hamelin descends beneath consciousness inasmuch as he only recognizes the elementary principles of consciousness. On the other hand, the purity of a continuous duration, already participating in the divine tension which it merely mitigates, elevates us to Bergsonism, to a status which is beyond our own existence. In either case, though in relatively opposed forms, value triumphs without anyone having fought for it.

Critical conclusion. A noology of dialectics and intimate processes must counterbalance a cosmology arising from and weighted down by perception. And this counterbalancing needs to be made not merely for philosophy's sake. It is not a question of denying that there are "things" in experience. When one sees impediments or breakwaters in experience, they often impose their solidity and opacity on us. But they can only occur in conjunction with all the movements of which they are the results, occasions, or centers.

Thus it is impossible to commit oneself to a science in which experience is never presented except as something external to a perception. Since 1750 psychology has been fascinated by the model of physics. It has been tempted by *behaviorism,* either in attenuated forms or, as now, in an express fashion. The results do not measure up to the expectation. But whatever the ultimate results, and whatever need there may be to desire such results, the very postulates of the adopted attitude exclude an indefinite field of descriptions which, in contradistinction to scientific anthropology, could be called *spiritual psychology.* Instead of making an extrinsic linking of events in space through the use of functional laws—something which can only be done when the givens of experience are relatively solid and ponderous—spiritual psychology looks for those dialectical and emotional operations which, in the midst of the total experience, affect intimate experience. The psychology of the animal and of the child, of the retarded and of the ill, studies life in subjects which are somewhat mutilated or undeveloped. Spiritual psychology must deal with life in subjects who are quite vigorous and well-developed.

Philosophy and psychology are not meant to neglect either intellectual or perceptual determinations, for these are the means and stages of thought. Nor should they sacrifice to determinations the moving beauty of experiences which any kind of analysis would destroy. Reality is neither so exact a closed system that life would die in it, nor so intimately plastic that thought could not find anything to grasp. The most naked intuition rejoins the most extreme abstractions. If this were not the case, one could neither think nor love. If the purity of every intuition were to ward off every determination, then the most naive and brutal positivism would present itself to supply the concepts needed for action.

One can now see the sense in which we accept the idea that philosophy must be experimental. If by experimental one means that philosophy must take into account all givens and all empirical aspects, or at least not antecedently rule out any aspects, we must agree. But if one employs the term *experimental,* deliberately or not, in such a way as to exclude certain modes of the contemplated or the lived, one detotalizes experience in a way which belies any claim of respecting experience. In particular, one should not have any partiality for or against the idea. Experience shows us the idea as so alluring and so sufficient that Spinoza had reason to deny the will because the will could add nothing to it. It also shows us the idea as so feeble that Bergson had reason to assert that it has to get its force from elsewhere, from either the body or the will or the soul. Intellectualism and intuitionism can thus replace each other, contradict each other, or converge into each other without these catastrophes forcing us to depart from experience.

By attaching physical causality to psychological causality, Maine de Biran has given an example of a philosophy equally capable of satisfying the requirements of either objectivism or subjectivism. We have only to deepen and enlarge his method by not restricting its thrust to the psychological self. But this enlarging can only be accomplished if no new fiat, running against the grain of the former, falsifies description by a contrary partialness. That is, the enlarging will only occur if we avoid adopting some postulate which would push us out of the self into some abstract or metaphysical reality. Contrary to all forms of a transcendental phenomenology, or all the givens of an ontology which claims to be isolated from the psychological subject, and, inversely, contrary to those forms of an anthropological psychology which claim to be self-contained, description cannot be inspired by any preoccupation other than to recognize and overcome these partialities.

This is the end of these critical considerations. They should be readily accepted in an epoch of philosophy of which one of the principal characteristics has been to give privileged status to dialectics of liberation. We have only to add here a refusal to give these latter dialectics the right to present themselves, in their turn, as exclusive. If they are employed alone, they can do no more than introduce nothingness. In fact, since a negative critique can never suppress that exigency of value which in varying degrees and modes inspires us all, such a critique ordinarily works to the advantage of some determination that is not discussed or is not treated seriously in discussion. Thus the most stringent critique ends up by putting itself at the service of the least critical partialness. Here, again, experience demands the recognition of the diversity of the givens which it offers to our description. The relation between determinism and indeterminism throughout history obliges us to take account of both of them. Thus it is for us to decide: Do we wish to mutilate or to respect experience? The breadth of the spirit is destined not to dissolve the spirit but to expand it. One must therefore make a place for the dialectics of convergence and consolidation even in the face of operations of negation and devaluation, for in all domains they manifest the conjunction of the value of creation with the value of criticism.

[V] THREE UNIVERSAL ASPECTS OF EXPERIENCE

14. *The beginning of description*

LET US NOW DESCRIBE EXPERIENCE. Every event can properly be considered either as localized, situated in such and such a place and thus exterior to other events, or as coextensive with the entirety of experience, proceeding from this totality and grounded in it. This latter view is legitimate since it is possible to link any event with all other events by means of relations which are either distended or compressed. This linking can occur whether the event in question has been made possible by or has been produced by the other events or whether it has made them possible or produced them. The legitimacy of these two points of view is exhibited by space and time, which are simultaneously the conditions for all discreteness and the contexts within which everything is embraced. One need only observe that it is easier to consider some givens as aspects of experience and other givens as parts of experience. The universality of the former kind of given suggests that we start by describing it.

Among the universal aspects which can be used to characterize experience, we will first pay attention to those whose evidence is most easily established. Since every description stands at the intersection of an authentication and an orientation, one can abstractly distinguish two kinds of evidence. In *coercive evidence*, that which is authenticated imposes itself on description. There is coercive evidence that it is daytime. A perception or an idea imposes its evidence when we are more passive than active in acquiring the evidence and when it is very difficult for us to dispute or undermine the evidence. In *assumptive evidence*, it is the description which engenders the described. If some coercive evidences come to us from the past, the affirmation that there will be a future is a typical example of those other evidences whose source is in the thrust of description itself. Everything would be coercively evident for a spirit which was nothing but a witness to the given. Everything would be assumptively evident for a spirit which was nothing but a creator. It is the conflict of evidences which gives rise to research.

Objectivism, as the very term *evidence* shows, has considered only the former of these two kinds of evidence. It constructs its theory of knowledge from the point of view of the known. But from this point of view one does not recognize what comes from the subject. Nevertheless the subject is always present in its preference for certain postulates which both make its perceptions and affirmations possible and, by implicit exclusions, turn the subject away from other perceptions and exclusions. Belief is what confers existence on the object of knowledge. Thus one should admit the possibility of conviction only when the two kinds of evidence converge, uniting what we know by virtue of the constraint of the senses and reason with what we believe by virtue of the thrust which carries us toward existence.

When an affirmation is such that it is practically impossible to refuse to admit that its content is authenticated, and further when we feel an almost invincible repugnance at the thought of not believing it to be true, then this affirmation harmonizes its own universality with the unanimity of spirits. It gives security to them and receives its own fecundity from them. We cannot always bring ourselves to the meeting point between validity, which manifests the contribution of the past to conviction, and value, which adds to validity the promise of a better future. But description must start from the objectively universal and subjectively unanimous affirmations if it wishes to proceed from what experience presents that is most impoverished and of the greatest extension to what experience contains that is most concrete and original.

15. *Three universal aspects of experience*

The convergence of the two kinds of evidence leads us to recognize three aspects of experience as universal truths and unanimous beliefs. It is impossible to avoid establishing or implicating these aspects in each and every description. Likewise, it is impossible not to hope to find them.

These aspects are as follows:

(1) Experience involves numerical and qualitative *multiplicity*, skips and gaps, discontinuity, things. In short, experience involves everything called the plural.

(2) This multiplicity is possible only in correlation with *unities* which cannot be further divided or unities whose amplitude simultaneously both surpasses and allows for the many.

(3) Finally, the union of unity and multiplicity is not a closed union, both because this union is not exclusively an order of presences and because every presence is the absence of something else. As a consequence, the consideration of *non-being* is just as rigorously imposed on description as is the consideration of being.

We will take up each of these aspects as it occurs and show that every description consists both in authenticating that some state of affairs is indeed the case and in requiring that it must be the case.

A

16. *There is multiplicity*

Multiplicity, in the sense of a given multiplicity, seems to be eliminated by all philosophies which claim to start from the continuity of being or of experience. This claim is belied by experience itself, whose multiplicity is presupposed in every description. Thus:

(1) There is no given, if by "given" one means an absolutely primordial nature or experience. No attribute has any meaning except by reason of the operation which leads to it. This is just as true of the attribute "primordial" as of any other attribute. Every starting point (and the given is a starting point for knowledge) presupposes both a regressive opera-

tion and the halting of the operation at a certain terminus beyond which it cannot be pushed because the law of the operation predetermines this terminus. Chemistry arrives at simple bodies because it limits itself to a chemical resolution. One is the lower limit of the division of whole numbers because no one wants to rupture unity. For Christians, the calendar begins with the Christian era. The final terminus of the regression is taken as the initial terminus of the progression. The final term is therefore nothing but the projection before oneself of a limitation which results from the relatively negative determination of the law according to which the operation is carried out. When this limitation is manifested in some way other than by closing off a path and when the operation can continue indefinitely, one does not reach a given, at least not unless fatigue intervenes so that another law interferes with the law of the operation in question. Every given, whether it is ontologized in nature or left in experience, is therefore no more than a relative given. It can have something of the absolute in it, but it is not absolute.

The given, which would have precisely the characteristic of being an irreducible unity if it were the only thing admitted, can only exist in connection with some operation, circumstances, and linkings. *Therefore the given is more or less fundamentally discriminated from some other thing, with which it constitutes at least a pair.* One could then make a cleavage between the given and its setting and supposedly place the given outside of experience and de-reify its setting. But doing this is doing nothing more than complicating experience. One will not have moved beyond experience. *Fascination* is the concentration of experience into the unity of a given which absorbs everything else into itself. But if fascination could be absolute, one could neither enter it nor depart from it; it would not even be mentioned. Mono-ideaism is a mental Eleaticism which, like Eleaticism, designates a fiction-limit. Even if one speaks of real unity and unreal multiplicity, one still discovers the presence of the latter in experience. One even endows it with a kind of unity by reason of the thought of real unity.

(2) Likewise, when one wants to make unity the essential characteristic of the given, one discovers the truth of continuity. Continuity replaces the given with an attenuated, extended, spread-out unity. To speak of continuity is to admit

multiplicity. For it to be distinguished from punctiliar simplicity, continuity has to present itself as a radiance or as a more or less homogeneous expanse in which punctiliar simplicity and continuity receive their fecundity from each other. An expanse as such cannot be given to experience without an incipient enumeration. And this enumeration, however slight it may be, causes a multiplicity of incipient actualities to emerge. Just as a piece of metal or paper is a piece of money only by reason of minting or of our using it for actual or envisioned exchanges, so unity only becomes continuity through a dilation which activates its abundance. Continuity must give off radiations.

(3) Further, no experience is the totality of experience. Each given is posited by being distinguished from other givens. An act which tried to make a given absolutely absolute, such as the act which would try to reach beyond the thought-in-itself to the real-thing-in-itself, would be an act of universal negation whereby everything else would be expelled from it. But expulsion presupposes some potency within that which it dispels. Continuity thus has reference to the discontinuity which it cancels and which cancels it. The description of continuity is also an evaluation. In opposing discontinuity, the trace of which persists in the affirmation of continuity, metaphysics tries to group the many into the one by means of systematization. Ethics condemns incoherence, war, and even the richness of experience. Art mollifies intimate discords through the admiration of harmony in beauty. Religion preaches the union of souls in the love of the universal God. None of this would make sense if unity had already turned everything around it into a barren wasteland. Metaphysics, ethics, art, and religion are objects of description within experience, but experience goes beyond them. These functions themselves get started by refracting unity in the very course of proclaiming it.

(4) Should one say that there are terms only by reason of the relations which unite them? One could say this, and the ideal of intelligibility often tells one to do so. But the unity of a relation is already an attenuation of absolute unity. Still, as Hume has shown, unless causality is to be annulled, the attenuation which suffices for the avowal of multiplicity has not defaced the purity of the one. Further, the terms can be attached to their connection only after having been distin-

guished from it and only if a trace of this distinction persists in the unity of the relation. It is Bradley who has shown most clearly the resistance which terms set up against their mutual interiorization. Either they have been and still are *terms,* or the relation without content is no longer a relation. The one is never anything but a pivot between one multiplicity and another. The very pleasure that one can draw from possessing the one is always an irradiation from it. It is not our intention to deny the value of unifying descriptions. But it is our intention to see whether these descriptions hold a preeminent position of value. And even if they do, unity still comes about only through a unification which involves plurality. What is the use of the relation if the continuity which it adduces does not introduce order into a previous discontinuity? If the relation does not do so, it would be idle to say that the scientist discovers rather than creates. The relation spares him none of the suffering necessary to obtain a unifying law.

What is true of multiplicity insofar as it is given to description is also true of it *insofar as it is required by description.* To describe is first of all to divide. To that which is described there are added both the act of describing and the describer. Description has value only if multiplication and differentiation have value. But how could one refuse to admit that they have value? The appropriate development of the population, fecundity, the proliferation of scientific laws, the discovery of previously unknown experiences, and the transcendence of novelty are, here and there, goals which are just as precious to consciousness as are the conservation of structures, the economy of thought, the reduction of the different to the same, the organization of ideas and acts, tradition, and security. The exclusive preoccupation with unity can be as lethal as is the caprice which flits from one element of a multiplicity to another. Both accident and invention have a common trait: they overturn all the established unities to which multiplicity has been subjected. Value is beyond the opposition of the one and the multiple just as it is beyond all other oppositions. To conserve or to organize can be either wise or routine and brutal. To innovate and to release can be either criminal thoughtlessness or creative revelation.

The confirmation of and the demand for multiplicity are encountered *in the joining of postulates to axioms.* In the limit case, the axiom would be the one. But an axiom only reveals the one in some very abstract manner. An axiom, then, is nothing but a condition of validity. Nothing can be done with the mere dead one. Postulates, hypotheses, and rules have to be added to it. A postulate is not merely a confirmation. Even if its verification in realized experience gives it a content, it is still independent of that content. Every geometry is independent of its subsequent applications in physics. A postulate therefore is a synthetic rule which both thrusts thought in a certain direction and encloses it in that direction. A postulate switches the train of thought onto a certain track. It provides an impetus to thought. But it adds the sentiment of a limit, of an impotence now or subsequently discovered. The arithmetical postulates of commutativity and associativity make calculus possible. But they limit its scope to those results which verify them. The Euclidean postulate opened the way for Euclidean geometry but made it seem arbitrary. A postulate therefore asserts multiplicity in two ways: (1) It contributes to the engendering of some definite possibilities; and (2) it leads to the presumption that other families of possibilities can be opposed to these definite ones.

The more philosophy is tied to concrete experience, the more it must gracefully accept multiplicity. It is true that philosophy begins with *a purification*. It sweeps away the pointless forms of useless knowledge in order to draw near to the intimate simplicity of things. But this simplicity appears real to it only because of simplicity's fecundity. Thus no one has posited the one without conferring on it the complexity of a whole or the generosity of a source. Bradley has radically distinguished the multiplicity of appearances from the unity of the Absolute since he excludes all possibility of passage from one to the other. Yet even he must admit that the Absolute is the absolute *of* these appearances. He would suppress the absolute if he juxtaposed an Eleaticism to a phenomenism. One would be unable to comprehend how the revelation of the phenomenality of appearances, i.e. their metaphysical negation, could be converted into the affirmation of the reality and unity of the Absolute. Bradley is so far from such a juxtaposition that he thinks that every judgment is a judgment on and by the Absolute. Thus, when he argues that appearances are "absorbed and transfigured" by the Absolute, he excludes the possibility of an intellectual continuity *for us* between the absolute and phenomena. But he does suppose an existential continuity between them. Further, he holds that the many are repetitious of the one, though he does so by showing that the one has no regard for human claims. This latter opinion, when taken alone, is serious because it compromises the superior value of morality over immorality, and ultimately compromises value itself. Still, it does not impair the solidarity of the one and the multiple. The triviality of this relation merely verifies its universality.

It is useless to insist further on this point. The pure one would suppress all description, for, on the one hand, a description makes what it describes proliferate and, on the other hand, it adds itself to what it describes. Further, a description becomes one with what it describes, either by identity of resemblance, as in the case of a copy, or by interiority of penetration, as in the case of an allusion. But a description is also distinct from what it describes, for the described is describable only if the description is added to it so as to orient it and draw it out within the meaning of this orientation. Thus, in response to whoever might try to reduce description to the unity of the object, as in the case where a man counts one,[1] it is enough to say that the attribution of existence to the one is nothing but the projection of an objective partiality.

B

17. *There are unities*

However important it may be to recognize the presence of unity at the core of experience, our discussion of multiplicity will remove the necessity for treating this point at length. Thus we will not mention this idea hereafter unless it is the occasion for some useful observations on other aspects of description.

(1) Multiplicity itself presupposes unity as an *element*. It is necessary to count one before counting ten. Number, properly speaking, is neither ordinal nor cardinal. It is both ordinal and cardinal. The tenth is a whole inasmuch as it is the tenth and not a new first, but only on condition that

1. Le Senne refers here to the activity of treating a given as something countable and thus as something that can be placed in a numerical series.—Trans.

the antecedent elements continue to be taken into account when it is called tenth. Ten is a special totality and not the pure totality of the one, but only if the spirit has counted up to nine and ten. Thus one can distinguish the cardinal number from the ordinal only because one can reverse the order of priority between the operation of addition and the total. When the operation is *for* the result, the number is called cardinal. When the result exists *through* the operation, which could not take place without giving rise to the result but which is not done with a view to obtaining its product, that preference is expressed by the ordinal number. Time, which distinguishes between its instants, and space, which makes a simultaneity of its parts, are unified. Standing between a fusion which would prevent one from thinking of them apart from each other and a duality which would destroy them in the very process of distinguishing them, the existential association of time and space maintains vis-à-vis both of them the unities which are the elements of a multiplicity and the unity which makes these multiplicities an ensemble. A counted multiplicity is not a canceled unity; rather, it is the mediation between an inferior unity and a superior unity, between the element and the totality.

One might object that a qualitative multiplicity, e.g., the rainbow or the coo of a dove, is a multiplicity without elementary unities. This objection is possible because such a multiplicity is an instability between the continuity of an ensemble and the fragmentedness of parts. Such an ensemble can be called a multiplicity, and felt as such, only by reason of the simultaneous representation of the extremities between which it oscillates. Experience is like quicksilver, capable both of scattering itself into slippery droplets and of mingling its parts in a liquid mass. In the case of a variegated multiplicity,[2] the elements are not distinct. Rather, they give rise to distinction. But it is necessary that some divisions be indicated, or no one would ever be able to call it a multiplicity. This is the ambiguity of the very notion of elements. If they are lost in the mass of the whole, they are no longer elements. If they are separated from the whole, they are different things. Not the least worthwhile thing about description is that it allows philosophy to consider both ambiguous states and ensembles fashioned through internal oppositions.

2. As for example, a rainbow.—Trans.

(2) Every multiplicity also presupposes unity as *totality*. Of course, there can be an infinite number of degrees and modes of this totality, ranging from the unity of a conflict, an equilibrium, or a collection to that of a structure, a system, or a solid. But whatever the mode of the totality, description is decisive here. Whether the totality is objective, as in an organism, or subjective, as in a stellar constellation, whether it has its meaning in the relations which the spirit posits as independent of itself or has its meaning in a decree of the observer, both cohesion and juxtaposition are wholes. The distinction between cohesion and juxtaposition rests on the theory which one formulates about them, on the expected resistance to or support of the elements for one another, and on the effects which are supposed to follow from them. The distinction indicates the sense of the connection between the whole and the self. In the case of solidity, the connection imposes itself on the self. In the case of juxtaposition, it requires nothing but a fulfilling of apperception. But the self always finds itself in the presence of a whole. A skeleton is a whole. So is a sunset. The grouping is sometimes more emotional than voluntary, sometimes more aesthetic than physical. That changes nothing of the intrinsic nature of the unity which the grouping has brought about.

Thus the idea of a multiplicity that is not even a collection is simply a *fiction-limit*. Unquestionably, nothing is more important in the movements of experience than these fiction-limits. The golden age, an absolutely smooth surface, a perfect figure, pure nothingness, etc., have played and do play roles in experience. They are defined in experience. But experience surpasses them by joining them with other things. This is what happens with a multiplicity whose terms supposedly are not reunited by the act which grasps them. It is useless to expand the terms. The act which grasps them would release them the moment that the unity, by virtue of which the terms are many, would explode, so to speak. Thus there is no multiplicity which is not in some way a whole. Pure pluralism is nothing but a subjectivization of monism.

(3) To be precise, then, the elements and the whole can be considered together only if they are dealt with in a description which alternates between part-to-whole and whole-to-part. Thus, in presupposing unity either as element or as totality, one presupposes it as *over against* multiplicity. The

circuit of consciousness corresponds with the connection of the whole to the parts. This is how it unfolds. Perception presents us with a unity which is distinct from others but is itself undivided. This unity imposes on us the feeling that it excludes us from itself. To look for this unity, then to find parts of it, is to begin to penetrate it. The self reverses its inferiority, in the face of the perceived, into a superiority when it separates the elements from the whole. The whole is then nothing more than a collection. This means that we can now painlessly separate the pieces of the broken solid from one another. Thus reassured, we will reassemble the parts so that they are a whole again, but we will remember the proper method for redissolving it. A whole, then, is nothing but an undivided unity accompanied by the memory and the presentiment of its division. It exists over against multiplicity. Description restores the means and products of concrete experience to concrete experience. It reveals the dialectics immanent in dynamism. Intellectualism is profound when it discovers that there are not only concepts to see but also dialectics to *espouse*.

Even when one shows that a notion involves *not merely a comprehension but a circulation,* one still risks reducing the inexhaustible diversity of the more complex operations in which this circulation is inserted. A circulation remains cinematic unless excitement, which intellectual or affective restlessness mixes into all the actions in which we participate, intervenes to give it dynamism. This excitement dramatizes the confrontation between the multiple and the one. As a consequence of this confrontation, experience either unites these opposites in conflicts or succeeds in coordinating them within a rhythm of mediations and immediacies. Every known or knowable category is an original connection of the one to the two. To each category there corresponds an intuition. Concrete extension corresponds to space. Duration corresponds to time. Production corresponds to causality. And so on. Or, better, to avoid again the problem that intuition can lead to merely looking on from the outside, let us say that some concrete experience corresponds to each category, and the list of categories is not closed. The description of experience, which is undertaken sometimes to enclose experience and make it determinate and sometimes to open it up by showing the inadequacy of determinations, must resign itself to do no more than delve into and examine carefully the richness of the lived opposition between the one and the multiple.

In the course of this narration, unity does not only present itself as a given; it is also required *as the ideal of a demand*. We will limit ourselves here simply to noting that within the extension of the notion of unity, the notion with the largest possible extension, one should not fail to distinguish cases which are often opposite to one another. We expressly distinguish *reductive unity*, which is obtained by precipitating an identity through eliminating the differences which diffract it, from *integrating unity*, which regulates an ensemble by compensating for the differences between the parts. To disengage a law from the cases in which it is verified is an inverse operation to that which brings two different but complementary elements into a whole.

C

18. *There is non-being*

Experience, as we have just seen, excludes the kind of pulverization which would scatter unity into infinitely many pieces and thus prevent any unity from being defined. Experience likewise excludes the kind of fascination which would make every unity suppress all other unities and would not permit any multiplicity to offer itself to description. We must now show that it is impossible to treat experience as a world which is all of one piece, a world which excludes all contingency and indeterminateness, a world which is a solid mass. The ideal of a totality which would dissolve all parts and of which man would be no more than one region has too often seduced human intelligence. It satisfies too snugly our tendencies to order, as if these tendencies were the only ones that counted. This ideal is confirmed so frequently in the success of particular theories that one cannot always use it for purposes of criticizing a transcendental myth which interposes its specter between experience and description.

We will dispel the specter quickly by confronting the characteristics which reality must necessarily have if it is to be definable in terms of a pure systematization with the givens of experience.

(1) Systematization could only be perfect—and if it exists

it must be perfect—*if it entails the non-distinction of the parts from the whole.* This is precisely what massive means: *solid gold.* The massive is that solid within which no function can be performed or even be conceived because thought could not find anything there on which to use its power of distinguishing. Looked at from the outside, the qualitative homogeneity would have to be absolute. Looked at from the inside, the interaction of parts which is indispensable for the cohesion of the whole must be so intimate that their multiplicity would vanish. It is not enough to say that a system presupposes a spatialization. A spatialized system would not meet the absolute requirement of unity which it should satisfy except by excluding extension. Extension allows for an aspect of exteriority between its points which one cannot completely reduce even by calling it "intelligible extension." Intelligibility presupposes an interiority of the terms which, precisely as such, renders those terms indiscernible. Consequently, pure intelligibility can only be ideal.

Does experience agree with this fiction? A simple glance shows that experience is always more or less liquid, relaxed, unfettered, and elastic. Hume has definitively opened up the description of experience by showing that necessity has meaning for the spirit only in conjunction with the separability of the terms it unites. Thus, there is no necessity if, by this term, one means pure interiority. Each given is the point of application of two contradictory attributes. That which is thought does not have the eidetic, formal, structural characteristic which "idea" evokes except when it tends to immobilize itself, and then only on the basis of a rather rough perception. That which is thought becomes a more or less stable equilibrium because it embraces a more or less profound conflict. Architectonic metaphors should have a less important place than orchestral metaphors in philosophy. If the ideal of intelligence could be attained, it would suppress intelligence. Intelligence is not an abdication. It is a life which adapts to itself what it discovers in order to invent.

The dialectic which protects us against the fiction of pure intelligibility situated at the convergence of intellectualism and realism is the dialectic which animates the idea of totality. A whole, we now see, would be a massive whole only if its parts were indiscernible. It would be a unity *which would preclude knowledge and action.* As soon as parts are defined, as soon as they are distinguished, the whole begins to disintegrate. This kind of whole no longer has the essence of a whole, for it can no longer integrate what it contains. Thus thought makes plausible the idea of system only because it reunites an alternation of almost pure unity and almost pure multiplicity with the name of a limit. This limit is the point at which the alternation of integration and disintegration becomes so rapid that the periodicity is changed into a thing. This is the case, for example, when a vibratory frequency becomes a sound or a color for us. In fact, sometimes a thing is presented to us as a whole but it pushes us back to the beginning of perception; at other times its multiplicity appears to us and we enter into it. But the perception which strikes that which, through a dialectical interpretation of what is remembered, we call its elements no longer grasps the multiplicity itself. Thus, if experience could be a whole, it would not be a knowing.

Likewise, thought, which can no more renounce its activity of distinguishing than it can renounce its activity of linking, immediately substitutes the idea of a systematic whole for the simple idea of a whole. And this substitution begins the fragmentation of the whole. A systematic whole is no longer a whole. It is either yearning for or hope for a whole. When our ignorance prevents us from using delicate and regulated means to penetrate into the whole, that is, when prior to every precise theory the whole is still nothing but the simple given of a perception, we have no other method to use but bombardment. Artillery is the principal tool in microphysics as in war. Both are aimed at cohesions, held together by a powerful energy, which have to be broken apart. From without as well as from within, the whole is thus inseparable from the multiple. *Every predicate is both inside and outside the concept.* And various dialectics, appropriate to the different situations, reduce predication to relation or relation to inherence.

(2) Now let us come as close as possible to a massive whole without claiming to reach it. Systematicity would still imply the *universal appropriateness* of everything which is defined therein. Pure necessity would exclude all disorder, all error, all misunderstanding. The only thing possible would be necessity's realizing itself. Never in any way would there be delay or anticipation of an event. An event would occur

only at that point of space or time in which it is supposed to occur. The here and the now would have the essence of things. Space and time would not be extrinsic to their content. Neither regret nor impatience nor demands nor restoration would have any place in this world. The relation of the one and the multiple would be transformed, in a Leibnizian manner, into a pair. This pair would juxtapose the eternity of the interiority of the one to the multiple and the parallelism holding between the elements of the multiple. Being would be a wheel, whose axis is eternity and whose rim keeps its spokes at a constant distance from one another.

When the description of consciousness is sufficiently advanced, it allows a philosophy to be understood by enclosing the dialectics of which the philosophy is the expression between the consideration of the "situation" which is imposed on the philosopher and the consideration of the "interests" to which his effort has adhered. But, in manifesting its scope, a philosophy sketches its own limits. Philosophy is not a method; a philosophy is one method. Philosophy is preserved by going beyond each philosophy. This is the place to stress everything which experience opposes to the postulate of universal *appropriateness*. If everything were "in its place" in experience, it would have been neither possible nor useful to produce so many philosophers simply to acknowledge that such is the case. Here again we run into one of those pieces of evidence in which the recollection of our disappointments flows along with the invincible thrust of hope animating our lives. Without this thrust, we would not look for harmony and we could not resent the lacunae in the harmony. Without these stalemates, we would not have to look for harmony. Philosophy could shunt aside contingence, and what contingence entails, by calling it appearance. But appearances are still in experience. Shunting them aside would amount to a purification only if the resistances which every appearance involves are dissolved. But if experience shows that the succession of appearances entails the eternity of appearance as over against reality, then contingence might be called provisional. But it will be definitively provisional. The description of consciousness is dominated by the opposition between aesthetic dialectics, which refurbish intellectual and qualitative images, and metaphysical or, if one wishes, ontological dialectics, which deal with consistent and profound givens. This opposition

presupposes that experience opposes the empty to the full.
Everything can occur either in season or out of season.

(3) In effect, we should note that this massive, set, rigid
world, which is always "up to date," *entails the partialness of
being.* The spontaneity of every thought, deriving power both
from its affective and intellectual thrust and from the clarity
of the analysis which distinguishes between one idea and
another, requires it to "land." Thought stops wandering like
a more or less randomly meandering stream so as to push
on to a term lying before it. In this term, thought overlooks
the progressive restriction of the experience which is imposed,
by an initial indecision, on the yield which ensues upon
thought through its own maturation. In this term, thought
finds being. Solidity is not always a barrier for us. It is often
the content of a possession and a condition for security. But
when man sets his foot down solidly he can lose the sentiment
of his intimate independence. This happens to those people
who, in Scheler's words, become the "servants of things."

Undoubtedly every philosopher, unless he wants to re-
treat to the condition of philosophy prior to the *cogito,* is
anxious to counterbalance the being of "that is" with the
existence of "I am." But even if one bifurcates the essence of
existence, still when one reduces experience to being, one is
simply taking note of that which is positive in each of these
two forms. And this is always a partialness. Every given is
positive by reason of what it contains and by reason of its
relations of solidity with all other givens. Insofar as it is passive, it is posited; insofar as it is active, it posits. But it is not
and cannot be either merely affirmed or merely affirming.

Thus experience forces us to recognize the intrinsic or received positivity of each given. But it likewise forces us, since
it goes beyond this given, to recognize that each given excludes
the other givens. There is more than mere juxtaposition and
contiguity in the proximity of two givens. Even when they are
encountered side by side, so to speak, their exteriority to each
other is only relative. If exteriority were complete, each of the
terms would be enclosed in itself. Each would be protected objectively against all action from the other and subjectively
against all comparison with the other. By having shown that
multiplicity is not reduced to its elements taken as separate
from each other, we have implied that the contiguity of two
terms cannot exist without some continuity. Each is in the

other without being the other. One cannot separate their identity from their duality without simultaneously annihilating them. It is impossible to express this ambiguity other than by making each term, and ultimately each point, both a presence and an absence, a being and a non-being.

Non-being is just as concretely experienced as being is. Every description of experience shows this. One can doubt this only if by an implicit purification he substitutes absolute nothingness for non-being. This is what happens when one affirms that only being exists. One hereby replaces being with the limit to which the idea of being is asymptotic. Experience always makes us feel the void, solitude, the past, the future, the lost, the destroyed, the forgotten, the discounted, error, the illusory—in short, the other-insofar-as-it-is-other. Every given irradiates something of positivity and something of negativity. An instant of time foretells other instants but does not embrace them. A piece of property both benefits and imprisons one. Every victory is also a defeat. A scattered deck of cards is not a peculiarly arranged deck. It is a disarranged deck. It is not what it should be. Suppose someone has not come to a meeting. How can what happens be described if one does not recognize a concrete experience to be lived through? If I do not meet in a certain place a person who is not supposed to be there, he would not be absent. Whether I call an image real or illusory, it is the same image, but the concrete experience of it is not the same. The most positive philosophers cannot eliminate all negative judgments. If they turn positive judgments against negative ones in order to neutralize the latter, the fact remains that the negative ones are opposed before they are canceled. When philosophy eliminates from experience the largest part of what humanity concretely experiences, then it is isolated from humanity. What is the good of defining reality in a way which excludes from reality what we feel every day? One can hide within the true and being as well as within the illusory and nothingness, for experience always brings into play both presence and absence.

Therefore, after this encounter between experience and the fictional hypothesis of a massive reality, we renounce any denial of non-being. *The other, which is the non-given, discloses itself between pure nothingness and the absolutely new.* It does not end up at either of these poles. If it did so it would be annihilated. Neither the dialectics of assimilation, which claims to attain identities without differences, nor the dialectics of rupture, which affirms the absolute incompatibility between the one and the other, can ever be pushed to its ultimate point. As we have already seen, neither unity nor multiplicity can be pure. And, further, the infusion of non-being into experience prevents us from construing unity and multiplicity as being in an order which could only become perfect by becoming massive. Both unity and multiplicity must be steeped in an experience which is never reduced to their positivity. The determined will always be inseparable from the undetermined.

In the interval between absolute nothingness and absolute otherness, non-being undergoes the most striking metamorphoses. Non-being always presupposes some antagonism between being and itself. But this antagonism is never more than partial. If the transition between the given and the other involved no jolt, however weak it might be, the other could not be opposed to the given. But behind the obstacle, which supervenes to interrupt the imperceptible course of the given and which forces one to think of the other, is this other the pure and simple suppression of the given? Is non-being a "pure loss," or is it some unforeseeable newness coming from the given? Even if this indecision is or ought to be resolved, it is still an occurrence within experience. This indecision is the domain which negative judgments try to deal with. These negative judgments range between "This does not exist" and "This is not that." But, in the first case, whatever "this" is cannot be denied without having been and having been represented. Therefore it has both some nature and some existence. If William Tell was not a man, he is still a legend. In the second case, "this" excludes "that"; the exclusion separates "this" and "that" but it does not annihilate them. Similarly, the other could always be linked to the same. In an existential judgment they are either united, for if A is B, there is AB, or they are separated, for if A is other than B, there is both A and B.

If non-being were absolutely non-existent, it could not prevent the existent from being petrified. If non-being were absolutely primary, it would annihilate the existent by phenomenalizing it to the point of suppressing it. Experience rejects the unknowable regardless of which of these hypotheses is adopted. If the second hypothesis is adopted, experience rejects the unknowable because the unknowable would offer nothing to be known. If the first is adopted, experience rejects the unknowable because the unknowable would bring knowledge to a termination in itself. This latter case is like the hypothesis of the massive whole. But experience instead is like the unsettled shores where the sea and the sand wrestle for space. Being, taken as solid, has to be able to prevail over non-being to prevent absolute non-being. But non-being or absence has to be able to undermine being, to corrode it without reaching the point of volatilizing it. As non-being is opposed to being, so are free dialectics opposed to necessary ones. This opposition, however, cannot be absolute, for necessity is concretely experienced and thought only in correlation with contingence. And in every dialectic there is a positive content which would be impossible unless there were being.

The dialectics of flattening. Description's recognition of non-being has importance because it warns us against the partiality which would come about if one abandoned himself to what could be called the *dialectics of flattening.* The basic characteristic of the dialectics of flattening is that it presents all reality as unfolding on a perfectly unified plane from which every accident or impediment, in short, every negative contingency, is definitively excluded.

Bergson has already denounced the devaluation of experience which results from reducing it to spatiality. But space can only play this role if it has been anteriorly despoiled of all its furnishings. The furnishings allow for voids and anfractuosities in space. In other words, space can play this role only if it does not allow for a heterogeneity whose law is too complex for us to conceive. Further, though spatialization is often equivalent to flattening, flattening itself can and does take on other forms. Finally, the seriousness of evil, with its dramatic ambiguity, does not receive in Bergsonism all the consideration which our harshest experiences demand.

Heidegger, undoubtedly following Bergson, also took note of and denounced one of the aspects of flattening when he pointed out the degradation which engenders the "one" (*das Man*). This leveling (*Einebnung*) of all the possibilities of being occurs when originality is reduced to the average, to the *durchschnittliche Alltäglichkeit.* "All uniqueness is silently depreciated. Everything original, day after day, is crushed under the pretext that one has known it for a long time. Things which were obtained only with much effort are made easily available. Every secret loses its power." [3] This leveling entails the suppression or the denial of value. But the realization of this effect does not free us from the duty to describe the dialectics which led to this leveling. While considering such consequences of flattening as the depersonalization of man, the debasing of effort, the reduction of value to utility, the hatred of nobility, or the reduction of creativity to wastefulness, description must further reconsider the operations which these consequences simply make manifest.

The essence of the "dialectics of flattening" is *the assimilation of experiences in which identity of content is connected to divergent orientations and values. This assimilation is brought about by considering nothing but the content.* Suppose that one man rolling down a slope and another in the process of painfully climbing up the slope meet at a certain point. If one were to consider the slope only at the place and moment of their intersection, the center of gravity of the helpless tumbling man could be theoretically interchanged with that of the climbing alpinist. What a gross reduction! One of these experiences manifests the defeat of the spirit whereas the other manifests its victory.

By leading to moral indifference, the dialectics of flattening, as expressed for example in the form "sometimes this . . . ," "sometimes that . . . ," robs morality of all sense of value. This is not the place to examine whether morality must be upheld for the sake of value itself, whether morality is the highest goal of man, or whether morality is a moment destined to be absorbed into some superior concrete experience such as beatitude or love or contemplation. It is enough to observe that morality is certainly a given of experience. Thus, if the flattening which tends to reduce morality's domain is presented as a dialectic, this dialectic itself must be recognized and perhaps associated with other dialectics. But it should not be substituted for them. And above all it should not be substituted for morality. What we are trying to do is to avoid ever eliminating any intellectual or emotional process of experience. To describe experience is already to promote it. Inversely, we seek to prevent either a part or the whole of the other dialectics from being ignored, discredited, repressed, or refused an examination by

3. M. Heidegger, *Sein und Zeit,* 3d ed. (Halle: Niemeyer, 1931), p. 127. [My translation from Le Senne's French.—Trans.]

reason of the tyranny of flattening. Philosophy is not designed to abolish anything; it is designed to spiritualize everything.

Further, in defending the omnipresence of conflict, we ourselves are brought to the crucial experience which manifests the indispensability of non-being for an impartial description of experience. But when one moves away from the special situation of the educator, a situation which confers on him the limited authority of an ethical rather than a military mode of commanding, one returns to other aspects of non-being. The most metaphysical aspect of non-being is that of mystery. Mystery is the relative annihilation of knowledge, the obscurity and ignorance which impede our glance equally whether we turn toward things or toward ourselves. Whether men take this mystery as the agony of the nothing or the vertigo of the infinite, in either case they eventually experience the terror of things or, more internally, the fear of themselves. To protect themselves from this redoubtable face-to-face encounter most men yield to the temptation of the dialectics of flattening, which arrest our view by throwing some distraction between us and experience. For common sense, this distraction is perception and business. For the scientist, it is the corpus of his theories. For the citizen, it is either his profession or the State. For the historian, it is the spectacular succession of events and doctrines which ward off this unrest. But this unrest is the very source of philosophy. To the degree that official optimism encroaches on philosophy, philosophy becomes anemic and dead. And at the same time that truth is dethroned by the cessation of thought, man imperceptibly loses the feeling of his own existence. His existence consists precisely in being engaged in what he does and says with all his powers and aspirations, in throwing into battle not only his head but also his soul. Civilization must not suffocate men. Even if it is not a question of reducing men to the isolation and brutality of the savage animal, it is no more desirable to lower them to the misery of domestic animals, to make them merely learned animals.

These reflections are worthwhile in themselves. They do not manifest the influence of non-being as an object to be confronted; rather, they manifest the *exigency of non-being as value*. The most violent movements of religious thought consist in deepening an existential void. This helps consciousness to hurl its effort beyond all determinations toward God. Despair becomes source. The growing horror of nothingness or of contradiction, which is the matrix of "annihilation" if it is not the matrix of resurrection, is transformed into stimulation so that man reaches God by the negation of the determinations which limit him. From Boehme to Pascal, from Kierkegaard to Karl Barth, these processes of rupture between the Infinite and the finite are processes which are diametrically opposed to the dialectics of flattening. They have had too much influence in philosophy to have had no value in experience. These processes of rupture imply that experience can be penetrated *by exigencies of openness as well as by exigencies of possession.* Further, they imply that non-being is imposed on philosophy no less as value than as given, however paradoxical it may seem to objectivism to attribute value to that which is simply a lack and to consider as given that which can neither be perceived nor thought.

[VI] THE UNITY OF EXPERIENCE

19. *A sudden turn*

DESCRIPTION HERE COMES TO ITS FIRST TURN. It is impossible to fuse the one and the multiple into a massive whole if non-being always makes the other appear and always intervenes in some measure to rupture the detected continuity of an object or an ensemble. On the other hand, it is impossible to make these three aspects of experience absolute strangers to one another, as if they formed three experiences. Non-being can only be relative. In experience there is no moat without a bridge. The one, the multiple, and non-being can therefore be nothing but parts and lacunae. All islands are accessible and all hiatuses can be leapt over. *The one, the multiple, and non-being therefore exist only in connection with a unity. Parts and lacunae therefore exist only in relation to a unity. This unity would be a whole* [4] *if non-being did not prevent experience from being compact and enclosed within definitive confines.* The content of experience is *with* the unity of experience. By *with* I mean that union of which *in, by, for,* and the other prepositions are nothing but specifications and categorical limitations. In opposition with every unity *in* experience, there is the unity *of* experience.

4. That is, a massive, undifferentiated whole.—Trans.

20. *The relation-soul*

One immediately sees that the Hamelinian relation infects precisely the three aspects brought to light in the description of experience. The possibility of distinguishing appeal from self-sufficient necessity, which would rule out the self, liberty, and idealism, presupposes the possibility of a separation between the thesis and what follows it. Suddenly unity loses its absolute indivisibility. Multiplicity appears through non-being.

But this does not mean that the unity of experience must be reduced to the unity of the Hamelinian relation. We will call the Hamelinian relation the *relation-norm*, or *relation-structure*, to distinguish it from the unity of experience, which we will call the *relation-soul*.

Hamelin in effect imposes on his description a necessary preliminary rule which is supposed to supply intelligibility. The relation is an idea rendered dynamic and mobile. But it is still an idea, in the sense that one looks to it for *the foundation* of experience and for the principle of a purification which would consign the irrational to nothingness and permit the rational to continue undisturbed to give incentive to intelligence. Hamelin thinks that the "mists of contingency" can be penetrated and dispelled by the intelligible sun. Does experience correspond to this supposition? Experience alone can give rise to a concrete conviction. Thus, though experience allows us to recognize the success of human intelligence, it likewise requires us to recognize its limits. Insofar as these limits are such that they can allow for utility and beneficence, experience suggests the feeling that this mist of contingency more closely resembles the London fog than it does a Mediterranean cloud, that it is an indestructible given of experience, and that its function is to dissipate in one place only to gather again elsewhere. This situation does not thereby entail the triumph of pessimism if this game of hide-and-seek is compatible with, and perhaps even the condition for, the expansion of the human spirit. It may be that it is neither possible nor desirable to banish this mist completely. Intelligibility can occur in such a way as to solicit and nourish our intelligence without overwhelming it.

This reservation in no way implies a condemnation of Hamelin's work. Skeptical and historical dialectics on the one hand, and Bergsonism on the other, in their respective fashions both run the risk of being partial by discrediting order in favor of becoming. A minute examination here would be premature; still one can recognize a threefold value in Hamelin's table of categories: (*a*) *artistic value,* inasmuch as the categories give thought a harmonious image of itself; (*b*) *deontological value,* inasmuch as the categories train the spirit in some dialectics which are more precious than others; and finally (*c*) *symbolic values,* inasmuch as they each supply a model of a concrete unity of the universe, a unity which is the ideal goal of intellectual and moral effort. Each table of categories is a finite view of a virtually infinite unity.

But one must immediately add that the very determinateness of the categories always threatens to make them passionate and dangerous. Even though this danger may threaten all philosophy, anticategorical as well as categorical, it is nonetheless true that a table of categories should be treated neither as the alpha nor as the omega of philosophy. In effect, the essence of a table of categories is to tend to reduce all dialectics to one. But such a reduction can only be accomplished by forgetting the infinite richness of experience. By what right, limiting ourselves here to Hamelin's case, does one reduce the spirit to being rational only when it launches out on the dynamism of the relation as in a ferry boat tied to a track? To do so makes the spirit stand over against experience as a witness whose activity is restricted to applying a regulation and whose knowledge is restricted to removing the obstacles which might shackle experience.

Respect for experience does not permit infinite reason to be reduced to the abstract universality of a single meaning which expresses the weakness at least as much as the divine unity of the human spirit. Truth cannot be the exclusive possession of a metaphysics transmuted into an intellectual ethic. Nor can reason be a militarylike rule. It is true that every idea is virtually infinite. But this is only a certain kind of infinity. This kind of infinity channels the spirit. If one wishes to stay faithful to the measureless variety offered us by experience one must oppose any restriction which forces thought to move in a rut and one must admit that the basic one [5] is not satisfied with aiming at a small target but radiates into every meaning. It must also be

5. Le Senne is referring to the fundamental oneness which philosophers have regularly tried to express. It is the oneness which ties reality, and thus the explication of reality, together.—Trans.

noted that when we bring in the spirit, we already refer ourselves to a teleological activity. To think is to think true. The unity of the spirit thus presupposes a specification of value starting with a unity which is as close as possible to having no specification. To make these admissions is to return to the unity of experience.

We must, therefore, go beyond the Hamelinian kind of relation. It is a relation which is only a thought, a norm, the principle of a structure of laws directed to dynamism. We should consider the Hamelinian relation as only one expression of the relation-soul. The relation-soul is equally capable of unifying both perceptual and conceptual forms, like the unity of a showcase or of a number; of unifying dialectics, whether they are regulated as in a chain of reasoning or free as in a search; as well as of unifying emotional processes, such as remorse or the presentiment of misfortune. *What relation-soul signifies over and above relation is the life of the relation.* By admitting contingency and liberty, Hamelin did indeed have to presuppose an existence distinct from the relation. In effect, he identifies spirit *and the absolute.* But this absolute is only a weak prop if it merely reigns and does not actually govern.

Experience forces us to pay more attention to the absolute. Marbe has shown the psychological utility of the notion of *the attitude of the spirit.* It has a universal truth. Weaving together the relation of the thesis to the synthesis involves an attitude, a *superrelation* of the relation to the unity of experience. But there are an infinite number of other relations in this superrelation. Hamelin's One can grasp the distinction of terms and separate them. It can distinguish between terms and connectives. It can transform the connective into the reason for conflict between terms. It can subordinate one term to another. It can stretch a relation to one of its extremities, etc. And, in general, with these elementary operations one can perform complex ones. Hamelinian description is comparable to Bergsonian description from the standpoint that both show an ascending experience. But the former comprehends this ascending experience in its dialectical essence, whereas the latter grasps it in emotional intuition. Experience goes beyond these parallel descriptions, both of which are antecedently oriented by a certain notion of value. Obstacle, periodicity, disorder, and defect are experiences which impose themselves on description just as imperiously as do rational construction or creative thrust. One must not concern himself solely with the reduction of all operations to the monotony of a rhythm. Hamelin's *Essay* is a normative description.[6] This determination is the source of both its value and its insufficiency.

Against such a position it is especially necessary to introduce the *existential aspect of experience*. This is the aspect whereby experience surpasses and dominates every given existent. For example, the experience of inventing is quite different from confirmation and the dynamism of the intellectual givens which analysis can recognize. Dialectically, one could essentially reduce invention to relational synthesis and even think that this synthesis is categorically effective. Nonetheless, invention presents itself as a gestation in which historical factors are inseparable from categorical factors. But let us now go on to the crucial experience. In thought there are always moments when the ideal continuity is broken, when it no longer exists, or when it does not yet exist. This is the fact which Hume forced philosophy to admit. Elements are scattered, misplaced, lost in other ensembles. Or they are nonexistent or absent either because they have been removed or because they have not been formed. *Where could these dislocated members be except in a representation about which all that can be said is that it exists, since this existence is greater than all the terms which are used to think about it?* In spite of the Kantian critique of the ontological argument, synthetic intellectualism postulates the adequation of the spirit, of representation, and even of experience itself to thought. Only reluctantly does Kant impede this adequation. He impedes it as little as possible, and in fact censures the impeding. Even if he were ideally right in holding that what experience embraces is in principle reducible to an objective principle which is its universal law, *reducibility still presupposes a distinction between the given prior to reduction and the given after reduction.* This fact is enough to make the objectivization of the relation-soul in the relation-structure no more than only one process among others which have to be verified and evaluated. What is such a relation-structure worth if it cannot find some matter to inform and control?

In short, the Hamelinian relation is the unity of intellectual

6. This refers to Octave Hamelin, *Essai sur les éléments principaux de la représentation* (Paris: Alcan, 1907).—Trans.

terms or, if one wants to reserve this word for psychology, of *ideals. The unity of experience or the relation-soul is the unity of the relation-norm and existence. It is the ideo-existential unity.* This latter unity excludes the monopolization of experience by an intellectualism which persists in the claim to reduce philosophy to mathematics or to dynamized necessity. It likewise excludes an anti-intellectualism which would understand philosophy as an exclusively existential analysis and would deny any kind of value to ideas. All strength is not reduced, Spinoza notwithstanding, to the strength of the idea. But the idea is never merely a quasi-empty flask which has to get all its power from outside itself. It is true—but, depending on the particular case, unequally so—that the right gives strength to its champions and that it also receives vigor from them. Existence sometimes opposes and sometimes identifies the existent and the existential.

21. *Transitivity*

Recognizing the unity of experience amounts to affirming *the universal possibility of passing from one given of experience to another.* All knowledge in varying ways links together the givens of experience. Experience entails its unity. But unless one applies the distinction between the ideal and the existential, one will forget that the liaison of givens oscillates or is distributed between their union and their distinction. It is a commonplace to say that to distinguish is nonetheless to unite. But this is not to unite as a unit. For example, when experience unites two terms for us, the allegation-of-juxtaposition consists in declaring that this union is not a necessity. That is, the union is not the objective interiority of an ideal one. It is not a union demanded by law.

When Leibniz reduced arithmetic duality to qualitative diversity by means of the principle of indiscernibles, he dialectically prepared for the reduction of this diversity to the multiplicity of an apprehension and thus for the reduction to the unity of a principle which was infinite when concrete. But this intellectually satisfying reduction dodged the difficulty that our perception grasps some dualities whose objects are distinguished by nothing but position. For us, two ten-franc pieces of money have to be interchangeable. It is not the same thing whether we have one or two such pieces. Thus the unity of an intuition cannot be confused with the unity of a logical principle. The unity of an intuition unites by embracing, while the unity of a logical principle unites by "naming." Starting with the paradox of symmetrical objects, Kant himself had to recognize the indispensability of intuitive unity. Whether one must interpret this unity as Kant did, and especially whether one must understand it as being both strictly human and specified in so definitive a fashion that we are enclosed in our humanity, remains to be seen. Nonetheless, the unity of experience is not reduced to intellectual continuity.

Terms, then, are logically or materially unified by the unity of experience insofar as it is ideal unity. They are logically or materially separated when they are united by the unity of experience insofar as it is an existential unity. The physical unity, for example, the meteorological and optical laws which allow clouds to be illumined by the sun, is a case of ideal unity. The view of the sunset is a case of existential unity. For the moment we leave aside all questions about value. If the unity of experience dominates everything, then absolute cohesion, which necessity alone could introduce into its products, is nothing but a limit. Inversely, existential unity could not achieve so definitive a representation that the laws could not suggest something else. The role played by the thought relation in the ideal order and by suggestion in the existential order is performed by infection of the ideo-existential order. But just as the unity of experience allows for both the disjunction of the terms of a relation and existential anarchy, so does it likewise permit the divorce of logic from existence. The cohesion between ideas and things can be fragile when it should be solid because the rest of experience modifies it. There are defects in the wheels of some machines and wheels can rust. For its part, existence can be illusory. Ordinarily, the existential unity of a dream does not equal that of wakefulness.

If it happens, on the contrary, that ideal unity and existential unity converge and intertwine, then experience becomes absolute. How could doubt attack ideas which are both coherent with one another and prescribed by existence? How could doubt disqualify existence with arguments which confirm it? Mono-ideaism and absolutely absolute intuition would each engender either intellectual or felt certitude if such certitude were possible. But such a certitude would be obtained by impoverishing experience. Experience would have to be divided into aspects, for its essence can be hypothetical and its existence deceiving. Beyond certitude, as well as beyond belief, we must therefore posit *conviction*. Conviction, if it occurs at all, necessarily results from an ideo-existential convergence in which dialectics and emotional processes each contribute the energies at their disposal.

Predominance. The foregoing discussion has shown that we cannot say that experience is either continuous or discontinuous. Experience is both continuous and discontinuous. Anticipating here the knowledge of value which we have not yet encountered in our description, we will state explicitly that when the description of experience forces us to unite two opposed aspects of experience into one single expression we will first name that aspect which we recognize as predominant and will treat only secondly the aspect which might be called recessive. Thus, in the case of the opposition just considered, *the continuity of discontinuity* can be concretely experienced wherever existence is sovereign over a manifold content. This is experienced, for example, in the consciousness of a man who adds numbers or who plays dice. On the other hand, *the discontinuity of continuity* can be concretely experienced in the case of disorder, where the anarchy of impressions imposes itself on consciousness despite the effort made by consciousness to bring unity into the disorder.

The same distinction which holds for the interplay between givens also holds for the givens themselves. The terms of all relations oscillate between a purely ideal nature and a purely existential one. Insofar as they are ideas considered independently of their infection with existence, they are depersonalized and tend to become pure logical essences. Insofar as they are clearly events, which not only are rooted in existence but bathe in it and concentrate the activity of existence in themselves to a greater or lesser degree, they become mental.[7] By abstraction any term can at times be called ideal and at other times existential. One hundred, considered apart from the one who enumerates, has arithmetic unities as ideal terms. One hundred persons, not as names or bodies but as mental existences,

7. Le Senne obviously means here that events are individual psychological occurrences which we each experience in a unique fashion, a fashion not reducible to some "essential, universal experience."— Trans.

constitute a relation to existential terms. The contradiction involved in a squared circle has ideal terms, whereas the contradiction involved in war has existential terms. But the intellectual suffering which results from the incompatibility of the circle and the square is existential, whereas the clashes of weapon against weapon, which manifest the hostility of the belligerents, are ideal. Logical identity brings together ideal terms. Love mingles existences. Resemblance is an existential given which can be formulated ideally as $R = I + D$, where I signifies identity and D signifies differences. At the beginning of the perception of resemblance there is an oscillation of consciousness in which both identity and differences make themselves felt, but they are not separated and defined. Existence prevails over ideas. But when existence is overlooked, then the concretely experienced likeness will be practically replaced by a group of symbols. In such a case, ideas prevail over existence.

22. *What the unity of experience is not*

By opposing the unity of experience to all the unities which are isolated or grouped within experience, one avoids determining this unity. Thus the only way to speak about the unity of experience is to speak negatively. Instability, indivisibility, independence, and indifference are all characteristics which apply to it when it is considered on the basis of what experience gives us. But this is, so to speak, its ideal minimum, for everything which experience presents further enriches the unity of experience. This ideal minimum is what negative theology achieves by denying to God all attributes in order to safeguard him from being limited by them, if indeed by the very term *theology* negative theology implies the mental reservation that God is not less but more than everything which one denies of him. The description of experience is the inverse of a dogmatism which at least appears to arrogate everything to itself so as then to extract whatever it wishes to consider. The description of experience arrogates to itself only that without which it could not describe anything. This dogmatism is monism at only one remove from its lower limit, the lower limit being the unity of the void. Such a void could be filled indefinitely without becoming full.

We want to prevent all unconscious slurring over this virtually infinite but actually impoverished unity. Therefore we turn away from those specifications of this unity which would simultaneously strip the unity of experience of the various kinds of promises contained in its virtuality and would locate this unity in a definite present.

(1) *The unity of experience is not a sum.* There is no such thing as a total of experiences. Experience cannot have a total since it is not closed in all directions. The closed is the correlative of the open. Further, it cannot have a total since the homogeneity indispensable for addition is nothing but the content of an abstract view. A total is the product of a totaling. It is comparable to the operation by which an architect assembles the products of a succession, namely, the deeds of his workers, into the relatively perceived and relatively thought simultaneity of the building's components. Totaling is a dialectic which the description of experience must confirm and evaluate. But description itself is not exhaustively described as a totaling.

(2) *The unity of experience is not the world.* World and unity of experience coincide inasmuch as the world, too, is unique. But it is unique only in principle. The act of cognition which apprehends it surpasses it, and consequently the world immediately becomes contingent and susceptible to completion or modification. In fact, the cosmological exigency calls for taking a stand in favor of rigidity, structure, determinism, prediction, and the exclusion of the contingency which is imposed on experience when disorder, fragility, caprice, unpredictability, and the exclusion of necessity have become too much to bear. At its limit, the cosmological exigency would require the reign of the object. But such a kingdom would be a wasteland. An inhabited world is no longer the world. In experience there are forms of every dimension and mode. But experience itself is unformed. Since it does not depend on any category, experience can have only partial limits. The categories themselves are merely limits of experience's unity. In effect, every limit is the demarcation of an inside and an outside. A limit divides experience in two and therefore cannot terminate it. Experience is one, but is not unified.

(3) *The unity of experience is not substance.* It would be worth seeing whether any great philosophy has betrayed the spiritual vocation of philosophy by making substance the necessitating unity which produces its attributes and modes with-

out either freedom or love or virtue. In every instance, according to Spinoza, the third kind of knowledge is the love of God returning to itself when intelligence becomes intuition. The substance has never been, at least for a philosopher freed from the direct or indirect burden of perception, anything but the objective symbol through which, at the very core of his experience, he converts the unity of the given into the unity of the giver in such a way that the ideal and existential values of this conversion are reconciled. Likewise, this conversion shows that substance is for us nothing but an ideal which, when used exclusively, tends to suppress everything opposed to substance, such as attributes, modes, contingency, error, and consciousness. Thus the unity of substance is essentially distinguished from the unity of experience in that the former is opposed to something, as one given is opposed to another given. But the unity of experience is not one given among others. It opposes itself to all givens without exception, whether they are intellectual, sensible, qualitative, or emotional just as it opposes itself to its own content.

(4) In using non-being to mediate the conversion of the givens of experience to the unity of experience we have excluded the possibility of reducing the unity of experience to the unity of *being*. In one sense, experience does not cease to be, since there is non-being only by reason of being. But insofar as experience would be nothing if it were merely pure being, identical with non-being, experience is always and from every viewpoint determined in some way. This determination is a relative limitation which gives rise simultaneously both to historical, positive being and to non-being. To make an exclusive affirmation that experience simply exists, one would have to terminate all possibility. One would have to exhaust all possibility. But because we have to designate this termination so as to be able to rise to the idea of the unity of experience, then the designation of this termination only occurs in such a way as to fall within experience itself and to lead us to confess that experience has no definitive limits, for finite thought is precisely the means for understanding experience. But if one calls *consciousness* that reflection which introduces into experience the name and idea of the total being of experience, then the idea of being and of each being is simply a means whereby experience objectifies the unity of both intuitive consciousness and reflective consciousness. Intuitive consciousness existentially encompasses re-

flective consciousness. Reflective consciousness ideally projects intuitive consciousness.

If the idea of the unity of being is an objective mediation within experience, it can be either of service or of disservice, depending on whether it intervenes as a barrier in the face of which every effort surrenders or as a direction to be pursued. Philosophies of being are beneficent or harmful either in themselves or in the use one makes of them. But they and their usage will both exist in experience. They open up experience in some directions in order to close it off in other directions.

When we initially subordinated the unity of being to the unity of experience, our intention was not to discredit being. The unity of experience is not value. The unity of experience permits the worst as well as the best. It permits war, the unity of belligerents, as well as unanimity, the unity of friends. By beginning with the unity of experience one begins with that which is most ample but which, if some value ought to be present, is most impoverished. And even at this quasi limit a vague recollection of philosophical experience is sufficient to convince us that one of the most important discriminations made in philosophy is between those givens which we must consider to exist and those which we must consider not to exist. A philosopher never praises illusion insofar as it is deceptive. He praises the being in illusion, not the non-being. Still, one who seeks the principle of value within being must not consider abandoning the unity of experience. Any value which cannot be referred to something within the unity of experience would be precisely the absolute annihilation of value.

If someone claims that the experience of being does not ground the being of experience and that the latter must be grounded, a sufficient reply is to point out that only *within experience itself* can the opposition between the ideal and the existential be posed. To ground is to make an ideal link between a principle and a consequence. To know the value of the operation of "grounding" one has to link the grounding operation to the existence in which it inserts itself so as to experience and verify the benefit which existence receives from this operation. The idea has to ground existence, but existence has to authorize the idea. When and whether these two actions confirm each other can only be apprehended through the study of experience. In every way the fact remains that being is simply *the common positivity of essence and existence* and that experience includes negativity as a given. Being can yield security and correctness. Non-being is needed to bring deliverance and perspectives. Experience must be both nostalgia and adventure.

(5) The unity of experience is not the unity of a *form*. We have already ruled out confusing the unity of experience with that of the world—understanding world as simply an existentially full form. We would not, then, have to rule out confusing experience and form except for the fact that the tendency to formalism is one of the most profound tendencies of the abstract spirit. The abstract spirit's need for unification by reason of some principle and by reason of a totality is satisfied by this tendency to formalism. *A form is a structure of directions*. But it is impossible to abandon oneself to these tendencies without some counterbalancing. Experience embraces both the unformed and the structured, the deformed and the normal, the material and the formal, confusion and order, the romantic and the geometric. In short, experience embraces both the existential and the ideal, both the seeking for, the absence of, or the disdain for the form and its possession. One can concretely experience a certain polemical joy in making some givens or aspects of experience a reason for denying others. But when one excessively accentuates that which makes a certain philosophy partial, and partialness is an inescapable characteristic of every philosophy, he deforms the face of experience so badly that the portrait is unrecognizable. The reduction of the unity of experience to formal unity can be shown as deficient by pointing out either the being of non-being or the non-being of being.

(6) The unity of experience is not the unity of an *equilibrium*. Undoubtedly the unity of an equilibrium is a better symbol for the unity of experience than are any of the others we are considering. Indeed, the unity of the equilibrium is rich; it infects a form with an existential halo. This is not the only case where science, which is the partialness of the ideal, reveals the inseparability of existence and the relations which constitute the ideal. For example, force is a mathematical product, mg, but this product signifies force only by reason of that which the recollection of action adds to it from felt experience. This is the truth in epiphenominalism, which describes consciousness when consciousness is merely the existential fringe of a historical or logical series of definite terms.

Thus in equilibrium one first of all finds the outline of an order. If we provisionally exclude all sympathy for the intense actions which are balanced in the equilibrium, and especially for the tendencies within these actions to go beyond the equilibrium, the equilibrium is still an organized ensemble. Like every other ensemble, it actualizes a concept. But we cannot let the matter rest there. An equilibrium is *more than an object of perception*. If it were an object of perception it would keep us entirely outside it. We have to go beyond pure objectivity. An equilibrium cannot be merely conceived. It is felt. One cannot think about the order it sustains without going back to a moment prior to its establishment to desire it, to institute it, and to begin to detect its collapse. An equilibrium requires compensation of actions, convergence of tendencies, extremely rapid alternation of incipient collapses and reintegrations, silently resolved combats, and mutual neutralization. Thus in the course of an equilibrium there is present both an almost instantaneous unification constituting a well-thought-out order and a more or less laborious or mitigated unification manifesting a thinking activity.

Nonetheless it is still true from the outset that equilibrium has meaning only in contrast with disequilibrium, and it is realized only to a certain degree. Further, with reference to the unity of experience it is like an object, a specification. If one were to make an equilibrium of the entirety of experience one would notice that experience must allow for *an aspect of compensation* so as not to be dislocated. But one might forget that this compensation can take place at different levels and that the progressions or the failures which make the compensation pass from one level to another involve something other than whatever equilibrium the compensation might pass through. Thus the unity of experience must be amenable to each equilibrium if the equilibrium is to exist. But it does not give itself exhaustively to the unity of an equilibrium any more than it does to any other specific unity.

(7) The unity of experience is not the unity of a *self*. One can be convinced of this simply by recalling that a self exists only by reason of the possibility of distinguishing itself both from a non-self and from another self. The very word signifies this. By being opposed to *I*, as *me* to *ego*, or *mich* to *Ich*, the word *self* has the character of an accusative, i.e., of an object. In effect, every self is posited with certain determinations which constitute it as a more or less solid nature and exclude other

determinations from it. The self is a landlord, always on guard.
Here is one self, there is another. Self thus presupposes a split
within experience. It accepts this and rejects that. From this
standpoint, every self bathes in experience by participating in
its unity. The unity of experience must embrace the experience
of both Peter and Paul. But Peter and Paul are carved out of the
unity of experience, as sectors apportion the surface of a circle
whose center remains common to all of them. There can be only
one experience. But Paul's experience is not Peter's, regardless of
what identities hold between them and allow them to intersect
or partially coincide.

(8) The unity of experience is not the unity of the *tran-*
scendental subject. This is not the place to explore the operations which define and limit the scope of the notion of transcendental subject. We must be content simply to point out its
partialness. This partialness is sufficiently underscored if we
remember that the transcendental subject brings together the
universal functions whereby subjects, e.g., men, are identified.
It is thereby opposed to the psychological subject, which is defined on the contrary by acts which express the singularity,
liberty, and eventually the awkwardness of each such subject. The transcendental subject is a specification of the self.
As such it is already more restricted than the self. Further, it is
opposed both to the matter which will fill its forms of apperception and to reality insofar as reality is independent of these
forms. And, finally, it is opposed to other things. The notion of
the transcendental subject has been a precious step in the
progress which has reinserted all of philosophy's givens, especially space and time, into the unity of experience. But proceeding from the distinction between what is necessary in knowing and what is contingent, the transcendental subject can
obscure the interaction between theoretic knowledge and the
other modes of the relation between the unity of experience and
its content. Where does the transcendental begin? Where
does the psychological end? The inventory of pure reason presupposes an invariability in the forms of knowing which the
profound sentiment of the dynamism of experience does not
allow one to assert without qualification. It is always some
individual man who defines the transcendental subject and who
derives from it, either through opposition or emanation, the
psychological subject.

(9) A universalized transcendental subject would be God

and its forms would be the general volitions of God. Thus one readily passes from the preceding hypothesis to one which would suppress every distinction between the unity of experience and God. We should clear up this confusion. If by God one means the Spinozist necessary and necessitating being, one denies non-being and excludes all indeterminateness, even that of an appearance. Such an exclusion does not fit well with experience, for experience is possible only through non-being. By contrast, if one seeks in God a free person who can love and be loved, one makes him, initially at least, one self over against others. In this case, what we have said in objecting to the reduction of the unity of experience to the self remains valid. In the absence of other considerations, it should be noted that the pure and simple identification of the unity of experience with God would ratify and divinize everything experience embraces, even the most cruel and heinous things.

(10) The foregoing shows why the unity of experience is not the unity of an *ideal*. Surely, insofar as it is unity, the unity of experience must countenance every ideal. But it likewise countenances not only inertia, which is the resistance of a given unity to its modification, but also war, which is the unity indispensable to the encounter between belligerents. The only way that the unity of experience could be exhaustively denominated as an ideal would be if it were nothing more than an ideal, nothing other than an ideal. But in fact the unity of experience also has to be expressed by givens, by obstacles. An ideal can only be defined over against an obstacle. A realized ideal would be the absence of an ideal. Finally, one ideal is distinguished from another. One ideal can compete with or battle against another ideal. Ideals, then, are encountered among the objects of experience and are thus in experience. They are surpassed and dominated by experience's unity.

We could indefinitely prolong the list of what the unity of experience is not without ever exhausting all the possibilities for reduction. Every definable unity could be unreasonably confused with the unity of experience. The unity of experience might well be considered as a center from which all determinations emanate were it not for the fact that it could be just as well presented as a point of origin or as an end. Each of these latter presentations would follow from a dialectic developed within experience. Consequently, each would be relative and just as partial as the dialectic of the radiating center. If one wants to call attention to the fact that each of these presentations is inseparable from the unity of experience, one could call them its *expressions*. Each expression could on occasion be treated pejoratively as debris, theoretically as a middle term, or more favorably as an ideal. An expression's worth consists primarily in what it reflects, always in an original fashion, in experience, namely, its unity. Every philosophy gives preeminence to one of these expressions. But it does so only by denying, i.e., repressing, the other expressions, sometimes temporarily and other times to the point of ignoring them altogether. Nevertheless, each of these expressions presupposes that the others are likewise definable within experience.

23. *How is the unity of experience to be denominated?*

The foregoing refutations forbid giving the unity of experience a name which might confuse it with one of its expressions, for its expressions are found within experience itself. However little one can say about the unity of experience, it is nevertheless necessary to make explicit that there is some interiority of experience in all occurrences, even in conflicts,[8] that experience is the relation between the ideal and the existential, and that experience considered apart from the content with which it is connected is without value.

This name cannot be the *one*. This would again reduce the unity of experience to a characteristic common to all its manifestations, namely, that of a unity within experience. More precisely, to choose to call the unity of experience the one leads too easily to the pure, separated, insular unity of the logician who tries to reunite everything by a progressively forcible elimination of differences. The unity of experience is the exact inverse of this constriction of experience. The unity of experience is open to all that is possible. It embraces negation and relative contradiction. It is closed only to absolute nothingness, because in closing itself to pure nothing it does not close itself to anything.

In choosing an appropriate word, it is essential that one maintain the sometimes unifying and sometimes discriminating

8. Le Senne means that there is no occurrence which is exhaustively constituted by external relations. No occurrence is so discrete that it is isolated from the unity of experience.—Trans.

solidarity between the unity of experience and the series or collection of experiences. The unity of experience is not a *one*. It is a *one of*. . . . To denominate this state, the word *I* is appropriate. This term *I* has the advantage of turning back toward some content. Further, it straddles both absolute impersonality and absolute personality. It participates in impersonality by reason of its indeterminateness. The *I* is as near as possible to the "there is" [*il y a*]. But it must never be confused with the "there is." Such a hypothesis would exclude the possibility of any content relative to the notion of person. *I* permits the notion of personality to appear, for it opens up the series of personal pronouns while distinguishing itself from the others by reason of the peculiarity of not referring the concrete encounter of confirmed or created experience to another, as do the pronouns *you* or *he*. The *I* is a unity of pure apperception. But it must embrace without restriction all that can be recognized, for it is not limited to the field of a formal a priori. The *I* surpasses every limit. Further, the *I* excludes the presupposition which would make it the subject of a purely theoretic cognition. The subject of the action and everything else, including the object or objects, are equally aspects of the *I*.

The indistinguishability of the I *and the ideo-existential unity of every relation*. The same *I* can equally well be either the first or the third person singular subject of a verb. In effect, *I* stands both for the "representative" or undetermined subject of the representation and for the interiority of every relation, whether the relation is ideal, existential, or ideo-existential. Both in the case of subjective apperception and in that of objective thought one finds a unity considered in abstraction from its terms. One sees this unity clearly when the terms change. On the one hand, the nature of squaring does not change, whether it unites 3 to 9 or 5 to 25. On the other hand, the content of a film which I perceive does not involve in its changes the unity of apperception as such. Thus one can equally well say that a relation is aware of its terms or that I am a connection between shadow and light.[9] These different languages manifest different attitudes of the *I*, but the *I* continues to dominate the unity of experience.

9. Le Senne is referring back to his example of a film.—Trans.

24. *The experience of the pure* I

The very nature of the *I* is such that apart from its encountering something or its being in reference to something, it cannot be the object of an experience. There is no supplementary experience of the *I* over and above experience. But a philosophy of description owes it to itself to look for what is given to us when we make the *I* something thought. Since one understands the pure *I* to mean experience without its content, one gets close to the pure *I* by going to the most pallid experiences, to those which the most passive apperception apprehends. These are the experiences which Maine de Biran interpreted psychologically as experiences of the self and classified under the rubric, *simple sensitive system.* These are experiences in which the self seems to renounce simultaneously both itself and things. By attenuating the vivacity of the impressions and letting them lose themselves in an impoverished contemplation, by weakening the interests which lead one to desire or to possess objects, by relaxing as far as possible all capacity to attend to and to will, by practically no longer loving any thing or person, even oneself, one enters upon a desolate experience in which the self loses its originality and its responsibility. Nothing is left except a vague apperception and an indulgence ready to tolerate anything. The pure *I* would be at the terminus of this indifference. It would find there, so to speak, its minimum. Its detachment would intermingle all of us in itself.

Must we accept this nothingness? One should distrust here the degradation which every return to the theoretic attitude imposes on what it is given to deal with. The *I* is indeed an apperception. But the scope of this term is unlimited and one has no right to restrict it to its most colorless acceptations. The *I* does not cease apperceiving when it is operating and creating. Though the *I* can be given other names when it is considered in its highest incarnations, we are not required either to restrict the *I* to the lower limits of such incarnations or to forget that the *I* does not cease to be what it was when it becomes better. In one sense the *I* is sufficient, for there is nothing but experience. This sufficiency, however, is an unfolding from *that without which nothing could begin* to *that in which everything is accomplished.* It ranges between a *non minus infra* and a *non plus ultra.* Even when experience is manifested as passing from a barely detectable emergence to the semiblind thrust of naive spontaneity, it is still experience.

[VII] THE UNIVERSALITY AND THE SUBLIMITY OF THE *I*

THE *I* IS RECOGNIZED as being at the foundation of the relation-soul. The relation-soul is capable both of expressing itself to itself by means of relation-norms, i.e., by means of ideal terms and connections, and of distinguishing itself from relation-norms by embracing the continuity in which they are situated. Therefore the *I* must be open both to the *dialectics of reduction* and to *processes of infection.* By reason of these two operations the *I* is both universal and "sublime." We are now going to pass from the consideration of ideals which define the sense of these operations to the acknowledgment of the universality and the sublimity of the *I*.

25. *The punctiliar one and the continuous one*

We begin this description with the *dialectic of reduction.* The human need for order, without which our activity slips into such insoluble contradictions that we soon become disgusted with putting forth effort, often leads us to give privileged status to the ideal. One identifies the real with the formal. Thenceforth the existential, taken either as objective gestations where everything is grounded in the ensemble or as the indistinctiveness of psychological sensibility, is no longer considered as anything but a confusion to be dispelled. When all these nebulous things are precipitated into forms, the forms clearly retain traces of the existential whence they have sprung inasmuch as they present themselves as pure facts. Thus, to use an approach which consists in separating a mixture into its elements, one is drawn to discover the simple. Then the simple is used to rebuild the complex, to resolve the forms in turn, and to look for that "first" from which everything else is supposed to come. At the end of such an endeavor one reaches two identical, formally isomorphic terms, the model for which is equality. At this point the difference among forms is volatilized by applying the same numerical designation to them. Thus one clears the way for what we will call the punctiliar, objective, abstract one.

Since Hume, the growing awareness of the irreducibility of existence to a concept has led intellectualism to make the idea mobile and to see existence as a relation. But this intellectualism loses all its explicative character and becomes an anti-intellectualism and a skepticism if it delivers the idea over to pure time. Intellectualism therefore is led to reunite relations in a manner comparable to that whereby it systematizes and reduces forms. Intellectualism is thus stimulated to go back to the primary relation, a relation which is primary only by reason of the mutual interiority of its terms. Because of this stimulus, though the objective one no longer presents itself under the form of the principle of identity, it is still rediscovered at the core of all relations as the principle of synthesis.

But, here as elsewhere, the objective one cannot be anything more than a mediating pivot between a regression and a progression. When all differences are deprived of their solidity in order that the one be reached, we concretely experience the triviality of the one. When the *I* looks for itself in this expression, it finds nothing but its ideal symbol. *The punctiliar one is the simple one, without parts and devoid of content.* The punctiliar one is supposed to explain, but it does not. Having been obtained by a progressive impoverishment of existence, it necessarily appears as inferior to everything existence encompassed before this dialectic came into play.

Thus it is inevitable that the *I* will be brought back to the other operation, namely, a *process of infection.* The progressive impoverishment already shows that existence transcends every abstract idea or thought relation. Existence would have no value if it could do nothing more than rejoin terms disjoined by analysis. The liberty of the *I* is manifested both in its power to create syntheses other than those given to it and in its capacity to reproduce discovered syntheses in places where these syntheses had not previously existed. This choice involves a contingence which can be accounted for only by going beyond ideal relations in order to consider their hyperrelation to existence.

More and more it becomes clear that to exist is *not to be composed of parts* but to be like *an ensemble, which in due course imperceptibly gains primacy over whatever parts it can be analyzed into. An analysis of it is always incomplete.* Gradually the *I* becomes an indistinct whole within which all parts are so intimately mingled that it would be absurd to want to separate them. Ideally, a picture is nothing but an intersection of chemical and optical laws. It exists, on the contrary, only as a totality to be concretely experienced. When Delacroix claims that nature is made of reflections, he raises the relation to the plane of art. But the harmony which results from these interchanges of impressions is no longer a harmony of nature to be thought through. It is either concretely experienced or it does not exist. There are no longer any laws to explain the existence of this harmony. Rather, its existence actualizes the laws. If one imagines this infection pushed as far as possible, then it is the entirety of experience which offers itself to the sovereignty of the *I*. To understand is now to love.

One cannot say that the continuous one which the *I* modifies and dilates at will is a term. In the direction of the objective one the dialectic of reduction cannot be completed because existence indefinitely gives it something new to reduce. The regression is asymptotic to this term. When the objective one is itself reduced to perfect simplicity, it brings analysis to a halt. In the direction of the continuous one, however, creation can be pursued indefinitely. Each of the ideal operations will simply add to the density of the continuous one because, from another point of view, they lose themselves in existence as physico-chemistry lost itself in Pasteur's consciousness. Must we conclude from this discussion that existence is self-sufficient? If that were the case, it would exclude all dialectics. Even Rousseau, who felt himself becoming extremely weak and uncertain when he passed from immediacy to mediation, was not able to abstain from reflecting, reasoning, and arguing. In fact, the very notion of infection refers to a more or less distinct though grounded multiplicity. An analysis of this notion would accentuate the distinctiveness of multiplicity. Existence overflows into ideas and relations. Though it is opposed to them it does not cancel them. Rather, it is opposed to them insofar as it surpasses them and ceaselessly adds to them.

At the bottom, there is necessity; toward the top, liberty. When the objective one is posited abstractly by momentarily forgetting existence, it provides a foundation for the future. But this foundation, by reason of the characteristic of the asymptotic ideal which comes into view, can only be conceived in its punctiliarity. That is, it can merely be named. When analysis turns its investigation toward it, when the investigation passes from this program of ideal unification, by means of the objective one, to applying this program, it seems to be getting closer to its goal. In fact, though, it encounters resistances and cohesions which are more and more solid. The further the metaphysical and mathematical analysis of notions extends and the more deeply the physico-chemical resolution of bodies and of physical functions is fathomed, the more resistant to resolution do the terms become. Toward the bottom, it is *the difficulty in breaking apart* which obstructs us. Toward the top, we are obstructed by *the difficulty of holding together*.

In the course of regressive concrete experience the punctiliar one presents itself as the ideal foundation for *necessity*. At the outset, the reduction was a triumph. But it was an artistic triumph over ideas separated from existence. Now the reduction is a laborious operation which nibbles at the solidity of things only by becoming increasingly painful and costly to maintain. We are led to say such things as: The fragility of the nerve tissue is comparable to that of artistic impressions. Or, the resistance of atoms to division is akin to the evidence of mathematical principles.

A consequence of this situation is that the less exalted the regions of experience into which we descend, the more imperiously are laws imposed on us. These laws indicate the limits which we cannot in actuality go beyond. They warn us that this is not the place for our liberty to provisionally exert itself, or at least that they can only assist our liberty if we respect them. If a saint can be crushed in an automobile accident, it is because the laws of mechanics must be obeyed. It is not because the saint himself is nothing but a mechanical aggregate. Necessity, like every determination, is both positive and negative. It is pure *permission*. Like every permission, it excludes what must not be. But it allows one first to choose between many possibles and then to choose between a specified possibility and an exploration. In permission, the objective one is rejected, for it invites the man who wants to exist, and to exist is to act, to redirect his aim toward an ever richer, simpler, and stronger existence. Blind alleys occur so that we may convert them into avenues. Perception occurs so that we may leap over it.

26. *The universality of the* I

The *I* is closed in the sense of the objective one and open in the sense of the continuous one. It has two characteristics flowing from this state of affairs. *Insofar as the objective one is the universal mid-point of all ideal mediation, that is, of all intellectual or perceptual mediation, the I is endowed with universality.* It is true that there is no aspect of experience about which it is impossible to think, if to think means to analyze or to construct a thought. In this sense intellectualism is unlimited. But because these operations always presuppose that the *I* is turned away from existence, this universality is nothing more than an abstract universality. The *I* must then have another aspect, *an aspect whereby it will apprehend existence itself or some particular existence as an unanalyzed ensemble. We call this aspect its sublimity.*

There is little to say to establish the universality of the *I*. This aspect of the *I* is the one which presents itself to those philosophers whose interest in analyzing and whose taste for ideas lead them to prefer movement toward the abstract one over movement toward the continuous one to such a degree that they have not been dissuaded by the stalemates arising from the partialness of the abstract one. Intellectualism is the easiest doctrine for the theoretician. But as we cannot completely lose the sentiment of existence, which the abstract cannot fully satisfy for us, intellectualism necessarily oscillates between a preference for space and a preference for time. It necessarily tends either toward systematization or toward history. The more the need for construction is subordinated to the need for analysis, the more order is presented as a scholasticism. In reality, every ideal order is nothing but a cobweb by comparison with the measureless richness of experience. It follows, therefore, that the multiplication of ideas appears to be more worthwhile than their unification.

But this proliferation, which was at first concretely experienced as a deliverance, is necessarily soon felt to be a dissolution. One and the same movement brings shattered societies back to authority, scattered science back to the theoretician who unifies it, and critical and historical intellectualism back to systematic intellectualism. Space and time call for each other and cancel each other. To the degree to which systematic intellectualism succeeds in organizing truths, it will verify the universality of the punctiliar one. At the same time it will verify the universality of the *I*. Insofar as the tendency to extend this verification is so ambitious that it surpasses all its applications, the *I* is universal in principle. Insofar as this tendency can surpass its applications only because of their limitation, it is always limited in fact.

Ideal experience always presents us with a variable degree of conjunction and of separation. Sometimes the ideas or the relations are isolated. Arithmetic began as a collection of scattered facts. Sometimes these facts are brought together in more or less vast structures which, however, come to a complete termination because of clues which lead nowhere. The beauty of the human body consists less in the harmony of its proportions than in the indefinite variety of attitudes and movements which make the body a kind of halo of possibilities. Finally, these structures are sometimes consolidated into systems. But existence always manifests the *I*'s independence of every order. It either shatters the systems, as happens when a war destroys a State, or it deserts them, as happens when a credal confession dies because faith no longer animates it. Every number is at the juncture between the axiom of the spirit's free mobility and its fatigue. Insofar as virtual universality is necessarily actualized in terms, every relation is crystallized and cut off in determinations. We will soon have to examine and describe these determinations.

One could compare experience to an unequally plastic and viscous mass which a somewhat torn net drags with it when it itself is not carried away by the mass. Here and there the mass submits to the directions and impressions of the net. When this happens a science of experience is possible. This is the case when the atomistic reduction of a perceptual complex of properties and elements is parallel to the dialectic of decomposition. But when the mass of experience weighs too heavily on certain stitches of the net and breaks it, then the scientist upholds the universality of the *I* by claiming that unknown conditions have been added to the known conditions in such a way that the former interfere with the latter's causality. This claim preserves the professional confidence of the scientist by permitting him to maintain his postulates in the face of the contradictions in experience. And this confidence will be verified, as far as necessary, when new theoretic successes confirm the universality of the *I*. But these new successes could not restore confidence unless experience as a mass has revealed, in belying a rational expectation, an absolute aspect of historicity and singularity by virtue of which it grants actual existence to the always hypothetical jurisdiction of laws.

27. *The sublimity of the* I

Every description enriches what it describes by being added to it as an effect, and specifies what it describes by retaining only one aspect of it. When the *I* identifies itself with the punctiliar one and thinks of itself in terms of it, the *I* then confers upon the punctiliar one a bare actuality. But it receives from this one the absolute simplicity which allows the *I* to be called a *center*. From this point of view the *I* is the thought *I*. Or, rather, it would be the thought *I* when it determined itself as a one, unless it remained independent of its own determination insofar as it itself determines and thus surpasses that determination. The *I* would be nothing but the objective one were there not an existential halo around that center into which each consciousness concentrates itself when it thinks about itself. This halo allows for a distinction between the thinking and the thought. Thus the weight which can be condensed at a body's center of gravity must also extend into the whole body. As a consequence, the *I* has to join to the aspect of universality an aspect of indeterminateness. This latter aspect is what we call its sublimity.

Let us present the *I* in another way. Hypothetically, let us suppose that experience is in the process of being impoverished. Indeterminateness falls from the infinite down to nothingness. When it has practically reached nothingness, then determination, which undergoes a parallel degradation, reaches its minimum. Its minimum is the punctiliar one. It is that which lets everything remain outside it, that which is a concept without content. By reason of the annihilation of the content of experience, the *I* is concentrated and rolled up in the punctiliar one. Something has to be thought for the *I* to exist. But the *I* cannot complete this movement of concentrating itself in a concept without content. If that were possible, then it would cease being the *I*. Therefore, the *I* becomes a center by reason of the reduction of determination to its minimum. But at the same time the indeterminateness inseparable from the *I* necessarily opens it up as a horizon. As Hume has seen, the *I* cannot be confused with any of the objects it presents to itself. Nor can it be confused with the punctiliar one, which is the ideal source of all objects. The *I* is always both *something thought and that which imagines*. Otherwise one could confuse it with one or the other of these aspects. The *I* cannot be somewhere without being everywhere. Before acting here or there it always acts in itself. Thus, insofar as it is a horizon, we call the *I* sublime.

The sublimity of the I is to be found in every segment of

experience, for sublimity is inseparable from the I. We will demonstrate this summarily by showing that some of the more important experiences cannot be reduced to their ideal content. Mathematics disturbs science by its concern for a beyond. This beyond is opposed to every determination precisely because it itself is not determined. Logic, understood as the determination of the conditions for the validity of an affirmation, is by no means self-sufficient. The *importance* of a theorem or of a method is always, sooner or later, found to reside in its reference to an unknown existence which owes its accessibility to some concrete metaphysical experience. If importance had value only by reason of its connection with the personal sentiment of the one who affirms it, we would no longer be in the realm of truth. Therefore, there must be in mathematics itself a mysterious accommodation of its forms of thought to that which goes beyond them.

Ordinarily it is the physicist who is the beneficiary of this accommodation. He receives the theories which come from this striving toward the absolute. But when the physicist looks for matter within these laws, he cannot push on to a rational relativism. He invariably believes in the existence of "something" on which the laws are imprinted. The fact that he often interprets this "something" according to the postulates of a materialistic metaphysics does not detract from this observation. Besides, it is "natural," i.e., easy, for a specialist to look within his own specialty for a term that helps him to point out precisely the insufficiency in his specialty. The opposition between the particle and the wave, and between the equilibrium and the field, among others, illustrates the duality of discontinuity and continuity which divides experience into models and zones. These models cannot be extracted from their milieu and these zones cannot be encompassed by a closed curve.

Insofar as one passes from the consideration of theoretic knowledge to the *activity* which subordinates theoretic knowledge to itself, the opposition between determination and indeterminateness *changes the objectivity of the opposition into spirituality.* The opposition is expressed ethically in terms of utility and disinterestedness. Utility, like science, which utility can only orient, goes from one thing to another. It does not go beyond either an intellectual or a practical mechanism of determinations. Thus it remains bound to the ideal. Disinterestedness, if it proves to be abortive, becomes disinterest. But when it succeeds it subordinates every determination to a sentiment of joy and happiness which we experience concretely but which we can refer to only indirectly. The study of the pure *I* does not let us reach any value yet. Therefore we stress here that the same uncertainty weighs both upon the determined, which can be either authentic or illusory, and upon the undetermined, which can be either a sublimity or a sublimation. Indeterminateness can be nothing or everything. It can be either the void in which one necessarily becomes lost or the fullness of soul discovered by reason of the impossibility of reducing the soul to a detail floating within indeterminateness. As the heavens are punctuated with stars and streaked with constellations, so experience presents us with givens and relations. But it submerges them in a continuity which is indispensable for discerning them. This submersion makes it impossible to be immediately able to decide whether the continuity is a confusion to be dispelled by revealing the mechanisms it hides or whether the continuity is the matrix of the detail it envelops. But in both of these hypotheses the sublimity of the *I* comes to light. Space as a system of distances and space as an empty environment are indispensable to each other. Conjointly they express the *I*.

Utility proposes to itself some determinate end. Disinterestedness aims beyond all determination insofar as determination is always somehow insufficient. Through utility, a man becomes a thing—he wants to possess. Through disinterestedness, which subordinates and surpasses utility, he becomes someone—he wants to be. *Personality manifests a kind of impregnation by the sublimity of the I*. Suppose that an unlimited intelligence, if such a supposition is possible, wants to identify and enumerate the determinations by which a man can be defined. It would fail to find its own personality in this enumeration. Even if one made this intelligence an essence of immense comprehension, it would still be merely a nature if there were no soul to bring the sublimity of the *I* to the fore. And the soul itself is both indescribable and prior to all determinations in the order of existence.

With reference to the mobile complex of determination and existence, both thought and love are initiated through a negative dialectic. Love discloses the insufficiency of conceptual and practical communication. It seeks a coalescence which is an interpenetration of souls. Love is anterior to the distinctiveness which allows for exchanging. It is not a kind of commerce.

If it could be perfected, love would make all cooperation super-fluous and, in fact, all concurrence impossible. In contrast to love, thought dissipates everything which obscures and beclouds perceptions and clear and distinct ideas. Through the identities it establishes when men encounter one another, thought makes industrial and juridical society possible. Thought's insufficiency appears in the fact that this encounter can just as well be the encounter of assimilation or war as of friendship.

Likewise, the sublimity of the *I* lends its mystery to love. By formalizing instead of ontologizing the transcendental principles of science and science itself, Kant recognized the place of *mystery*. There is human mystery by virtue of everything added in the subject to the categories, and transhuman mystery by virtue of the thing in itself. But this classifying genius claimed to establish a demarcation between determination and indeter-minateness. Instead of intermingling them as he should have, he juxtaposed them. He did not recognize that determination, which is never determined except to a certain degree and in a certain way, always involves indeterminateness; and indeter-minateness, in turn, cannot progress to a perfectly pure state of indistinction without annihilating itself. The development of science has revealed not only that contingence is inseparable from science but even that the role of contingence grows in direct proportion to the progressive complication of knowledge. Thus it is impossible to relegate either exterior or interior mystery to a restricted zone at the edge of which one stops as at the edge of the ocean. *Mystery insinuates itself into all the processes of thought just as experience itself is at the heart of the empirical.* Craft and genius come together in us as well as in our works. Two opposed dialectics alternately make the deed the goal of the man and the man the soul of the deed.

The highest degree of personality is *moral life,* if one gives the term *moral* its richest meaning. One can distinguish be-tween ethics and morality by opposing them, on the one hand, as the theoretical cognition of the rules imposed on men and, on the other hand, as the practical orientation of these rules. Since it is one and the same set of rules which is examined and organized, this distinction between ethics and morality presup-poses a source different from either of them. This distinction refers to an existence capable of diverse intimate orientations. Such an existence is the soul. The soul is superior to determi-nations, for it gives them their meaning. Thus the soul is that which constitutes morality. The essence of the soul is to surpass every essence. It is inaccessible. Two acts which have the same ideal content can have opposite values. Obedience to determinism can be an act of either passion or reason. Abstract intelligence takes no account of intimate existence. For it, passivity with regard to duty, inspiration, and grace is identical to passivity toward matter, society, or impulse. We are incapable of pronouncing an irrevocable verdict on others' morality, or even on our own. Not the least precious index of a man's morality is the fact that he always doubts whether he is moral and that he asks himself how he should be moral.

Thus, to confuse morality with legality is extremely damaging. When a judge conforms to the legislator's decision and attaches a sanction to an act, he brings together two determinations. His decision, with its sanction, disregards the specific morality of both the sanctioned act and the agent. Similarly, an interpenetration of sensibilities takes place at the core of all disputes. And if one ought not, by reason of a partialness for intuitionism, always claim that intellectual reasons are nothing but a matter of publicity or a special pleading for intimate preferences, it is true that discourse attempting to express a sentiment has sometimes been incapable of suggesting the sentiment. The moral life, which is nothing less than life at its highest point of intimacy and efficiency, stands between sufficient demonstration and intuition *ex nihilo*. The moral life embraces the sublimity of the *I*. Not the least defect of vulgar positivism is its reduction of experience to that which is determined.

In these observations, which are meant to reveal aspects of science, personality, and morality that reflect the sublimity of the *I*, we have basically considered only ascensional or rising experiences, experiences inspired by duty. One should not conclude from this that noticing the sublimity of the *I* is just a way of introducing value surreptitiously. To do so would be false to the indifference of the *I*. The *I* embraces and presents for description both sublimity's positive form, value, and its negative form, nothingness. Every specification, taken by itself, is both deprivation and invitation. A specification blocks out that which it is not. But it also gives itself so that one can grasp it. This happens, for example, when an event which seems to prevent success becomes the cause of success. Likewise, the privative expressions of the sublimity of the *I*, such as absence, void, forgetting, or ignorance, manifest sublimity in experience no less rigorously than does happiness, which is not this or that particular good, or sanctity, which is not this or that action, or any delightful and precious experience which has to be concretely encountered in order to be known.

Thus sublimity is intermediary between what is less than and what is more than determinations. As such, it entails a consequence which is important for all experience, namely, that it is constantly wavering. One can speak of the nature of sublimity by reason both of the determinations which are outlined in it and of the *de jure* universality which allows these determinations to appear. But these determinations never attain more than a semiconsolidation. Indeterminateness remains, sometimes to darken the determinations with its shadow and sometimes to illumine them with its brilliance. Thanks to indeterminateness, the *I* of experience from the outset sets itself in opposition to pure dogmatism by reason of its essentially critical power.

28. *The* I *is thought and forethought*

All that we have to do now is to bring together what might be called the two complementary aspects of the *I*; thereby we will obtain a miserably reduced but nevertheless balanced view. In the ideal order, the *I* manifests its omnipresence through the universality expressed by the punctiliar one. The punctiliar one is both without parts and alternately either exterior or interior to everything thought. In connection with what is thought, the *I* exists and also is thought. In principle, there is nothing in experience which is not progressively reducible to determinations. From this point of view intellectualism is unreservedly true. But this truth leaves aside existence, and after Kant one may no longer leave it aside. If existence is overlooked, thought degrades itself into the determination of that which is thought. The indefiniteness of the *I* is sacrificed to its unity. A dialectic which consists in observing that there must be a unity of being and non-being, and therefore that being is the only thing which exists, not only contributes nothing to the relation between being and non-being but in fact drives non-being back into the realm of the forgotten. Such a dialectic might have some worth as a dialectic of security. It could uphold the being necessary for confidence in the face of a skepticism which tends to dissolve confidence. But the opposite dialectic is of no less importance to liberty.

In effect, if one focuses the description of experience on determination, one degrades the unity of experience in such a way as to make it a unity within experience. Every localized unity "sifts" the I, but none should be allowed either to exhaust it or to capture it. If a localized unity were to exhaust the I, experience would thereafter find nothing but nothingness, the absolute limit of non-being. If a localized unity were to capture the I, experience would thereafter find only the thing, the absolute limit of being. Thus it is that another's death appears to us as the sum of a cadaver and an absence. If there were only a cadaver, death would establish the reign of nothingness. Nothingness is that which is nothing because nothing can spring from it. The thing is that which is nothing because nothing can be related to it. Nothingness and thing, then, suppress being both as position and as copula. This nihilism and realism can be cast aside simply by returning to experience. If experience were reduced to determination, to what is thought, to the one as its source, there would be determination and that which is thought. But there would be no experience of determination and of that which is thought. *The I is always the unity of a thought and a forethought.* The sublimity of experience manifests the infinity of experience. The infinite is sometimes the *apeiron* (the indefinite), that which is never determined, the miscarriage of order in the abyss of the monstrous and the unformed. At other times, the infinite is the inexhaustible principle of everything which is finished and perfect. Thus at each instant determination must be united with value. Only thus can determination mediate the expansion of experience.

3 / The Transition from Spontaneity to Reflection

[VIII] Naive Spontaneity

When we look for some experience in which we might draw near to ourselves from the side of the pure *I*, we are led to those moments of slackened apprehension in which the content of experience is homogenized to the point of resisting every distinction. One can progressively pass from this minimum possible activity to an experience whose essence is to continually increase in intensity without the continuity ever suffering any check sufficiently serious to arrest its thrust. This latter kind of experience we call *naive spontaneity*. One can call it either *natural,* to indicate that it remains easy even when it is violent, or *given,* to note that it expresses more the benefaction of the past than the inventiveness of the future.

Even a summary study of naive spontaneity calls for critical reflection. The integration of the events which occur within naive spontaneity is so intimate that this self-satisfying experience ordinarily escapes being described, and it would not be easy to recognize its characteristics if the memory did not recall this integration during subsequent crises. It follows that we must not accept uncritically our memory of this integration. The faculty of memory is the spirit itself, when a determination mediating the spirit's movement has been situated by a judgment of existence in the series of events which symbolize the past for it. All the functions of the spirit must therefore be found in the memory, where a process of utility or animation, of propaganda or artistic modification, adapts this past to the present intention. That which is remembered is ideally identical to a past perception, at least when the memory is accurate. But it is always existentially different.

Here, relative to spontaneity, the present intention is not utilitarian. On the contrary, the intention is often a disappointment aroused by the stalemating of a project, and generally the collapse of the determination. When the determination collapses we are thrown back upon both ourselves and what we remember of spontaneity. Using Kierkegaard's profound distinction, it is a question here less of the *faculty of memory*, which leads us back to a determination, than of the *re-memory*,[1] which utilizes the continuity of spiritual existence. The past is not cut up. No enumeration is attempted. Remembered spontaneity presents itself to the self in its undivided totality. One need only take cognizance of the regret accompanying the re-memory of spontaneity to realize that we look to spontaneity both for consolation and for a promise. Unless some re-memory illuminates an ideal, it is a mere idea. It could not be desired or even conceived. An ideal has the power to allow for hope and activity only because it has been lived. Paradise Lost guarantees the Promised Land. In the course of a crisis, the recollection of spontaneity justifies hope in its reviviscence. If I am born once, why will I not be born twice? But the partialness of the man who turns back toward spontaneity necessarily and immediately leads to a transfiguration which gilds the remembered spontaneity.

It is criticism itself which forbids critical partialness. The recognition of this transfiguration does not entirely discredit the recollection of the spontaneous thrust. The unity of experience prevents the distinction either between a past determination and a present determination or between a prior concrete experience and an actually occurring concrete experience from being able to rupture their continuity absolutely. If the memory were always other and nothing but other, there would be no memory. Whoever claims that this is the case experiences a memory of having conceived it. Remembering spontaneity must therefore prolong it while transforming it. And it is permissible to try to discern what there is in present experience that continues the prior experience.

Four methods can be used to detect this continuity. When

1. Le Senne is here contrasting *mémoire* and *ressouvenir.*—Trans.

the four methods concur, the objectivity of the description is assured. The first method has to be intuition. This is the concrete experience by which knowledge in every domain pierces through appearances to the depths. Intuition is completed, made precise, and, when necessary, corrected by the second method, namely, sympathy with what others have concretely experienced. This sympathy is made possible by the descriptions which others give of their experiences. But so much for the existential methods. Finally,[2] one can recognize that every intimacy has to manifest itself through spatial and social effects and that this manifestation extends in scope from thrusts which are most simple but also most charged with the future, from thrusts which individuate life, to the most powerful and most complex social expansion. When one sees this, then an exterior description will grasp from the outside what interior description has felt or intimated from within.

29. *The description of naive spontaneity*

Intuition lets everyone recognize naive spontaneity under ever novel forms. There is no one, whatever his activity, who does not distinguish two kinds of periods in life. There are those periods of painful living in which difficulties require the will to repeat itself at each instant in a willing to will. And there are those more or less prolonged moments in which our will intermingles itself so exactly with a superabundance of energy in motion that we cannot say whether we undergo or whether we bring about our expansion. On the one hand, there is effort, labor, duty, and almost always the threat of discouragement. On the other hand, there is a thrust which overwhelms us at the very moment that we are overjoyed by it, a thrust whose ardor we ratify at the very moment that it sweeps us along. This thrust deserves to be called *spontaneity* because it unites the power of nature with the joy of liberty, and it deserves to be called naive because it comes to us as a gratuitous gift which we have only to accept with ingenuousness.

2. Though Le Senne says there are four methods, he appears to mention only three. I think that the identification of spatial effects of intimacy, on the one hand, and social effects of this same intimacy, on the other hand, are to be taken as two distinct approaches to discerning what the present continues of the past. If this is correct, then Le Senne does have four "methods."—Trans.

The rhythm of naive spontaneity. Whatever its form, naive spontaneity employs only one rhythm. This rhythm has three tempos. At the outset, it starts off easily and slowly. The organism puts an organized and easily used energy at the disposition of consciousness. The least blunt determination can set off the liberation of this energy. This liberation takes place by an increase of energy. A progressive mobilization brings into play a growing multiplicity of forces and means until this ascent reaches its apogee. This is the second tempo. Up to now, the wear and tear of the means used by consciousness are much more than compensated for by the intervention and influx of new confluences. It is almost impossible to believe that spontaneity is wearing. It bears all the characteristics of a generous exuberance, giving without reckoning the cost and never economizing. Finally, however, this spontaneity does no more than balance the debits and credits. It no longer gushes forth; it counts the costs. It no longer creates; it maintains. Spontaneity, as it were, reaches a plateau. It maintains itself without labor, but it cannot elevate itself without resorting to effort, without questioning itself, without turning the millstone of the will. Victory is replaced by triumph. And triumph lasts until the first signs of a weakness heralding the exhaustion of the means and forces involved brings about restlessness. The undividedness, which was thus far the essence of experience, makes one fear a dehiscence. The two terms of a relation are substituted for the free motion which would result from their convergence. On the one hand, there are indications of the resistance of an external world which separates itself little by little from the self in order to erect barriers to it. On the other hand, the enfeebling of the internal power involves the shrinking of subjectivity. Subjectivity abandons experience in its near totality in order to localize itself in the self. Does this happen because things increase their pressure? Does this happen because of a progressively deteriorating responsiveness? An obstacle punctures the continuity of experience and points up this disjunction in experience.

Thus the universal schema of the naive spontaneity which we will always consider to be the soul of youth is as follows: expansive mobilization, a more or less durable plateau, incipient malaise. It would be arbitrary to limit the scope of naive spontaneity to only its most violent forms. Every concretely experienced dynamism is located in the interval between pure action and pure contemplation. Insofar as the dynamism manifests the unity of the *I*, the multiplicity which gives it its content tends to be displayed in the unity of a spatial intuition. But an experience which would be sheerly simultaneous could not even exist. The simultaneity of two givens demands their distinction, and their distinctness necessitates a circulation from one to the other. A multiplicity is always temporal as well as spatial. It is always numerable as well as recognizable. All contemplation, then, involves some action. Inversely, an action in which the self were not somehow contemporaneous with the successive stages of the action would be scattered. There would be chapters without a book, sentences without a chapter, words without sentences, letters without words. Every action, therefore, also involves some contemplation.

What is true of all dynamism is also true of spontaneity. Sometimes spontaneity will come about primarily from a pure liberation of material energy. This is simply the lower limit of spontaneity. But doubtless it is this character of animality which it has by reason of its proximity to nature that makes us so often consider spontaneity to be a privilege of infancy. Sometimes, on the contrary, spontaneity will set itself up, so to speak, halfway between instinct and love, by taking the form of an affectivity involving the entire soul. Sometimes, finally, it will refine itself and spiritualize itself into a freedom which is most intimate and most unentangled with matter. In this process an extraordinarily facile and abundant ideation and a completely unadorned imagination will seem to coalesce almost entirely into an immobile contemplation.

There is a large range of nuances between the spontaneity of the child running to play, or the warrior rushing toward victory without even thinking about the resistance of the enemy standing between him and his goal, and the joy engulfing the poet or artist in a flawless and painless conception. But the differences do not dissolve the kinship among all those whom spontaneity unites in one and the same experience of happy power. The ingenuous intoxication found in the power, suppleness, and precision of the movements of the body overwhelmed by the joy of living is identical to that found in the efflorescence of ideas which offer the spirit apparently inexhaustible promises of intelligence. This intoxication is identical to that found in a gentle spirituality where all sacrifices appear as graces and all hopes as possessions. The transfiguration by memory completes the purification of the experience of spontaneity. It overlooks the impediments that perception, which is always angular, places here and there in spontaneity's path. But the recollection of spontaneity would not have such charm unless precisely these accidents had added to spontaneity the measure of seriousness needed to release it from the tenuousness of a dream.

The confrontation between direct and indirect intuition. This summary description refers to indirect experience. The mediation between the self's experiences and those of another is easily found in the identity of the discourses which manifest the identity of souls. Those men whose character can be described as "sentimental" give the most sincere and the most precise testimonies concerning naive spontaneity. Their aptitudes for meditation and self-analysis, their attachment to the past, and their interest in affectivity prepare them for the retrospective description of the modes of naive spontaneity. Of all the modes, none is more precious to them than freely given spontaneity, for their most serious and pervasive fault is the impotence of their wills. When the will is incapable of buoying up a depressed sensibility, spontaneity is the only salvation. These men know the worth of grace because they so often are without it. In them, spontaneity reveals one of its essential characteristics, namely, that of being the activity of a self which the self's will does not control.

Thus Maine de Biran has often called attention to the contrast between the intimate debility of his mature years and the memory of his youth during which a thrust filled him with a joy in being alive which was so intense that it was a kind of metaphysical support. The "good moments," in which "the internal expansion," the "lucidity of ideas," [3] reminded him of the times when he believed that he was "capable of all that is best and most exalted," [4] became more and more rare. He writes: "I sometimes remember the impressions of my youth in that season. I was so happy with the air, the sun, the greenery. I was so expansive and so good. I nourished myself with such

3. Maine de Biran, *Journal intime* (1817–24) (Paris: Plon, 1931), p. 7.
4. *Ibid.*, p. 333.

delicious sentiments. I took so animated an interest in everything around me. Today. . . ." [5] He eventually tried to substitute the help of grace for this spontaneity now lost and beyond
resuscitation. But he had remained closed up in his psychological self too long. Condemned as he was to take hold of himself only in an effort definitively directed against the non-self,
this aspiration to divine life could not progress beyond its
initial stages.

With Rousseau, on the contrary, the power to recover lost
spontaneity in recollection and, when necessary, in "sylvan solitude" did not disappear with his youth. The very expansion of
this spontaneity converted the affective *cogito*, through the
mediation of the idea and sentiment of nature, into the divine
cogito. *The Profession of Faith of the Vicar of Savoy* is simply
the description of this happy expansion. The intellectual recol-
lections of Descartes, Clarke, and Condillac receive existence and
value here from the movement of the entire soul. First, the
Cartesian *cogito* is transported into the heart of affectivity.
Doubt becomes restlessness. Evidence becomes sincerity of
heart. Likewise, conforming to the expansiveness of sentiment,
spontaneity must itself dilate to the dimensions of the universe lest the bluntness of a perception or the hostility of a man
shatter the free flight of the spirit. The angular forms of towns
are unfavorable for this. It is in the presence of the established
continuity of the country that spontaneity deploys itself without difficulty. It is there that the self concretely experiences
those "delicious transports" which reveal its unification with
God. For God is found in the womb of animated nature. In this
Einfühlen (empathy), the *I* resolves the opposition between
God and the self and rediscovers its own unity. The will is suppressed. Experience is transformed from opposition to consciousness. Rousseau, the hero and victim of affective spontaneity, sometimes received happiness from it. But the defects
in his social and practical life that manifested the infirmity of
his will prove that, Guyau notwithstanding, freely given spontaneity cannot be confused with the ultimate expansion of experience.

Collective spontaneity. The most powerful social thrusts
simply manifest mutual sharing and the multiplication of private spontaneities. *To say that there is a collective spontaneity*

5. *Ibid.*, p. 30.

*in which individuals participate is the same as to say that there
is a convergence of individual passions.* Existence infects the
one and the many. The same ardor animates those men who
concretely experience their union with God through the thrust
of religious revivals, those who in military undertakings concretely experience the creative power propelling life to conquer
the world, and the crowds which in revolutionary movements
are invigorated by a social hope. But when ardor is stalemated
and a barrier stifles ambition and converts the conquest of a
goal into a mere dream of the beyond, consciousness asks itself
whether this spontaneity was divine or natural, valid or deceptive. Now there is simply an undivided power in which multiplicity, which can introduce the element of reflection, appears
in outline merely to nourish and aid action.

Vital spontaneity. Through regressive simplification and
condensation, one can descend from the level of these complex,
multipersonal thrusts which are definable in terms of their
ideal. These thrusts are always on the verge of passing from
activity to aggressiveness. One can come down from them to
that undifferentiated power which deploys itself not only in the
core of the highest forms of life but even in the very lowest
forms. Clear thought distinguishes and enumerates the manifestations and effects of these forms. But it itself emerges from
an intensive coenesthesia whose almost total lack of differentiation is nearly reducible to natural energy and which expresses
in its own way the unity and indeterminateness of the *I*. This
coenesthesia is also found it the *hormē*, to use von Monakow's
term, which is essential to all life. It is found in the tropisms
and instincts which specify life and in the growth of organisms.
And it is also found in the expansion of a concept or of a
hypothesis. Nature is to spontaneity what persistence is to perseverance.

30. *The undividedness of the* I *in naive spontaneity*

The essence of natural spontaneity is *its anteriority with
respect to all the disjunctions which subsequent reflection can
bring to it.* In naive spontaneity the *I* is still undivided. The
blows directed against its simplicity are still so mild and so
fleeting that they can neither interrupt the course of spontaneity nor restrict its scope. *Spontaneity at this point is not
within experience; it is still experience.*

(1) *Self and non-self.* Spontaneity is initially indifferent to the notional distinction between the self and the non-self. It is immediately united to the *I*, which it expresses as dynamic unity. The independence of the *I* manifests itself negatively in spontaneity as the *Ungrund.* The negativity by which the *I* can indefinitely rise above every condition is unlimited. So is the affirmativity by which the *I* anticipates the beyond of every finite reality. Schopenhauer's mistake lies not in having recognized the universality of the will-to-live, but rather in his burying it in blindness. The will-to-live is at some point capable of suggesting goals. Then it is no longer blind. Consciousness cannot be anything but light. But this is as yet only a glimmer which permits neither the theoretical discernment of the necessities within experience nor the profound collaboration of the reflective will with the spontaneous thrust.

At the source of spontaneity, intellectualism and romanticism are mixed together. How, except verbally, does Bergson's *élan vital,* which is diffracted into structures, differ from the generative activity which starts with an idea's unity and unfolds its comprehension? Specifically, if one considers a relation as a negation of distinction, as a composition of terms, or as a demand for something else, the relation can be taken as the ideal symbol of spontaneity. At its starting point, spontaneity would be the pure power of liberty. At the apex of the thrusts which ravish the ingenuous soul, should one say that the soul is carried away or that it creates? Neither the one nor the other. Or, rather, both the one and the other. Subsequent reflection, in reflecting on spontaneity, looks for a duality not to be found except in its products and in reflection on those products, as one might look in the ovum for the parts of the adult. The power of a force which gives itself to us gratuitously is mingled here with a certain freedom. Buoyed by this confluence, the self expands without any further hindrances other than those needed to feel the efficacy of its will. The relation of the self to the other does not simply depend either on the self or on the other. Thus consciousness concretely experiences neither the solitude of an abandoned man nor the indifference of a desert in the contemplation of which consciousness would lose itself.

In such an experience what would be the non-self? Could it be an undetermined existence? Consciousness could not by itself oppose to its own concrete experience of spontaneity the existence of a completely undetermined thing in which it would posit a reality of which it itself would be the product. Doubt would first have to lead consciousness to distinguish both between determination and existence and between extrinsic existence of the thing and the intrinsic existence of the self. In brief, doubt would have to cast its incertitude upon the ensemble of experience. There is no doubt without an indication of a duality of terms. There is no duality without doubt being born. At the source of that experience in which the incoherence of the ideal entails the beginning of the exhaustion of existence, there is the growing feebleness of spontaneity.

Can the non-self be matter? One could take the word *matter* to mean that which is added to the laws in order to confer on them an existence independent of us. In spontaneity, the laws, if there are laws, are intermingled with the content of experience. There is no reason to posit a substantive existence outside a thrust of consciousness which is not subject to any resistance. The self knows matter and body only through the accidents which they impose on it. Spontaneity converts past accidents into prefaces to its victory, masks present accidents, and cancels future accidents. The "emergences" themselves must erupt into spontaneity so that it can expand and have something to conquer. They intervene to testify to the accommodation of being to consciousness.

(2) *Self and God.* Following the postulates of theoretical knowledge, the scientist rids mystery of all spirituality by reducing it to material existence. Material existence is enslaved to the relation, and the relation in turn is objectivized in a structure. This process kills God. But in common with the opposite attitude, which affirms the primacy of the spiritual by affirming existence, this scientific attitude likewise allows one to set universal existence in opposition to the self. But how could this opposition take place during the experience of spontaneity? Spontaneity is an expansion which immediately shatters any limit in its path. Retrospectively, naive spontaneity can just as easily be cherished as the glory of God or as the salvation of man. While it unfolds, spontaneity recognizes neither God nor man, and by this fact it again expresses the indifference of the *I*. It is a passion, but without heat. It is like a mechanism of the heart. It is a fire consuming more than it warms. It is not a love. In eliminating unhappiness, it eliminates pity. This is why spontaneity so easily turns into war.

Spontaneity is suspect and subject to the verdict of reflection. Alain's philosophy has the irrefutable value of forbidding the abolition of judgment. It is judgment which attributes spontaneity to God or to the self, depending on whether the postulates are submitted to or chosen by reflective consciousness. Maine de Biran, who became progressively more unhappy after 1813–14, reveals in his *Intimate Journal* under the date of February 18, 1818, the postulate of his unhappiness: "Everything that is spontaneous is organic or mechanical, even when it is the thrust of genius." [6] Spontaneity is thus discredited by being reduced to the body. As always, the body can account for insufficiency, but not for value. Biran always believed himself to be enclosed within Biran. But by what right does one *reduce spontaneity to the body? Spontaneity can neither arise nor deploy itself except through the concurrence or the permission of everything which experience presents.* One might as well maintain that a book of Kant's is totally explained by its printing—this is a typical form of scientific explanation—or that for a rose to be radiant there is no need for fresh air or sunlight or for one to let his gaze rest on it.

A religious consciousness, on the contrary, will interpret the duality following in the wake of spontaneity as the separation between God and the self. But it will do so by admitting the presence of God in a bygone spontaneity. There is the myth of the golden age and the dogma of a lost Eden. Likewise, there are expressions referring to the memory of glorified spontaneity. In conjunction with these expressions, the passage from the *I* to the self is understood as a fall. The fall brings us back to that physiologism which in Biran so often contradicts the hypothesis of "the hyperorganic center of consciousness." Both for one who thinks in terms of the fall and for Maine de Biran, man is delivered over to his own impotence. If he yields to this view he will be destined to be more sensitive to fear than to love, to be more preoccupied with protecting himself than with developing himself. Nonetheless, prior to those movements of reflexive consciousness, spontaneity proceeds unreservedly toward an ever greater fullness and power.

(3) *Self and other-self.* Retrospective judgment, by repressing the division between the self and God, can look for their union in the undifferentiatedness of naive spontaneity. Similarly, one can judge that naive spontaneity coordinates all con-

6. Maine de Biran, p. 84.

senting selves into one and the same thrust of consciousness. Children playing a game together, the members of a crew filled with the same enthusiasm, the curious who are oriented toward one object of attention, and believers bound together by one faith are both one and at the same time many. There is no way to separate what distinguishes them from what unites them. It is true that two men in front of a picture both see the picture and see two views of it. But that does not make three "seens." It is also true that sympathy must intertwine two souls if it is to exist (and its conception entails its existence). But it must keep the souls distinct lest it annihilate one of them with the other. In its early stages, individualized spontaneity increases its power with all the energies and with all the encouragements and impulses which life and other selves cause to converge in it. Conversely, in the thrust of a crowd the reciprocity of action stimulating its members molds a growing energy into a common charge.

One has to expect the scientist's analysis to subdivide and reduce the *Miteinanderfühlen* (community of feeling), using Scheler's term, to mere mechanical interaction. Scientists are condemned by their profession to make spatial maps of *communities of souls*. But this very analysis presupposes that its matter has already been given to it. The *what* specifies the *that*. The determinations of existence would not even be smoke without existence. At the same time that spontaneity is distributed among individuals, not as portions but as participations, it still possesses its own proper individuality. This individuality differs from the individuals found within it, but it is inseparable from them.

Naturally one should not assimilate this unanimity to the identity of a collective representation, as Durkheim has done. Sociology was born in admiration of physics. It has been an effort to transpose an attitude and some postulates and methods of demonstrable validity in the realm of matter into a domain where they can succeed only if man is first materialized. Every connection between two men is an existential connection in which identity only intervenes as a means of communication. There is a unanimity among men when this communication permits their *existential* identification in one and the same thrust. The sociologist transforms this connection of two existences into a connection between two depersonalized, objectivized, thought terms, matrix element 22 and matrix element

23. He forces them into the extension of a connection whose identity defines the group. This identity is called collective representation. As a consequence of this naturalization, the identity makes the sociologist a witness and makes the human matrix elements into slaves. The existential has been definitively degraded into the ideal. Every self has been dissolved into a mechanism which excludes vivifying spontaneity and, generally, consciousness.

(4) *Time and eternity*. Let us conclude our argument by pointing out the spontaneity which is anterior to the duality of time and eternity. We will not, however, try to give a description of time at this point, but will only recall that time presupposes that there are givens to encounter.

When time is thought, that is, made an object of thought, it presents itself as a relation between its instants and their law. If, in effect, the instants were without interiority, they would be a plurality of worlds, each a stranger to the others. The impossibility of such a situation rules out the possibility of a pure empty multiplicity. But if there were nothing other than the interiority of their law, initially this interiority would be no more temporal than it would be anything else, and, further, time would be purely a possibility of time, a virtuality of succession. It is therefore necessary that *the two terms of this relation*, the generating succession and its ideal eternity, *even or especially when analysis distinguishes them, be given in an existential unity*. This existential unity is the sublimity of the *I*.

A concretely inexhaustible variety of experiences of time comes from the fact that the *I* sometimes accentuates succession and sometimes abstract eternity. Human unhappiness with time begins when a barrier interposes itself between a present instant and a past or future instant and prevents the self, which is encouraged by the abstract unity of the law of time either to remember or to look ahead, from reaching either the past or the future instant. The human being then concretely experiences either regret or impatience. A self which is enslaved to determination makes use of abstract eternity to universalize its actual experience, and it will make either regret or impatience its definitive condition. Abstract eternity is simply a man's ideal expression to himself of his own eternity. Regret is expectation of the past. Impatience is expectation of the future. But, as Jung has said, "To expect is hell."

Spontaneity is directly opposed to the foregoing experience of time. Initially the *I* does not oppose itself to time as a relation-structure, the objective terms of which would be ideal eternity and succession. Besides, spontaneity does not have the leisure to feel obstacles as such. There is no serious hindrance except the discouraging hindrance. Spontaneity still knows no lassitude. As a consequence, within undivided spontaneity, *the existential unity of the I is not distinguished from the ideal unity of the law of time which engenders every instant one after the other.* The *I* becomes one with the eternal idea of time, as the locomotive is one with the railroad track. That is, the *I* or its material symbol, the engine, supplies the energy and the track supplies the direction. Further, since the content of experience is docile, there is a necessary harmony between the rhythm of perceptual events and the rhythm of desires. The past arises without restriction in present activity. Regret therefore is excluded. The future repeats a mobilization ever more powerful and ever more efficacious. Desire is fulfilled almost as soon as it is born and thus knows nothing of impatience. The *I* lives with history without ever being ahead of it or behind it. As a locomotive in starting increases its speed with each stroke of the piston, so the thrust has no time to become slack because its most recent effects press it on further. Everything comes about at once. Eternity and time no longer are opposites. One could say that there is a preestablished harmony between the subjective course of wants and the objective course of opportunities. But this dual series does not presuppose a reflexive operation. There is no need for the intervention of a reflexive operation.

31. *Against the psychophysical reduction of naive spontaneity*

In the course of this sketch, we have just seen that spontaneity could eventually be linked to the self, i.e., to a consciousness now rendered human by virtue of its being conditioned by an organism. Thus one might consider spontaneity as the body in action. One might claim that, though this connection presents itself to thought only after spontaneity has died out, the connection was already there while spontaneity was in force. We now have to show that such an interpretation is arbitrary.

First let us make the general observation that the *I* is related to every experience. There is no reason to shrink the *I* to the dimension of an organic self. Spontaneity does not furnish such a reason, for it engulfs every obstacle. It sweeps along in its movement not only the whole body but also all the supports which the body receives from the world surrounding it. Or, better, during the period of spontaneity, the body is the world. The distinction between the two terms, body and world, practically disappears in their solidarity. The duality of subject and object does not yet exist. There is only the *I*.

One can doubt the *I* only because of an individualism which makes man a metaphysical shooting star, an insular kingdom. Individualism imposes itself on us so one-sidedly that the mutual and universal participation among men and things appears to us as nothing more than an aberration of which primitive people are victims. Whether this view of participation is in fact primitive, it still must be acknowledged. Participation always occurs in conjunction with distinction. Without distinction there would be nothing but an identity. But this conjunction is precisely the opposite of an absurdity. In the ideal order there can be no truth except through the interiority of the terms of judgment. And in the realm of existence there can be neither individual nor social life except through the interpenetration of organs and functions and the communication and sympathy of individuals. One need only glance at the human body to find traces and hints of all the participations which unite a man and a woman to previous generations, to each other, and to their children. And at the same time these traces show them to be united to all of nature. Matter everywhere and always bears the mark of spirit. How could one explain in bodily terms alone that which precisely reveals the necessity of linking the body not only to the past but also to the future? If I consider only the physical content of the musical note A_4 I can define it by 435 vibrations, for there is an adequation between the whole and the sum of its parts. But how would I explicate in terms of vibrations the characteristics A_4 acquires when a man hears it? The body is a part of experience, which is not the sum of its parts but their relation; and in every relation the connection and the terms are in reciprocal and unstable dependence.

When one claims that spontaneity is organic he does so by means of retrospective or preventive negation. He wants to avoid calling spontaneity either cosmic or divine. One might call it cosmic to refer to a confluence of universal causes. Or one might call it divine if he wanted to express its superiority to the matter which it involves in its movement. Spontaneity might just as well be called organic, as life might be called surgical. At some time organic causes have affected or will affect spontaneity just as surgery affects life. Spontaneity is organic, but it is also sylvan, playful, and lyrical. What matters is that it is not merely organic.

There is nothing more dangerous than that debasement of the most profound or most noble experiences which imperceptibly results from reducing them to the postulates of a professional method. It does not follow from the fact that the beating of the heart is indispensable for the generosity of the hero who braves danger to rescue a child that generosity is merely something physiological. Everything that eventually enters into spontaneity—whether it is the lake of Geneva for a Sénancour, or the net, balls, and sky for the tennis player, or her son for the loving mother, or the thought of the enemy by the conqueror at the beginning of a war—every object oriented in a certain way is indeed indispensable for spontaneity. The physiologist translates all these conditions into physiological terms as if the proximate conditions, and especially as if a certain few of these conditions, can be considered independently of the remote conditions. For him these are sensations, which he calls photoreceptions, sentiments, which he calls hormones, and actions, which he will classify as excitations or inhibitions.

Must we accept this restriction, this schematization? Where it is useful to the scientist and pertinent to his proper objectives, certainly. But does this schematization not risk leading to the restricting of his intelligence? A recorder of mortgages could conceive the whole world as a string of occasions for making and registering mortgages. The vocation of philosophy is at once more delicate and more ingenuous. Philosophy should break up all partial approaches and all deformations by leading men back to the experience of reality as it is given.

If that which is altogether simple, which recognizes itself as a totality, and which opens itself to the future, is spiritual, then spontaneity is spiritual. The utilitarian does not love his goals. They are only means. A means would not be sought unless impotency pressed one to accept some mediation. Naive spontaneity, which effortlessly succeeds in increasing itself, loves itself. Love is that which creates itself without restlessness or searching. It finds in itself all the means of its progress, but it has no need of isolating anything from it. When Rousseau concretely experienced the thrust of his spontaneity, he had the analytically thinkable conditions without which the thrust would have collapsed onto itself. Undoubtedly he had to sleep well. But if a preoccupation with these means had turned him away from the thrust which sustained them he would have lost the experience of spontaneity. He would have substituted thought concerning the conditions for spontaneity in place of spontaneity itself. *The indiscretion of science lies in introducing technique where technique has no place.* There is no scientific theory of happiness. There is only a theory of unhappiness, for a scientific theory recognizes a cause for those things which do not happen as one expects them to happen. Where the causes dissolve into the unity of the thrust, there are no more causes. Spontaneity is a dynamic confluence in which we participate, as lovers in the course of sexual fecundation participate in the universal energy which inspires life and in the love which irradiates it. Nothing is more superficial than to see here a mere physiological act.

Spontaneity in its subsequent stages can be conceived as the encounter between a nature which determines its content and power and a self which witnesses its play. This would be unintelligible unless the variety of spontaneity's forms could be analyzed. These forms stretch from necessity to liberty, but they are never exclusively one or the other. *Every given is simple: but it tends alternately to opposite extremes.* Reflection introduces a division into the concept itself. In experience such a division occurs only with reference to the terms of the extension of the concept. There is no invariable dog which sometimes takes the form of a basset and sometimes that of a spaniel. Where would description find such an invariable dog? But the dog tends toward the basset or toward the spaniel. Spontaneity fans out like a peacock's train, spreading from movements nearly reducible to the materiality of a physiological operation to aspirations which would escape from experience if that were possible. The frisky joy of a healthy young animal, playful ease, and certain intellectual skills manifest an almost totally mobile consciousness. These moments are as far removed as possible from the almost purely spiritual free flights of the spirit such as those known to the mystics.

It is not astonishing that a physiologist yields, willingly or not, to the temptation to take the thrusts constituted almost exclusively by the body as paradigmatic of everything. There are a number of reasons which lead the scientist to degrade and impoverish spontaneity. For example, there is the weight of perception. There is the habit of seeing the living only from the outside. There is the cynical contempt of those who see man as a mere object. There is the scientific necessity of beginning with the simple and the lowest and leaving out of consideration all contingent events, including free acts. And, further, there is the intellectual bias of confusing a fact with one's abstract expression of it. This last-mentioned bias would lead to the conclusion that there is nothing to be found in experience as such but singularity. Thus the scientist encounters only cases of rudimentary spontaneity. And these cases verify the postulate of the dialectics which led him to them.

The example of sexual thrust, which we used above, best illustrates this description. The sexual thrust starts as an organic function which is almost indistinguishable from a biological mechanism. It develops into so deep a participation that bodies fade into the background. They become only unnoticed conditions for the thrust. From one term to the other the quality of spontaneity should express the extraordinary diversity of components unified by this thrust. In particular, spontaneity makes it possible for the spatial changes constituting the physiological outline of possession to appear as the event which the concrete mental experience merely reflects. Or, on the contrary, spontaneity can appear as the mechanical expression of a power whose goal lies well beyond the event itself. Spontaneity is more organic at the lower ranges, and, if one wishes, more religious at the upper ranges. Does one have the right to replace it by its own lower limit? Evidently not, for this limit is only a fiction. It is, then, not permissible to deny the authenticity of the most intimate spontaneities. Nor is it permissible to forget that the most material spontaneities would be completely unknown, and consequently nonexistent, if they were exclusively material.

Now let us return guilelessly to experience. When the joyful child runs out into the sun, he does not see his perception of the sun. He sees the sun. The perception of the sun must transcend intermediaries and reach some identity with the sun in order for there to be a perception of it. And since the child concretely experiences warmth as well as the sun, his perception is true. When the intoxicated lover satiates himself with the memory of the first acknowledgment he received from his beloved, there is no reality for him in this act of memory except what she has placed there of herself. When the researcher has his spirit illuminated by the first glimmerings of impending discovery, his thrust transcends psychological consciousness and hurls itself toward some point of absolute reality. The physiologist tries to show how it is that personal consciousness depends on the body. He ends up by forgetting that consciousness does not depend upon the body except by reason of a double analysis which has to yield two series in order to make body and consciousness correspond. If one claims that these series are independent of everything else, then this is a marriage of ghosts. But if these series get their reality from the comprehensive unity of experience, then it is because the spontaneity of the *I* inaugurates, indeed precedes, the analysis. Analysis is only one of the ways in which the spontaneity of the *I* progresses. A sunset is not a mere decoration except for one who does not love beauty. Childhood is not lovable except to one who loves the virginity of a life as yet undamaged by any disappointments. Something of the guilelessness of childhood is to be found in the most noble moments of experience.

32. *Why is naive spontaneity not endlessly followed?*

Obviously one can conceive of naive spontaneity indefinitely following its own course and growth. Indeed, nothing is easier to conceive. For the universalization of a concrete experience or of an idea to follow from the spontaneity of the intelligence guided by this idea, all that is needed is that the abstraction shatter everything which could lead one to doubt it or force one to modify it. In contrast to the determined generalization which consists in proceeding step by step from one application to another to verify its precision, undetermined generalization is a pause in the void. One affirms that everything will always happen in the same way because one does not make the effort even to imagine some other possibility. Thus a single concrete experience of spontaneity could lead one to think that spontaneity will never cease during the course of concrete experience because it is essential to spontaneity that it project hope ahead of itself. Later, one might think that spontaneity will never end because it is replaced by the idea of it-self. The sluggishness of our spirit all too easily universalizes this idea. Let us recall the critical reflections with which we began this summary description of spontaneity. We point out within experience itself what it is that makes this kind of uni-versalization a fiction. Every description is authentication and evaluation. Therefore, reasons for causal impossibility coincide here with reasons for ultimate impossibility.

(1) Every description mixes the pure with the impure. There has never been pure spontaneity. Pure spontaneity is only an existential limit which a soul presently torn by crisis converts into an artistic sentiment which eliminates from it any possible mishap. A more extended description which studies diverse forms of spontaneity, therefore, would discover all the things which either degrade or enrich pure spontaneity in order to make it a lived spontaneity. In effect, if spontaneity could be perfect, by definition there could be no departing from it. But the description of spontaneity is legitimate only if spontaneity is departed from. Spontaneity is not perfect. There is no liberation of energy which does not presuppose something like throwing a switch. And so the cumulative or compensatory mobilization which takes place in the course of spontaneity presupposes a succession of jolts. To be sure, the obstacle always remains inchoate, nascent, menacing. It is dis-solved as soon as it rouses spontaneity. *But this rousing is enough to show that analysis intersperses spontaneity like filigree.* Spontaneity's continuity is the summation of a series of acts scarcely separate from one another. But these acts could not have been posited unless gaps were introduced be-tween them. These gaps differ in depth and durability, but they are always prone to become deeper and more lasting. The jolt which transforms the experience of victory without pain to that of pain without victory will be retrospectively recognized as the last of a series of hindrances whose seriousness becomes ever more profound. Thus Baylen was a foreshadowing of Leipzig.[7]

Just as spontaneity is insufficiently integrating, so is it also insufficiently comprehensive. It never completely escapes from

---

7. I have not been able to determine exactly what Le Senne is alluding to here. Obviously he is thinking of military battles, the first of which was won with difficulty and the second of which was a major defeat.—Trans.

the law of all experience, which is that it oppose an interior to an exterior. *Its expansion is not sheer creation; it is conquest.* Every conquest necessarily presupposes the prior relative exteriority of a given. Here, as everywhere, apperceptive consciousness is accompanied by reflective consciousness. The halo surrounding each spontaneity begins to isolate the spontaneity. Then it is before the *I* like a cinematic spectacle. No action is so captivating that we do not sometimes feel ourselves brusquely torn away from it or swept away from its ravishments or called upon to question its value. For a moment during these strange absences, the *I* appears to the self and becomes an object for the self to view. Then it hurls itself back into the ardor of living. But this brief interruption cannot occur without some apprehension casting its shadow across spontaneity.

When spontaneity reaches its plateau, its defects are aggravated. The success of spontaneity extends its domain. It encroaches and expands. It touches more and more objects. Spinoza defined progress in the knowledge of God as the knowledge of an ever greater number of singular things. *This spreading out is a reason for increasing weakness.* All our energy comes to us from sources, from pockets. The sources are subject to drying up. The ore is subject to being exhausted. Even when victory nourishes victory, the deposits of latent energy are limited and they become more and more difficult to reach. A universally verified dialectic ends up by turning all ambition against itself. The more it suceeds, the more it exhausts itself. Joseph de Maistre wondered at the triviality of the causes which ruin the most powerful enterprises precisely when their triumph seemed definitive. This happens because these causes enter into play as apparently negligible extra weight. But when they are added to a heavy load, they break the bearer's back.

(2) It is fortunate that such is the case. At this point description should stress the split in spontaneity. It should do so to prevent precious modes of experience, having certain characteristics in common with spontaneity, from being confused, through a kind of degradation, with spontaneity. This degradation could occur because spontaneity is a kind of natural symbol of these modes. It is in the depths of these modes that spontaneity should rediscover itself and spiritualize itself as an existential component of them. *The insufficiency of spontaneity results from the passivity which a structure imposes on it.* Two factors come together in the sentiment of liberty: the

alternative representation of a number of possibilities, and the concrete experience of an increasing tension. If one of these factors overwhelms the other instead of joining with it, moral liberty is lost. The dilettante fails to create because of an intimate debility. Lacking suppleness, the passionate man necessarily transforms his exuberant energy into clumsiness. Spontaneity always risks being passionate. It is both given and overcome. It proceeds from the past and presupposes a previous merit, but it scarcely involves that merit any more. It has previously required much searching, effort, and skill to bring about the conditions, to organize or reveal the resources of which spontaneity is now the beneficiary. Heredity and heritage, extra- and intra-organic antecedents converge. Both intelligence and will have contributed to all these accomplishments.

At this point, intelligence and will are the servants of a thrust whose material and affective energy is sufficient to sustain its vigor. It often happens that reflection ceases to bring about the precision of means indispensable for success. As a consequence, the constrictiveness of the structural determination leads to the dissolution of the clearly considered determination. The will yields to sentiment instead of specifying and directing it. If spontaneity almost exactly resembles Paradise, the reason is that it presents itself as a receptiveness more than as an invention. Every kind of intuitionism runs the dangerous risk of confusing a biological thrust with a spiritual inspiration. We are neither angels nor beasts, but are both angels and beasts. Though the body is an indispensable instrument for the spirit, still it must not impose its baggage on the spirit.

Here we should distinguish between two often confused meanings of "direction." We call the first meaning *the direction of the beaten path;* the other, *the direction of control.* Wherever the first kind of direction is imposed, action is channeled in such a way that foresight could anticipate its course by determining the path it is following. The traveler on a fast train cannot get off before the first station. The traveler who presses forward into a tunnel will only come out through the other end. One has decided to board the train, to enter this passageway. The essence of decision is to bind the one who makes it. The direction of control, the kind which a tourist imposes on his automobile or a hiker in open country imposes on his feet, presupposes, on the contrary, the almost uninterrupted possibility of changing orientation. Direction of control excludes any alienation from liberty. Though every human activity takes place between absolute necessity, which the direction of the beaten path approximates, and perfect liberty, which governs the direction of control, it does not follow that certain actions are not nearer one or the other of these poles. Caprice, which sacrifices power to safeguard independence, arises from a preoccupation with avoiding all direction of the beaten path. Spontaneity, by reason of the energetic mass which fills it and the restriction which a strong affectivity imposes on the field of consciousness, always brings together a one-dimensional perspicacity and a blindness to everything else. It is open in one way and closed in all others. And the more pressing the situation from which it has arisen, the more the probity of its action will be judged with all the impulsiveness of a fixed idea. Only with difficulty does spontaneity escape from the defect of blindness and the reproach of lightheadedness.

This is why *it so often happens that spontaneity changes into aggressiveness*. The first reaction of a spontaneity animated by a powerful affectivity against an obstacle which resists its impulse is a negative reaction. It tries to smash the obstacle. If the obstacle persists, the will which has put itself at the service of spontaneity begins what we will call the *process of assault*. When the thrust is insufficient, will is employed to build it up. The will recoils to be better able to spring. On the one hand, it repels the intimate factors which could abate the mobilization of energy. On the other hand, it creates the convergence of the most stimulating ideas and images in the hope that the conjunction of these factors, both reinforced and harmonized with one another, will overwhelm the obstacle. Spontaneity is religious by reason of that process which looks to contagion to sweep the obstacles away, rather than to criticism to dissolve them, or to reflection to change them. But spontaneity reverses the religion of love into hate by seeking its own proper development through the negation of the rest of experience, up to the point that the obstacles, ever more difficult to overwhelm, turn spontaneity back on itself and disorganize the structure whose coercion spontaneity had vaguely submitted to in the very course of its dynamism.

Thus we conclude that spontaneity must be surpassed. It is not morality. Morality absolutely demands the concourse of all the ideal and existential factors of experience. Therefore it cannot be reduced to any one of these factors. From the beginning of our description, this conclusion could have been foreseen. Each time that memory retrieves the past, the occurrence which would try to occupy the fullness of consciousness is localized in a region, in a part of consciousness itself. The smallness of this region reveals how far short it falls of being adequate to the unity of experience. What a poor little thing is the idea of an occurrence or the lived recollection of an old love. Similarly, if spontaneity can end up as the idea of itself, it is because sadness, courage, effort, philosophy, in short, searching cannot be definitively excluded by it. Thus there is no cause for surprise that after having benefited from the prior morality, which finds its triumph in spontaneity, spontaneity must be quenched in view of a morality capable of new creations. Spontaneity is in a hurry. The infinite is not.

This conclusion does not take anything away from the previous descriptions. It would be just as partial and as dangerous to exclude spontaneity from experience as to recognize nothing but spontaneity. Not only has spontaneity provided the joy of the most ardent periods of our life, but it has a glory compared with which the prescriptions of prudence and the works of civilization are miserable and comic, and it suppresses death for a time by suppressing fear. And even when it becomes weak and feeble it supplies everyone who sets himself off as a distinct entity within experience with the energy needed for critical reflection and skepticism. For if one does not get a clue from the skeptic, who plays off determinations one against another, one would concretely experience the joy of the kitten playing with balls as something merely boring.

It is true that mechanized and domesticated spontaneity could become so feeble, its goals so limited, that little by little the maintenance of life would turn into decadence. It is at this moment that spontaneity's worth will make itself evident to everyone. If instead of looking for a passageway from naive spontaneity to an illuminated and generous passion one would try to get rid of all spontaneity in a people or in an individual man, or at least would try to make the spontaneity anemic, one would see the most noble creations of experience withering away or being aborted. And soon life itself would lack that sap which is indispensable for its maintenance, to say nothing of its growth. For life, one must first love *that adhesion of the self to the self* which defines the hegemony of existence over all determinations.

[IX] THE FISSURE

WE HAVE NOW ARRIVED at the critical turn. Naive spontaneity, where we have left it, no longer enjoys the continuous growth in power which it had in its youth. It has even reached the point where the mobilization of newly liberated energies no longer suffices to compensate for the outlay of energy and for normal wear and tear. The sentiment of victory which accompanied the expansion of spontaneity has ceased. The conquest can do no more than exploit the results it has achieved. Between the encountering of a difficulty and its solution, the delays, whose causes are more and more serious, get longer and longer. Spontaneity used to have, using Klages' expressive term, a "magical" efficacy. Spontaneity had to do no more than wish for something and what it wished for was given to it, as happens in dreams when hunger is enough to suggest the view of a well-stocked table. But the dream was real. Imperceptibly now, on the contrary, the real becomes a dream. The value which a man or a people had is volatilized. Imagination has lost its power to inform.

33. *The fissure is instigated by an obstacle*

Everything is ready for the *I* to crack. Within experience, where undividedness still prevails over discontinuity, a sadness announces the "emergence" of a determination. Through the encounter between a confluence of material forces and a convergence of reflections, a determination comes to be and to be considered a cause of detainment. *The obstacle shatters, at least as far as possible, the unity of the I*, which has by now become a productive thrust rather than simply pure apperception. A violin string breaks while the violinist plays, hears, and lives the sonata. A word revealing indifference rends the lyric heart of a lover. An accident to someone dear destroys the joy of living. A fact interrupts the elaboration of a hypothesis by contradicting it. The thought of death routs one from all hope. Under ever new guises, the same disillusionment converts the presumption of an indefinite ravishment into impotence and apprehension.

Between the uneasiness of naive spontaneity in its decline and the discrimination of the obstacle there must be a last, brief

period of *astonishment,* whose evolution passes from a be-
dazzling which allows for scarcely any thought to the perception
of the astonishing thing. Without this period of astonishment
the solidarity between the unity and the sublimity of the *I*
either would permit the ideal given entirely to eclipse the existential emotion or would permit the emotion to bring about
the repression of the ideal given. It is easy to explain astonishment as the confused consciousness of disarray produced by
the retrogression of spontaneous energy stumbling against an
obstacle and dispersing both outside and inside the body, according to mechanical effects. But description must first recognize the felt existence of astonishment which is found at the
crossroads of the effects of this retrogression and the rest of
experience, included within which is the indeterminateness of
the future. Astonishment is not exactly described if one forgets to show that in it there is an indeterminate restlessness
about what is going to happen. The reduction of astonishment
to intelligibility, whose motto *nil mirari* (let nothing surprise
you) is a moral expression, presupposes the experience of astonishment. Opposing itself to the retrospectiveness which must
characterize theoretic knowledge since it deals with that which
is determined, astonishment, which results from our inability to
reach a new determination, must open itself to the indeterminate. *Astonishment can be defined as the knowledge of the unknown when the unknown presents itself as the womb of a
determination whose nature and existence do not depend on
us.*

The sedimentation of astonishment into the obstacle is
achieved *by the acknowledgment of the obstacle.* While spontaneity held sway, existence was included in it. But at the
moment when astonishment solidifies into the obstacle, existence seems to desert spontaneity, to rush out of it. At the
same time, the uneasiness is given precise expression by the ex-
clamation, "Then that is where anxiety comes from!" The uneasiness can now be designated. *Existence becomes the support of determination.* Existence imposes both the nature
and the presence of the obstacle on us. The determination is
the red fire which comes out of the haze, the official notification
which crystallizes the presentiment, the ultimatum which gives
meaning to a period of diplomatic tension, the first clap of
thunder in the Pastoral Symphony.

In place of the diffuse unity of uneasiness there is sub-

stituted the localized unity of a *fact*. Every fact in some respect
bathes in a concretely experienced existence which surpasses it.
Only on this condition is it a fact, for the determination which
constitutes the ideal content of the fact would be a mere possibility if it were not felt as *adhering to existence*. In saying of a
determination that "it is a fact," one obviously adds nothing to
the content of the determination itself. But inasmuch as such a
statement must add something, since a determination which is
a fact is distinguished from that which is not a fact, this sup-
plement can be nothing other than existence. Nevertheless, the
fact cannot be confused with existence; for not only is a fact
determined to be this particular fact and not some other one,
but this fact also imposes itself on existence. The fact makes
existence be as it is. There is universal agreement that one cannot make a fact not exist or make it be other than as it is
given. The more the fact ruptures the ideal continuity, the more
it is unintelligible, but also the more it manifests its character
as a fact. *Therefore what there is in the fact is the obstacle.* If
the fact can be subsequently presented as a given without affective connotations, this is because theoretical knowledge has
dehydrated it, as it were, metalized it, made it a coin whose un-
oxidizability allows it to be passed from hand to hand without
its being perceptibly changed.

34.   *The subdivision of the* I

For the distinction between the interior and the exterior to
appear in experience, it is sufficient that an obstacle emerge
and consolidate itself. The lowliness of the subject replaces the
sovereignty of spontaneity. *Insofar as I originate with the sentiment of limits which I cannot believe that I have imposed on
myself, I become myself.* My life discovers itself in humiliation
and my liberty begins with the search for independence which
the pressure of an obstacle provokes. It is in the midst of sadness
that the self points to existence. And the very word *subject* acknowledges the misery of its initial condition. To be subjected,
to undergo, to be submitted, and similar expressions reveal the
subjection of which one complains. *The dualism of subject and
object loses its dramatic essence in the field of theoretic
knowledge.* But theoretic knowledge does not make the object
anything other than, as its prefix indicates, an attentuation of
the obstacle. Likewise, the subject remains nothing other than

someone condemned to submit. Realism merely intellectualizes this experience of inferiority by formulating the principle, that is, by postulating that the object has within itself the power to impose itself on a subject which it is independent of and that the subject can be nothing other than a witness condemned to waiting and to submitting itself.

The *I* cannot be reduced to this humiliation. Every limitation can only be a middle term between a "this side," which is circumscribed by the limitation, and a "beyond," which is unlimited, for this line of reasoning would hold good for every other limitation: for example, an island bounded by the ocean. If the *I* were reduced to the pure experience of limitation, it would not know limitation and would not feel the limit as an obstacle. Here again the existential character of this experience must be emphasized. *To feel a determination as a limit is something other than to know it in its nature as a determination.* Napoleon, on the evening of Waterloo, "concretely experienced" his defeat; and this means that he was not related to his defeat and the thought of it as he was related to the thought of the Roman defeat at Cannes. *To be limited, then, is to have a presentiment of something beyond the limit.* This presentiment does not, however, arrive at some other specific determination hidden by the obstacle, for a hurdled obstacle is no longer an obstacle, not only because it does not hinder anything but also because the striving which is indispensable to hurdling it is no longer required. What, then, is offered to the consciousness aspiring beyond the limit? What is that which is neither a limiting determination nor a sought determination? Whether one calls it the unknown, the future, the beyond, the thing in itself, God, or any other name, *it is first and foremost the annulment of determination.*

One will perhaps be surprised that we make this annulment of determination something which can present itself. Description, in this case emotional description, obliges us to do so. And this requirement simply specifies what has previously been said about the admixture of non-being in experience. What could waiting, the sentiment of ignorance, the fear of the unknown, the discovery of mystery be for us if not absences felt as such but present by reason of being felt? That observation or introspection which bludgeons the ambiguities of consciousness, casts away the clouds, suppresses the twilights between day and night, and forces one to decide, to formulate, to take one's stand, to dissolve anything whose existence can only be expressed by means of negative expressions, is crude observation or introspection.

Now is the annulment of determination absolute annulment? This hypothesis too is excluded by the recognition of other universal aspects of experience. Absolute annulment would have prevented the determination from appearing; it would have had to be inexorable, unremitting; it would not even have allowed for a will-o'-the-wisp. The self cannot admit absolute annulment, for the obstacle itself, the more brusquely it affects the self, has the power to convince the self that it is something. That from which the obstacle separates the self is not the abyss, pure annulment, annihilating annulment. The annulment in question here can only be a positive annulment, a grand indeterminateness of determinations, from which the cohesion of the obstacle can emanate. But likewise it must be able to yield either our presentiment of intelligence, which will relocate the determination of the obstacle in an ideal system, or our presentiment of happiness, in which the I will rediscover the undividedness of spontaneity not merely renewed but purified of the reason it came to a halt and purified of the natural conditioning which constitutes its fragility and danger. It is this positive annulment, this superdetermination, which is the reason that the obstacle is not a mere cloud about to be dispelled but rather does count as obstacle, and the reason that presentiment is not a mere word but does count as concrete experience. Further, superdetermination is the reason that the promise contained in the striving inaugurated by the obstacle cannot be vain but rather can be worthwhile. *That superdetermination, capable of emitting all determinations and incapable of being exhausted by any of them is, therefore, value.*

Value's indeterminateness prevents one from confusing value with the non-self. The non-self, or, better, the non-mine, by contrast with those determinations whose relative disposability I make use of, is that body of determinations whose provisional or partial nondisposability I concretely experience. Or, if one prefers, every determination is at one and the same time both obstacle and means. Where the character of means prevails over that of obstacle, the self recognizes the determination as "his." In the contrary case, the self recognizes it as "not-his." If, however, one wishes to consider in the non-self not the determinations which the self opposes to his own possessions, as the external might be opposed to the internal, but rather the existence which not only bears them but also abides in them and is the indefinite but absolute foundation for the determinations, one will find that this existence is not given to us. This existence remains undetermined and leads us back to that positive annulment in which we have just recognized value and which is no longer either "mine" or "not-mine."

Both value and determination must be attached to the *I*, for nothing can have meaning in experience without being *with* the *I*. The *I* must therefore have some other aspect than that which determines it as a self. Since value is, with reference to determination, unlimited and primary, the *I*, insofar as it is the self of value, should be called God. *What we designate by the word God is an undetermined source, but a source in which existence makes us participate when existence is animated by value.* A God reduced to determinations would be matter, that is, a world or atoms. A God exterior to experience would be an absence which would be mere absence. In either of these cases, God would not exist. God, then, must be distinguished from determinations even if the determinations necessarily proceed from him. Nevertheless, God must be given in experience. Thus he can be nothing other than the *I* of value. Value manifests him in that it is always absolute, always sacred. But inversely, value presupposes him, insofar as the unity and the infinity of the *I* must intervene to prevent value both from canceling itself and from being canceled from outside. Duty is the ideal expression of value; value is the interior of duty.

The *I* therefore has *two branches.* It is both self and God. But since the *I* as the unity of experience is eminently and in its source indivisible, it is in its joining of the self and God that the *I* allows for and opposes its two aspects. The *I* concretely experiences its closedness insofar as it is a self, and its openness insofar as it is God, an openness which the definitive inadequation between the self and God's infinity unceasingly points out to the self. Therefore no radical rupture intervenes between God and the self. And if morality is bipolar, if it is capable of being either creation or disintegration, ascent or descent, it is so only because the self can either oppose itself to God as to an object in which the self now sees nothing but a nature, or it can unite itself to God as to a friend. The self will be, from its point of view, a relation between a certain concretely experienced embodiment of divine immanence and a partially perceived exteriority of divine transcendence.

Daily experience corresponds to this subdivision of the *I*. Insofar as I am determined by some particular perceptions or postulates of thought, some specific point of insertion into the ensemble of spatial and temporal experience, insofar as I am impotent in proportion to what limits me in these matters, I am merely a self. *My experience stands out within infinite experience.* But if the *I* feels itself to be limited, if it can think its limitation, that is, both affirm and subordinate its limitation, then this *I*, which excludes from its experience what it calls the non-self, includes the non-self in its experience by reason of what it knows about the non-self, by reason of the presentiments it has concerning the non-self, and by reason of the hopes it has concerning the non-self. The *I* would not protest, would not hurl itself against determination, if it did not believe that there was a beyond which is accessible and congenial to it but which is provisionally withheld from it. Thus the *I* must be, under another name, the soul of value just as it is the subject of obstacle. Our salvation is the pure interiority of the Spirit to our spirit. But one can scarcely call this interiority an identity, for identity, or unity of sameness, assimilates determinations, forms, or qualities. Even more, this interiority is not the abstract identity spoken of by the logicians. The *vinculum substantiale* (substantial bond) between God and us is not an umbilical cord; it is value which mingles us together, as it is love which mingles together a mother's life with that of her child.

The admirable analyses of Hume in his celebrated pages on "personal identity" lead to the following conclusions. First, by showing that there is no permanent determination which would correspond as a given impression to the idea of the self, Hume implies the existential character of the *cogito,* which he calls "the smooth and uninterrupted progress of the thought." [8] Then he tries to find out how this continuous experience, which he has to call the *I*, since it is a web of concretely experienced relations, engenders the idea of the self by neglecting the slight

8. David Hume, *A Treatise on Human Nature,* ed. L. A. Selby-Bigge (Oxford: Clarendon Press, 1960), p. 260. [Le Senne's footnote says that he used the Renouvier and Pillon translation into French published in 1878.—Trans.]

differences between successive perceptions, by orienting their eventual convergence to one identical end, and by recognizing among them a solidarity comparable to that of animal or vegetable organisms. The initial *I*, or the continuous experience, cannot be called psychological in the human and limiting sense of the word, for this term is only appropriate to experience already connected by the self after the self has come into being. This continuous experience is without specification, without confusion, the object of all knowledge and all belief, and the source of all realization. In brief, it is experience insofar as experience is divine.

Hume's description, then, is not simply the transition from substantialism to criticism. It is the entrance into a philosophy of the relation between the existential unity of God and the determined unity of the self, which has its proper existence distinct from the coarseness of its knowledge, a knowledge which is condemned to mix together, through an identification devoid of subtlety, the diverse givens of experience. The idea of the self is nothing but the intermediate ideal through which the *I* passes on its way from undivided spontaneity to a particular sentiment of lowliness. The value of this sentiment will vary, depending on whether the sentiment sets in motion the degeneration or the free flight of experience.

35. *Disjunction and diffraction*

The subdivision of the *I* can be considered from two aspects. One could say objectively, if "object" does not signify determination, that in the content of experience a *disjunction* introduces itself which opposes that which is determined to value. From the point of view of the *I* itself, abstractly considered apart from its content, one could say that there is a *diffraction,* corresponding to disjunction, which distinguishes between the self and God. Description starting from the *I* as ideo-existential relation must advance as and with the *I* itself in the knowledge of experience. This advance takes place through a twofold study, a study on the one hand of the proper and contrary characters of determination and value, and on the other hand of what constitutes and distinguishes the existence of the self from that of God. The second part of this book is devoted to this twofold description.

From these two aspects it is obstacle, newly emerged, which

instigates all philosophy. It must do so. Every philosophy, insofar as it is and cannot fail to be primarily a conceptual expression of experience, is a mediation. Every mediation obviously presupposes that the two mediated terms have been provisionally separated and relatively prevented from reuniting. How could what Hamelin calls the appeal be distinguished from that necessity which makes one term the beginning of another term if, like Hamelin, one forgets to consider the obstacle? For the notion of appeal to make sense, the exigency for the other must be counteracted by some source of delay and, on occasion, of nonfulfillment. It follows, then, that the description of the obstacle, of its particulars and of its transformations, must be taken up by philosophy. The obstacle is that which imposes on us the sentiment of exteriority. It is that which awakens in us the consciousness of our weakness. It is that which provides us with an intimacy by reason of the turbulence which it instigates. It is that which enables us to pity others. And the obstacle always remains present under the dualism around which all philosophy turns. It scatters unity into multiplicity and explodes infinity into a swarm of determinations, determinations which are the incessantly renewed expressions of the obstacle.

36. *Two observations on the obstacle*

We begin our study of the obstacle with two preliminary observations:

(1) The first observation consists in cautioning that it is not yet time to ask *where* the obstacle can come from. The obstacle just appears by surprise. It emerges. It issues forth. It is as yet hardly thought about. Or it is merely thought about insofar as every designation entails some rudimentary thought. At its outset, perception is an almost pure emotion. To the degree that this provocation is defined, localized, and intellectualized, the self, which is discovered in the overcoming of the obstacle, reacts by means of some dialectic or emotional process. One or the other of these reactions will define and entail an attitude with regard to the obstacle, and from this attitude a theory will evolve its postulates. But this attitude presupposes the obstacle. The obstacle has preceded it and is independent of it. *Thus the obstacle is a given which can be eliminated but whose elimination cannot make it something which did not have to be eliminated.* There is something of the absolute in the obstacle, in the sense in which a universal trait of science confirms an absolute. Thus a quantity is called absolute insofar as the effort to make it relative has not succeeded in subsuming it under another quantity, as, for example, mass cannot be subsumed under velocity. In this sense, the absolute is a halting point. And however one assesses it, it will still turn out that one has been brought to a halt.

If every philosophy is a "theoretization" of the obstacle, it would be necessary to pass all philosophies in review in order to understand the modes of the obstacle. Agnostic realism makes the obstacle the reason for affirming the irreducibility of a thing in itself to experience. And, as a consequence, it discredits the self enclosed within phenomena. This is a process by which the sentiment of existence is objectivized in a pre-ideal and pre-conscious existence because this sentiment is accompanied in us by an experience of the obstacle which condemns us if we do not surpass it. This shows that the thing in itself, the absolute, independent of all categories, is, in its position vis-à-vis the categories, identical to the *I* vis-à-vis its experiences.

On the contrary, idealism inaugurates the mediation which makes the obstacle intelligible by transforming it into ideas and then into relations in order to end up converting it into a "glorious body" of the disencumbered spirit. By revealing the idea in the heart of the thing, then by revealing the dynamism in the heart of the idea, it discovers the spirit itself at the root of those obstructions whose constraining force the spirit concretely experiences. But the uninterrupted confrontation between realism, whether materialist or spiritual, and idealism is enough to reveal that the idealist dialectic is understood only through the obstacle. If one method alone were sufficient, it would have suppressed philosophy long ago. The conflict between the two has made philosophy progress.

The most concrete functions of consciousness with regard to the obstacle have more technical and less exaggerated reactions, for the infinite puts a profundity into each given which can only be touched but never fully exploited. Science, following the direction pointed out by idealism, intervenes only after the process of assault has been stalemated. It consists in turning the obstacle around to discover another occurrence, the "cause," which, by virtue of a law linking it to the obstacle now become object, will allow the obstacle to pivot by changing it into an instrument. The essential method of science is mediation by the ideal. Imperceptibly, through this method, the obstacle is dissolved into determinism. The obstacle was merely something awkward.

As science changes the obstacle into idea, so art changes it into image. A transfiguration which deepens the operation memory has initiated in everybody makes the obstacle a touching episode whose only value is to offer the spirit the occasion to play with the determination. In the absence of a liberty which is definitively measured by its creative power, the obstacle will give consciousness the pleasure of a liberty over phantoms. The worth of these phantoms resides in the sensible qualities they convey, such as the sensible qualities conveyed by the painter's colors, the shades of flowers, and clouds. Religion, whose vocation is to maintain the transcendence of the infinite in all the dialectics and processes of the spirit, cannot admit the obstacle without assigning it some value. It must alternatively consider the obstacle either as the effect of a human fault or as a divine warning. In their respective ways, *these operations each bring about the spiritualization of the obstacle*. This spiritualization dissipates the obstacle as obstacle, and an obstacle made in order to be dissolved will seem to have been nothing more than an appearance. It will suffice, then, for only the final term of this extenuation to be retained; and the retrospective error which consists in "flattening out" experience by eliminating the rough spots from it will come to be symmetrically opposed to the equally grave error which consists in looking into the obstacle for the point of an immeasurable irrationality. It is the obstacle which gives all thought its seriousness. It itself must be taken seriously. It is neither everything nor nothing, but makes it possible that there be something.

(2) If one should not volatilize the obstacle, neither should one solidify it. In its most striking form the obstacle is a barricade, a barrier, and we ordinarily use the mechanical image of the collision to symbolize our experience of the obstacle. This image is appropriate in the sense that the self, which becomes conscious of itself in this collision, does not feel itself to be harshly limited except through the collision of one of its members, e.g., its arm, with which it instinctively or deliberately identifies itself, and something which it locates in the realm of the non-self, e.g., a wall. But this simple case is only one of the occurrences which can impress itself upon us. Separation, es-

trangement, ignorance, emptiness, catastrophe, and poverty are obstacles coming about more from absence than from presence. Mechanism is confirmed when the movement of the human body is halted by the opposition of a greater force. And by reducing the experience of the limitation of the self to that of a collision, one paves the way for the reduction of human activity to objective causality. But this mechanism is partial, for it does not recognize that which non-being adds to the experience of the obstacle as a conscious occurrence.

Let us consider, for example, *intimidation*. No hurdle bars the path of an act. If the notion of the act had not been conceived, one could say that the absence of cause prevented the act from taking place. One is incapable of pronouncing a forgotten name. But he who is tempted to perform the act has conceived it. Even more, in pure morality, he conceives it as having no objective sanction attached to it. Will one say that he foresees the remorse that this act would inflict on him? The psychological conditions for such a position would be sufficiently destroyed if these disadvantages did not attenuate the eventual profits of the act in question. Before him there is nothing but a void to fill, but he abstains. One always speaks of decision as if it consists of comparing determinations. But decision always finally rests on problematic presentiments.

To take a case less extreme than that of pure morality, let us consider a sale. A customer and a vendor are discussing it. The merchandise brings into play two antagonistic apprehensions, the fear of missing a profitable transaction and the fear of not concluding the transaction at the most advantageous price. These two men are faced with nothing but absences, nothing but wagers on the future. A balance swings. One can determine its successive positions. Here one can define the alternative proposals, but these determinations only express the results of existential oscillations which make each of the negotiators pass from feeling superior to the other to feeling inferior. In turn, each ventures and each regrets.

Thus one must not draw the obstacle to that limit where *the solidity of a determination is about to reduce a man to the condition of a thing.* No one can concretely experience the closedness of certain directions except in perceiving the openness of others. The completely closed self would be the self without God. Or, and this amounts to the same thing, such a self would be matter. The obstacle, therefore, is always *the connection of a coercion and an intimidation.* As coercion, it reenters the system of determinations which compose the ideal. As intimidation, it presupposes an orientation of existence, an emotional evaluation of which judgments of value are only the public face. Certain pressures will be more compelling, others will be more threatening.

This is the case because even if the obstacle, in specifying the *I* as self, imposes itself on the self, the obstacle still depends on the self insofar as the self contributes to the importance of its aspects. The alpinist can simply renounce climbing the Meije in favor of climbing Mont Blanc. The Meije is no longer an obstacle to him. What is evidently true of obstacles in the realm of play is true in another way of the obstacles in life. But one could classify them by reason of the hold they exert on the self. What the word *obstacle* indicates will always be the aspect or the degree of the grip by which the obstacle imposes itself on us as that which does not depend on us.

Situations and structures. One can thus represent the self as being at the intersection of two ideal ensembles. That ensemble through which it concretely experiences difficulties, in short *a complex of obstacles,* defines its *situation.* The self refers this complex to the non-self. The most serious of these situations are those in which the efforts of the self to extricate itself make the situations worse. For such situations we can use the general term *bondage.* The most favorable situations are those on which we can draw whenever we wish but which permit us to withdraw and to escape when they tend to entrap us. For these situations we use the term *unimpeded mobility.*[9] Between bondage and unimpeded mobility, description must recognize the degrees and modes of situations which, when they are real, weigh unevenly on our actions and our thoughts.

Every collection of determinations which, on the contrary, puts at the disposal of the self a multiplicity of means and directions, with which and depending on which its success will be easy and efficacious, constitutes the self's *structure.* The body is only a part of this structure. A bicycle, the telephone system, a grammar, and so on, eventually complete it. The body is not altogether a part of the self's structure, since illness or infirmity and organic activity which do not depend on us make the

9. Le Senne uses here the word *survol,* literally "overflight."— Trans.

body partially an element of that which is not-mine. The boundaries of the mine and the not-mine therefore vary. *The self which localizes the I in the encounter of the mine and the nonmine has the unity of a connection.* This unity is ideal because situation and structure are determined. But their ideal expression omits all the existential processes, e.g., fear, hope, a taste for danger, presence of mind, utopian absence, etc., processes from which, unlike definite determinations, we cannot distinguish ourselves and which provide savor to our existence. Absolute determinism results from a twofold *dialectic:* (1) the dialectic of *leveling,* whereby one confuses situation with structure in an objectivity emptied of the significations of value by means of which we distinguish between situation and structure; and (2) the dialectic of *completion,* by which one extends determinism to every dimension of the universe. To recognize the operations which construct absolute determinism is already to surpass it and to discredit its ontological claims.

4 / Determination and Value

[X] DETERMINATION

Transition. Experience is subdivided into the experience of determination and the experience of value. The experience of determination is essential to consciousness insofar as consciousness is limited and subordinated. Determination is the object of a mode of knowledge which can be called *discrimination,* or, in more current usage, perception, for every object, whether it is more sensible than intellectual, or vice versa, is always both sensible and intellectual. Thus it follows that the actually thought idea of "five" is just as much the object of a perception as is a sighted pile of five pebbles. The experience of value which is essential to consciousness insofar as it is pure and intuitive is the object of a mode of knowledge which does not allow for distinct parts and can thus only be called a *concrete experience.*

To give precision to this opposition, we will successively look for the essential characteristics both of determination and of value. It might seem evident that the characteristics of determination must be defined by affirmations, whereas those of value, in order to respect its indeterminateness, must be expressed negatively. But since the distinction between determination and value is inseparable from their solidarity, this affirmativeness and this negativeness temper each other. Thus Descartes counted privations and negations among the "simple natures." And, on the other hand, intuitionism necessarily presupposes that the content of intuition is nuanced by virtue of the effect of certain determinations so that the intuition, mute as it is, is not likewise empty.

37. *Essential characteristics of determination*

We will begin with the affirmed, the discriminated, and the description of this disjunction.

A

Determination is introduced by obstacle and emerges from the relatively undivided continuity of naive spontaneity. Thus its first characteristic is that it is *localized*. One can call this characteristic *thereness*. The self points, and what it points to is what is this and nothing else. A determination therefore exists only by reason of a more or less profound cleavage between it and every other determination and between it and indeterminateness. It is insular. By making the act of intercalation the essential act of description as he understands it, i.e., of scientific description whose task is to establish series, Royce makes the category of the "between" the first of the scientific ideas. For *B* to be recognizable between *A* and *C*, *B* must not be confused with them in the passage from *A* to *C*.

One could thus say that *determination is an interrupted relation*. As in those chemical reactions in which some bodies have no time to become established because each of them is being decomposed as soon as it begins to be formed, a relation whose fecundity is undisturbed will immediately change each of its products into the subsequent product. For an infinite spirit, the law of the progressive development of quantity or magnitude requires the development to take place in infinitely small but infinitely rapid stages. The most recently produced quantity is almost indistinguishable from the immediately preceding one. But when an obstacle or a volition provoked by an obstacle intervenes, the activating dynamism stops and a number comes up, as the movement of a die has to stop for a face to show us its spots.

Thus, only that which is determination could be a thing. Determination is the subject and the attribute of every use of the verb "is." Should the self let itself be fascinated by determination, determination will become, or rather will have already become, a thing. But this possibility is excluded since the determination exists only by offering itself to the *I*, which always surpasses it and which, by reason of its immanence in the self, prevents the self from becoming pure matter. The self can at least be approached from this limit. On the other hand, common sense retains an overwhelming sentiment of the solidity of determination, of its inertia, and of its resistance to modification. These characteristics are all the more obvious because they are consolidated by abstraction, which, by removing the determination from every environmental influence, changes it into a universal essence. Science, in turn, has emphasized all the experiences of regularity, e.g., astronomical periodicity, the persistence of earth's solids, and optical rigidity, at the expense of contingency, liberty, and the spirit.

Though this solidity allows determination to become an obstacle, it eventually also confers value on determination since it allows the self to satisfy its needs for security, possessions, trade, and order. It does not, however, follow that the positivity of determination is without its counterpart. By bringing doubt, i.e., the conflict of determinations, to bear upon the meek self which had treated all determinations as absolutes, the Cartesian *cogito* initiated the extenuation of determinations. In science, it produces ideas from these determinations; in art, it produces images from them; in ethics, ideals; in religion, creeds. None of these processes of spiritualization would be possible if the positivity of determination was absolute. In opposition to materialism, which transforms determinations into things-in-themselves, and in opposition to positivism, which limits determinations to merely being recognized, one has to underline the negativity of determination resulting from its localization.

Every determination is negative in four senses:

(1) It is negative inasmuch as it is *omissive*. It is what it is, but it is not what it is not. Of course, the diverse is not the contradictory; but the other, if it does not suppress sameness, is the omission of sameness. It amounts to the same thing to observe that determination excludes certain other determinations or to note that the self has and will always have no more than a limited capacity. The interiority of God to the self, which is identical with the unity of the *I*, manifests itself here through an aspiration, without which this limited capacity would be merely a capaciousness without being a defect. As

nothing is grasped in our life if we do not presuppose in man some concretely experienced indigence, every determination is a little more than the nothingness of other determinations: it is their absence.

(2) When it is merely omissive, determination postpones but allows for, with due regard for objective coherence and within the limits of the subjective capacity of the self, access to other determinations. But when the actions which impose determination on the self not only consolidate it but maintain it as it is given, determination becomes *prohibitive*. The delay involved in passing from one place to another is made worse by the delay involved in an obstruction to be overcome, or at best circumvented.

It is at this moment that determination's aptitude for *playing the role of matter* begins to appear. By making time the fluid stuff of a becoming which manifests the eruption of eternity even if it degrades it, Bergson has divinized suppleness. If it is true that matter is inertia, brittleness, and indocility to the spirit and to value, it is nevertheless not so much its solidity as the inopportuneness of its consistency that makes us feel it as matter. For where this cohesion is possession, springboard, or assistance, where it serves the vocation of the spirit, it does not oppose itself to the spirit. It is only when this cohesion is intemperate, ungracious, and oppressive that we acquire the sentiment and the concept of matter.

It is appropriate to stress that determination is matter only when it resists the self and refuses to be informed in accord with the self's sentiment of value. When a thing is a docile instrument, as happens in the highest creations of art when my body does nothing but put into play the energy it contains and the images the soul wishes—this is especially verified in dance—determination is then no more than the content of the spirit. What the spirit discovers in beauty is precisely itself. Since matter in itself is the spirit denied, there is no more matter when matter manifests the spirit. Matter can only be found when determination is prohibitive.

(3) The situation is even more serious when determination becomes *polemical*. Not only does the determination prevent one from reaching another determination, but it also begins to repress the movement which would transform an incipient determination into a mature one. As one determination cannot affect another one without being affected itself, the antagonism

between two determinations presupposes the unity of the relation between them. But in the present case the opposition prevails over the union in such a way that unity is reduced to a minimum. Each of the two determinations appears to the self as incomplete. This can only happen by reason of their conflict, for a determination which is of itself always limited can only appear as limited to a self who first represents it to himself, then forms the ideal of a richer determination, and, finally, concretely experiences the obstacle constituted by a second determination which is incompatible with an evolution from the first determination to the second.

(4) Finally, since negation is not so much the quality of being denied as it is the act of denying, one must take into account the fact that determination can subsequently become the point of application of a tendency. That is, the determination can become the instrument of an effort which imparts to the solidity of the determination by which one tendency resists another tendency the supplementary energy of an action oriented toward repulsion. Determination then becomes *tyrannical.* It is here that the danger bursts forth of objective "leveling," which *considers the idea independently of the position taken by the self in its connection with this idea.* One and the same idea can function in many ways: (*a*) it can be a principle which the self makes a rule of its activity; (*b*) it can be a given which the self makes the object of its analysis or which it tries to link to another given; (*c*) it can be a means of reconciling the situation which is imposed on the self with one of the self's intentions; (*d*) it can be an argument by which the self promotes the success of one of its projects over those of someone else and consequently a means of managing others; (*e*) it can be an excuse by which it justifies to another a harmful act, and so on. Thought is never exclusively the intuition of a determination. It is also an activity which deals with the determination as a soldier deals with his armor. Up to now, philosophical description has more often subordinated thought to the idea than the idea to thought.

It is appropriate to insist on the negative aspects of determination, because the objectivism of logic deals only with the positive aspect of it. As a consequence, there is a general misunderstanding of the range and nature of negative judgments. It is here that a description which does not limit itself to concepts, to their objective identity or their objective exteriority, but goes on to the dialectics of which these concepts are ultimately the products, traces, conditions, means, etc., presents itself in all its value as the introduction to a study of thought, in opposition to the exclusive consideration of what is thought. The exclusive consideration of what is thought is nothing but the intellectualized version of a fascination with the perceived.

From these analyses, it follows that the relationship of limitation between determination and the self, a relationship which derives its nature from them at each instant, operates in two ways. Insofar as determination is negative, defined, and circumscribed, the self surpasses it. Once again, it is impossible not to recognize the existential unity of the self and still to comprehend how determinations which are disjointed by nature can be juxtaposed. To juxtapose is already to unite them, all the while acknowledging the contingency of the union, in an apprehension which simultaneously discriminates them. The dance of determinations, both submitted to and willed by the self, constitutes its intellectual life. On the other hand, insofar as determination is positive, it imposes itself on the self, affects it, and determines it before determining its own subsequent representations. From this point of view, determination limits the self. In the relation between the object and the subject, it is important always to note which prevails over the other, or, more precisely, how one prevails. One should grant that the subject has some limitation in virtue of which it is appropriately thought of as an object, while at the same time one must note that the object is only an object insofar as it is represented or representable.

Definition and *horizon* are the words which best express the manner in which object and subject limit each other. *Definition is the limitation of the ideal; horizon is the limitation of existence in the self.* But, on the one hand, the idea, the specification of the ideal, which likewise expresses the divine aspect of the *I*, possesses an infinite virtuality which makes it the expression of the Infinite-in-every-way. Limited existence can only hint at this. On the other hand, the existence of the self, encompassed at every instant by a horizon beyond which it cannot perceive anything, opposes to the relativeness of determination the absoluteness of existence. Determinations presuppose the absoluteness of existence as soon as they impose themselves on it, for the thinkable can only be thought in connection with the thinker. Object and subject thus surpass each other, but each does so in its own proper fashion.

B

In showing that every determination is necessarily both positive and negative, that it is and that it is not, one shows it to be on a scale which has an infinite number of gradations. Every determination falls between absolute, perfect determination which leaves nothing outside itself, between the superior and inaccessible limit of determination, on the one hand, and pure indetermination, determination's lower limit, if one can call a limit that which is no longer something thinkable, on the other.

Determination cannot be characterized by an absolute cohesion which would prevent its being analyzed, or by an annihilation of cohesion which would deprive it of any nature whatsoever. This median condition reveals itself in the second characteristic of determination, namely, that it is always *the relation between an opacity and a transparence.* Insofar as it is determination, it is analyzable; insofar as it is intelligible to a certain degree, thought can touch upon it. As such, determination is intellectual. But though intelligence makes some penetration, it soon collides with a resistance which prevents pushing the analysis any further. Determination is transparent, but like all transparence, this presupposes a foundation. If in fact apperception were absolutely foreign to determination, if apperception slid over determination as over an absolutely smooth surface, it would not be the apperception of that determination. But if determination yielded indefinitely to analysis, the self would no longer apprehend this same determination, and finally it would not apprehend any other determination in this one.

Every determination can thus be called both intellectual and sensible. A determination is defined to a certain degree when it is seen. There is no sensation without perception, no perception without sensation. $\sqrt{2}$ is thought insofar as one begins to enumerate decimals, but one always stops. In the same way, when I perceive a book, or a color, it is because the analytic resolution is never completed. The analysis soon collides with an opacity. Every sensible object is intellectual in that it presupposes a certain degree of determination so as to be this particular object and not some other one. Every intellectual object is sensible, given, mentally perceived in that the analysis which begins the reduction of the object comes to a stop. In the case of green, I think that it would vanish if I closed my eyes or if certain radiation were impossible, but insofar as it is green, it is given. In the case of 11, I begin to think 10 + 1, but 11, 10, and 1 present themselves to me as beings. Either the distinction between the sensible and the intellectual calls attention to the inequality in the relative importance of the two aspects or it signifies the diversity of the attitudes of the self in regard to determination, through which attitudes it inaugurates certain operations on determination.

This is why it so often happens that the philosophical passage from the perception to the idea, from the realism of the sensible imagination to an idealism of the intelligible, changes nothing essential to the attitude of the self. In either case it is equally possible to enclose oneself in determination, to hold fast to the thought of a determination, to sacrifice the existential to the ideal. There is no essential difference between the sensible operation by which a perceptual composite is decomposed and recomposed and the intellectual operation by which a complex idea is defined analytically or genetically. The difference between philosophies consists more in the difference between the dialectics which animate them than in the objects which are the occasions, means, or traces of these dialectics. The objects are always both given and thought.

C

These are the same characteristics that one finds under another aspect if one completes this sketch by taking note of the *insufficiency* of every determination. Through its emergence, its isolation in an experience which always surpasses it, the determination reveals that it is only a momentary pause on a journey. It exists only by being shot through with existence, which not only makes it more than a mere possible determination but has to confer its very possibility on it. A determination's possibility, in order to be such a possibility, must be started, imagined, foretasted, in brief, must be given in an existence. Existence adds to determination the sentiment that, as a determination, it is incomplete. If the case were otherwise, determination could not be concretely experienced as something which halts the spirit. If a determination could be the absolutely last term, that beyond which nothing more would be desirable, far from interrupting, i.e., from frustrating satisfaction, it would fulfill and satiate desire. Experience would end there. It would condense itself into the determination. This would be the end of the world. And since it would be impossible to conceive how an absolutely sufficient experience would not from the outset immediately substitute itself for everything which would have tried to appear before it, all experience would be annihilated in the absolute one.

38. *Appeal and influence*

The insufficiency of determination takes two forms which it is of major importance to distinguish. The first is the insufficiency of every determination *relative to another determination.* The second is the insufficiency of determination *in general.*

For the former, we will use the Hamelinian term *appeal.* Whether one presents determination as an intersection of relations which have to be interrupted if there are to be terms, or whether one shows the aspects according to which determination is negative, one always admits that a determination is not a thing, that this island is a port of embarkation, that it is an occasion for a self moved by an aspiration immanent in existence to proceed to another determination. The number two appeals for three, for qualities, for a reason to be represented, for an arithmetician, for the letters of the Morse code, and so on indefinitely. Appeal is the principle of all circulation traversing determinations, whether this circulation takes the form of reasoning, of association, of suggestion, or of history.

In using the term *appeal* we must make sure that we do not impose on it the restrictions which it bears in the rational construction of Hamelin. Appeal, according to his doctrine and usage, is a univocal, "univalent" appeal. Relation appeals for number, and directly it appeals only for number. The order must not be jumbled. But this privileged, normative description presupposes the antecedent intervention of a rational preference which eliminates from the description of experience almost all its riches. To open up description one must free appeal from this restriction. Appeal, as we understand it, is in itself *radiating*. If one calls thinking the "going from one determination to another," he will eventually think in every sense of that word. From an illness, appeal can lead me to its cause, to its effects, to the nature of illness, to the frequency of this particular illness, to society, to the problem of evil. In short, it can lead me everywhere else.

The sole limitations to which appeal must submit comes from its own definition. *It moves from one determination to another, but it remains enclosed within determination in general.* Its universal postulate is that *one determination determines another determination.* This is the law of a "spread out" thinking which is incapable of disengaging itself from the thing which is thought so as to return through an existential conversion to the thought which transcends this thing. This is a consciousness which is conscious of things and not of itself. It remains imprisoned by the relative as a locomotive is in a network of rails. It does not know the *cogito.* But it is philosophically impossible to enclose oneself in relativity. Relativity inevitably leads us back from the relative, not to the idea of the absolute but to the absolute itself. Over and above all relations, the absolute is within all relations. After having spelled out the categories, one must enter into the indivisibility of existence which sustains them. At that moment, appeal, whose movement is ultimately nothing but the projection of infinity into exteriority, reveals its actual insufficiency.

Thus, since appeal permits circulation only through the existent, one must add to appeal the element of *influence,* which is the passage from the existent to existence. When a man reasons mathematically, appeal allows for the succession of mediations from premises to conclusion. But this reasoning is also lived. The mathematician concretely experiences the impressions of satisfaction when his deductions converge, of joy and fatigue alternating during the course of his work. A sentiment of security and hope settles itself in him to the degree that his thought progresses. In the course of his reasoning, appeal is the determination of one of his steps by another. The influence of this sequence of determinations is the suggestion of concrete experiences whose proper character is always to be beyond determination. Language shows these experiences but it does not convey them.

For every philosophy which is interested in nothing but determination, and thus risks reducing itself to history, to science, or, at the most profound level, to metaphysics, every consideration of influence must be swept away. When one makes determination everything, then existence and the spirit can no longer be anything but holes, voids. The knowledge of the self becomes the cancellation of the self. This partialness can only lead to frustrations. This kind of philosophy, as a net lets water escape, eliminates precisely that existence whose irreducibility to determination the *cogito* and the Kantian critique of the ontological argument have definitively established. What matters absolutely for every man is that he is not what he has but he is what he is. What matters is not determinations but the concrete experience which the influence of determinations gives rise to in him. The miser does not love his gold; he loves his love for his gold. If a picture is merely a display of colors, there is no artistic enjoyment of it. A sweet-smelling flower is a chemical body; but what the woman who smells it loves is the perfume which exists nowhere but in her heart.

Thus the influence of determinations is consciousness itself insofar as it is pure. I distinguish myself from what I can see, touch, count, discriminate. I do not distinguish myself from admiration, joy, or fear—in brief, from the undivided concrete experience that I have of such feelings. When a man imagines that he could have been born somewhere else or been otherwise determined, he verifies that he can separate himself from what he has, namely, from all determinations, but that he cannot separate himself from the existence by which he feels the determinations. It remains to be seen whether the determinations which he can suppose himself to be deprived of are not the most superficial, and whether his existence does not in its own right entail the laws of his determinations which permit them to be his.

If philosophy refuses to have recourse to any consideration of influence, it cannot get free from an inextricable difficulty. One condemns oneself never to leave determinations. One betrays and ignores consciousness. If one wishes to return to consciousness, it seems that one must blot out all determinations. This is what takes place when one introduces the pure self. But an agnosticism of the pure self is no less frustrating than is the forgetting of the self. The two dialectics end in the same nothingness. The spirit seems to be condemned either to grasping itself only by alienating itself into some object or to rendering itself unknowable to itself if it does not wish to betray itself. By throwing up a bridge between determinations and existence, the influence of determinations on the self, and in an inverse sense the emission of determinations by the self, restores *the connection between terms separated by the preceding dialectics*.

The *I* is the *ideo-existential* relation, and, consequently, so is the self. Not only is conscious existence as such directly and concretely experienced; because the influence of determinations touches it, existence can also be thought indirectly. Sometimes it can be reproduced by a figurative description. Sometimes it can be shown by an allusive description. Two men can agree on what they see. They can also agree on what they concretely experience if they precisely specify the situation in which they have the concrete experience. Smelled perfume escapes discrimination. But since the concrete experience results from the influence of chemical perfume, the concrete experience can at least be designated by means of the determination which causally contributes to provoking it.

It cannot be otherwise. So long as one remains on the ideal plane where one determination determines another, one eliminates consciousness itself. Consciousness is the negating of determination which joins either an ordered or a haphazard sequence of objects in order to confer existence on them. Neither the luminous ray, nor the optical excitation, nor the encounter between extrinsic action and centrifugal action, all of which allow perception to occur, is perception itself. The postulate of mechanistic determinism is that the cause suffices for the effect and the effect is everything that the cause can yield. How, if there are only determinations, could one add to causation the seeing of this causation? Thus experience requires that description recognize both appeal, of which causality is one mode, and influence. Appeal makes one leave behind some particular determination. Influence makes one leave behind every determination. Kant has established the irreducibility of existence to a concept. Bergson has given solidity to the sentiment of existence by requiring that its duration furnish its own content. One must pursue this work by multiplying the allusive descriptions which will permit one to conquer the domain of existence. But this goal does not require one to renounce the study of determinations. Experience presents them to us as linked with existence itself.

[XI] VALUE

BY PUSHING US BEYOND DETERMINATION, not in determination's accidental character but in what is essential to it, influence leads us to existence considered absolutely. Without existence, determination would not be something existent but rather something non-existent. That is, without existence, determination would have no consistency, no efficacy, no influence, in short, no value. Negatively presented, as it necessarily is by a thought naturally turned to the thing which is thought, to the definite, to the determined, *value is the cancellation of determination*. One immediately sees that this relative cancellation stretches from absolute nothingness to absolute existence. But determination itself forbids us from taking the cancellation of determination to be pure nothingness, for if there were no principle of existence in experience, determination would be less than virtual. Since determination is given as existing, even in a dream, and since it is worth something, value is a positive cancellation, or, if one prefers, value is more-than-positive. This cancellation is positive insofar as it posits determinations, and more-than-positive in that existence itself is, according to its value, susceptible to elevation or degradation.

39. *Essential characteristics of value*

The essential characteristics of value must be correlative to those of determination, but they are correlative in the way that the existential is correlative to the ideal. We will consider these characteristics briefly.

A

In opposition to the localization of determination, value is atmospheric. In general we will call *atmospheres* those nuances, hues, or colors of existence which specify the sublimity of the *I*. Influence concerns one or more of these atmospheres insofar as they are conditioned by determinations. But insofar as value is necessarily absolute and primary, this specification is a limitation, a negation, a shadow cast over value, as color is light which is obscured and disturbed. So it is impossible to reduce value, absolutely considered, to the degrees and modes which would arise from its encountering determination. Because of its negativity, determination can never completely lose its character of being an obstacle.

Value has to be called atmospheric, *because it is not composed of parts* and it is not enclosed within circumferences. Value impregnates. It diffuses itself. The pre-Socratic classification of elements, if one proceeds from earth to water to air and finally to fire, is a precious symbolization representing the passage from solid, hostile, material, angular determination to more and more subtle forms of spirituality. Descartes has written in the *Olympica:* "As imagination uses figures to conceive bodies, so the intellect uses some sensible bodies, for example wind or light, to express spiritual entities." [1] It has already been noted that determinations can and must have, over and above their nature, the value of representing spiritual atmospheres. Matter is canceled spirit. But this negation is suppressive, destructive. On the other hand, spirit is canceled matter. But this negation is propulsive, exalting. And as this propulsion can be continued indefinitely, matter is elevated by and with spirit. Art gives us an example of this. In the course of an artistic transformation, as a slight amount of fluorescein colors all the water in a large pond, so determination is spiritualized in a felt atmosphere.

Everyone's experience testifies to the fact that value is an atmosphere. Where could goodness, generosity, pity, inspiration, genius, nobility, sincerity be localized? Science, which goes from determination to determination, never finds these qualities on its path. Will I place the sadness which a landscape inspires in me in this cypress or in that cloud? Whatever influence these objects contribute to the scene, *sadness could never be inspired in me unless my entire experience were*

1. "Ut imaginatio utitur figuris ad corpora concipienda, ita intellectus utitur quibusdam corporibus sensibilibus, ad spiritualia figuranda, ut vento, lumine." Descartes, "Cogitationes Privatae," *Oeuvres,* ed. Charles Adam and Paul Tannery (Paris, 1896), X, 217.

transformed by it. As soon as there is perception, perception manifests the union of determination and atmosphere. If the perceived is what it is only by being distinguished from another perceived, it is the content of someone's perception only by virtue of the atmospheric totality of the self who perceives. The self always blinks in perceiving. It sees and touches a thing, but it does so by feeling itself as existence. A number, which results from the degradation of an atmospheric ensemble into an ideal totality, is never anything other than a numbered thing surpassed by the numberer who situates the number in experience. Only in experience does the number find its importance.

One can best verify the atmospheric essence of value in the two extreme cases, the most favorable and the least favorable. The first is found in those experiences in which we denominate a reality which can belong neither to any one definite determination nor to any organized totality of these givens. Let us consider "disarray." Disarray is not a property of a specifiable perception or of a specifiable idea encountered in its tumult. Nor is it an order among all perceptions or ideas, for disarray precludes order. Is it the simple juxtaposition of such things? No, because an objective multiplicity is felt as disordered only to the extent that it frustrates a demand for value which one cannot define by a determined order, for the representation of this order brings the disarray to an end. Let us go now to the essential point. Disarray is always linked to a difficulty in discriminating. Disarray prevents determinations from achieving that solidity which would make at least some of them havens for attention. Can we deny, however, that disarray is an experience as surely, as easily, and as generally recognized as is 321 or the musical note *re*? On the contrary, for a deaf man does not encounter *re*, nor does a man who is ignorant of arithmetic think about 321. But both of these men, and every consciousness, we feel sure, have and do concretely experience disarray. How could science, which retains within its scope nothing but systematized determinations, have a place for experiences which exclude both order and definition? But there are few experiences which are more important for peoples and for individual men. Disarray can prepare the way either for revolution and suicide or for heroism and regeneration.

Let us now go to the contrary case, where the harmonious

order of determinations *seems* to exempt consciousness from adding anything. The highest form of this order is *beauty*, the truth of which is nothing but a simplified pattern. Is it possible to confine beauty to the level of determinations? If it were possible, there would be no difference between the exclusively sensible perception of the form taken as beautiful and the sentiment of beauty. But there must be a difference, since one man can perceive a form which suggests artistic emotion to another man without concretely experiencing it himself. Beauty therefore does not reduce itself to determination but involves a sentiment, an atmosphere, an existential life which results from determination's influence and adds to it.

From the opposition between determination and value, it immediately follows that *value would simply annihilate itself if it reduced itself to determination.* When one speaks of the value of a determination, this value is added to the determination itself. A share of stock is not identical to the legal certificate which stands for it. The title can remain materially unchanged and yet its value may change from moment to moment. When one considers the exchange value of a coin, the coin has value only by reason of the desire to procure something else by means of it. The coin is a relative value. But a relative value in itself would be nothing but a negation of value. For if the means which I seek to procure for myself have no value for me beyond their utility of leading to an end, they are in themselves neither desirable nor lovable, and I can only detest having to make use of them. They are, in short, without value. *Either value is absolute or it is not value.* What is merely valuable for something else is not valuable. It is perhaps the gravest and strongest sign of human limitation that man necessarily reduces value to values. By making itself plural, by falling to the level of the ideal, value becomes a matter of quantity. This reduction could be of help to commerce. But in commerce itself, value will animate it, when it does animate it, in proportion to whatever aspiration worthy of being loved is put into the commerce by the soul of the merchant.

By reason of this essence of being absolute, value is susceptible to all the dialectics of rupture which manifest the incommensurability and heterogeneity of the infinite to the finite. Even though the rupture can never be a complete rupture, even though experience can never be broken in two, the transcendent character of value can be located as near as possible to absolute exteriority, without, however, reaching that point. It is indeed true that value hovers infinitely above us, that it necessarily gives rise to a quasi despair of reaching it, that it will not be the captive of any human technique, and that we always have to fear being unhappy and malevolent. It is this aspect of value which manifests the severity of duty. Duty in morality is quite similar to what pure revelation is in religion. But what good is this severity if transcendence were not to change itself into immanence? Every revelation is destined to serve as mediation from the absence to the presence of God. The Infinite cancels the finite but also emits it. Instead of being a justification for our lowliness, value must become our soul, since God gives himself in love. The dialectics of rupture have to be succeeded by the processes of union. Where value intervenes, the ideal relation of the finite to the infinite is converted into a mode of life by which the help of the Infinite permits us at each instant to surmount the finite.

Just as a determination is an interrupted relation, so an existence is a break in value. In itself value is necessarily one and infinite. For if it were self-contradictory it would cancel itself, it would be prevented from appearing, and consequently it would be worthless. The only way value could be limited would be if it were subordinate to some other reality. But then the name *value* would be transferred to this other reality and the latter would be infinite. Thus pure value has to be thought of as an expansion, an inexhaustible diffusion. But since experience has imposed on us the distinction between determination and value, pure value is only a limit of experience. Value is not suppressed but rather is diffracted by its encounter with determination. It is not limited but channeled. Obstacle intervenes everywhere as a cause of separation and retardation, without the separation being able to be a fracture, without the retardation being able to be a definitive stoppage. From this universal fact it follows that the unity and infinity of value must be parceled out into individualized, and more or less stifled and segregated, atmospheres. The term *value* is only relatively appropriate to each of these atmospheres. They are both values and non-values, according to their degree of nobility. It is better to call them existences.

Existence is indeed a value, and in fact it is the only value, since, like Roland's mare, which was sober, obstinate, etc., but dead, everything which could be valuable would be worthless if existence is not given to it. But when we think about existence, we are considering a diminished value which has become the object of theoretic knowledge, a value of diminished warmth, of meager expansiveness, a value already about to fade away. *Existence thus presents itself in the interval between infinite value and nothingness, sharing with them the common essence of canceling determination.* Just as every determination is definite, so every existence is limited. Value has to thrust determination into relation and to inspire existence to create lest determination become routine and existence a vanishing illusion.

Value is knowledge of the Absolute. Either there is no value, or value necessarily dissipates every kind of doubt concerning itself. This is what nothingness manifests by counterproof. Where there is nothing, there is no place for a dispute. This is what every existence confirms over and above itself, for even if the content of this existence were a relation, it is still an absolute fact that it is represented. We pass from the relatively absolute to the absolutely absolute at the moment when existence without limits, indefinitely dilated by its own proper expansion, mingles itself with value considered in its pure source. This is what description shows when it reaches the highest experiences of our life. The lover who rejoices in the presence of his beloved when love mingles their souls, the artist ravished in the contemplation of beauty, the hero carried along by the joy of noble action, the scientist entering into the understanding of what he had hitherto not known, Pascal on the night of November 23, 1654—none of these have to ask themselves whether their experience is valuable. They are beyond both doubt and death. Furthermore, we should avoid making this value an object to be viewed, a backdrop unrolling before an intuition. The experience of value can be a life of dialectics and processes in which value is omnipresent, as a storm unifies all the eddies which constitute its turbulence. When value triumphs, determination and existence conspire to bring the triumph about.

B

We have seen as a second characteristic of determination that it is found at the point where opacity brings reflection to a halt. Indeed it is essential to a determination, to a term, that it be given a set position. The determined is the abstractly definite. Its localization renders it independent of its surroundings by separating it from them. If this independence could go so far as to separate the determined from existence, then objectivism would be true. What establishes the falsity and abstractness of objectivism is that *determinism cannot extend to eternity except by losing existence.* As soon as it is defined, a determination appears as eternally possible. But this eternal possibility can still be an eternal absence. It can always lack historical actuality. Insofar as knowledge bears on determinations and is indifferent to value, it achieves universally utilizable results. It matters little to knowledge whether alum or African boars have existed or have disappeared from experience. As essences they share in the eternity of the sphere. But to know is also to act. Knowledge discriminates, but still it is either worthwhile or not. And when knowledge is important, that is, when knowledge is not a mere routine but is a creation, it is because the sentiment of value has led it back to existence and to its own vocation.

Since what is "set in place" is, in its nature, immobile and without real connection to other things, without a vector of importance, value, by opposing itself to the "set in place," must have the twofold character of being *bipolar and oriented.* One could show this first of all with reference to the most simple connection, i.e., identity. Identity can be either fixed or mobilized. Identity is either a being or a method. In the first case, it is a determination in which two almost forgotten terms are blended together. It stands in full view. It is like an object in front of the self to such a degree that the self almost obliterates itself in it by its perceptive attention. In returning to life, the self must mobilize identity. Identity then becomes more than a trajectory; it defines an operation. This operation thereafter can be applied equally well to different matters, and the spirit can move from one comparable thing to another and from them either to their identity or to their differences. In these two circulations identity becomes bipolar. And, depending on whether the intention of the spirit is looking for things which are comparable or are diverse, identification or differentiation will awaken a preference or a repugnance. We will have passed from the level of determinations to the concrete experience of value.

In saying that this characteristic of value is bipolar, one is simply admitting that given of description which shows that *every positive value is correlative to a negative value*. Truth, love, beauty, generosity, simplicity, hope, life, and enthusiasm exist only in opposition to falsity, hate, ugliness, avarice, deceitfulness, fear, death, and discouragement. Likewise, when determination is affected by a trace of value, it cannot become precious without running the risk of becoming dangerous. For that which lays the foundation for security consolidates blindness; that which offers itself for possession begins enslavement; that which satisfies the seeking prepares for the routine. But this bipolarity belongs properly to value, not to determination. Determination in itself is independent of the value which comes to it from its relation to existence. A wall is a wall whether it protects or imprisons. A luxury does not change whether it brings one delight or reduces one to slavery. A fact has its content whether one subsequently judges it true or false.

The transition from formal and analytic intellectualism to dynamic and synthetic intellectualism replaces the idea with the relation and thus projects the dynamism of value onto the plane of the ideal. Reason, in becoming, by force of its nature, the law of construction, is polarized like value itself. Thus this projection mediates the infusion of value into intelligence by helping to mobilize and orient intelligence. One does not have the right to conclude from this that the determination on which intelligence comes to bear is in itself polarized. Reason, however it is theoretically defined, has been charged with value by an act which is applied to it but which transcends it. This is shown by the fact that reason could remain a necessity indifferent to value without changing anything of its nature. Sometimes value animates and inspires intelligence. This is the case which the classical theory of rational liberty considered. Sometimes value casts itself at cross purposes to that which a more or less canonical intelligence produces, so as to upset the elements and reshape their order. Sometimes, on the other hand, value pursues its goals with intelligence serving it only in a subordinate and mediocre fashion. Intellectual value is only an instance of unrestricted value. It would be the very death of intelligence if intellectual value should claim to monopolize absolute value. Intelligence has value only because of the soul's value. Intelligence either expresses and contributes to the value of the soul or it degrades both itself and the soul.

One cannot be content with defining the poles of value, for that would again substitute a discrimination for a concrete experience. No idea of value is value itself. The idea of value helps us not to deviate from value. It turns us away from a temptation which would reduce life to negative value, that is, to nothingness. It mediates an existential conversion which goes beyond this ideal aspect of value; it introduces us to participation in infinite value and permits us to nourish ourselves spiritually with value. Again, it is always possible for any idea of value, and even for any of the particular values themselves, to degenerate into intellectual and emotional passion and disguise an intimate action which is in reality a debasement. From the point of view of man, all the indices of truth and value are simply approaches and aids to a sense of value whose security and delicacy has to grow with the actual participation in absolute value.

C

We have not claimed that bipolarity and orientedness are two characteristics of value, because value's bipolarity is simply an aspect of its being oriented, and its being oriented is merely an ideal translation of its existential nature. Determination is insufficient, because it stands in wait both for an indefinite complement from other determinations and for existence from value. Value, which gives determinations their connection and order, and which adds existence to them by giving existence to itself, must be *sufficient*. Sufficiency excludes every maximum, since a maximum would be a stoppage, a suspension of efficiency. If the human soul is not made to transform itself into a thing but rather is made to know creative life, the essence of which is not to suffer loss from what it produces but to enrich itself by giving, then such words as "expansion" or "generous exuberance" are best suited to express an experience which is a mixture of appropriation and openness. In the course of such an experience value gives itself to us before manifesting its presence to others through the determinations which it causes to emanate from itself. From the vivifying presence of value, depending on the solidarity of the existential and the ideal, a contagion of joy and vigor diffuses itself and pours forth a shower of ideas and things. One enters into value through duty, but one goes out from duty into value.

To make the sufficiency of value clear, one has merely to underline the insufficiency of determination. By noting immediately that determination's isolation, its distinction, assures its abstract universality throughout space and time, we ourselves are now given the right to say that determination is *the instrument of every definite transmission.* No definite transmission is possible except through an isolating protectiveness which, by leaving determination in almost exclusive dependence on its origin, prevents the determination from being disturbed. From this point of view, determination is always capable of becoming social. The science of determinations is society itself. Science makes society essentially military. As Spinoza and Pascal have seen and noted with equal clarity, society is force. The essence of the State is sanction. It acts on bodies with material means. It expects docility in each man's intimate existence with regard to the determinations, laws, taxes, decrees, prohibitions, and regulations by which it deals with him. At its lowest level, society is an army, which is simply mobilized science and industry. At its highest level, society is the teaching which fashions spirits in conformity with official programs. The voice is also a material action. When a man wants to brutalize the intimacy of another, he shouts.

Further, the ideal of all social thinkers, whatever name they give themselves, is always, if they are not conspiring against society as are liberals and anarchists, that mode of value which is the order of determinations. That this mode of value, like all modes, is to some degree indispensable to liberty and to happiness cannot be contested. Creativeness presupposes some security, and since creativeness is not caprice, it presupposes some continuity. But experience is not a world. Every mode of value is transcended by value itself. A consequence of this fact is that history manifests a labor of Penelope in the course of which structures incapable of being perfected are erected and renewed. War, which is the conflict of such structures, and decadence, which is their profound collapse, confirm the truth of the legend of Babel. Even universal empires, as certain scientific or juridical institutions, the *jus gentium,* international parties, and churches already are, might remain or do remain on the fringe of the humanity which they embrace without seizing.

This is because these abstractions, e.g., State or society, can do no more than receive and transmit existence. As existents, they are intrinsically insufficient. Value comes to them from men, whose innermost consent or hostility will make them either flourish or perish. States or social structures are not self-sustaining. If people are no longer willing to risk and sacrifice themselves to maintain such structures, a trifle will knock them down. Their collapse reveals the existential self-conceit of pure determination. Laws which are not applied, rules which are scorned, arms which are not taken up by courageous men, a population in the heart of which love of universal consciousness and devotion to its future no longer entail the joy of begetting and creating are merely determinations in the process of dissolution.

One must not react against the idolatry of the theoretical and the juridical by hurling oneself into an idolatry of the self. The limited existence of a man is possible only through absolute existence, which is value in its unity and infinity. But though man's existence receives its positivity from absolute existence, man's existence still restricts absolute existence by its negativity. Besides, these two partialities, either in favor of the sufficiency of the idea or in favor of the sufficiency of the self, proceed from the same passion for determination which is considered sometimes in itself and sometimes for the self. In the former case, one abstracts from concretely experienced existence. In the latter case, one forgets that the self entails, from the lower standpoint of the theory of knowledge, the *I,* and from the higher standpoint of metaphysics, God. Forgetting value makes thought oscillate from the exclusive consideration of the law to the exclusive consideration of the caprice and pleasure of the self. Two alternating abstractions do not make an existence.

Thus, one must go beyond the opposition between determination and self. This means, first, that one must recognize the relative value of each and must raise above this duality, as above every other duality, the sovereignty of infinite Value, in which determinations find their ideal principle and the self finds its true happiness.

tanto ch'io giunsi
L'aspetto mio col Valor Infinito [2]

Since the idea, on one hand, and existence, on the other, surpass one another each in its own manner, there is a value in the idea which the self must respect, just as there is a value in the self which the idea must serve. The heart of man is small enough so that he must do through duty what he cannot do through love. Individualism, which consists in denying every rule because it is a rule, betrays personalism in every case where the moral or juridical rule favors the expansion, happiness, and beneficence of the self and of others.

But this critique of an anarchical romanticism, such as that of Stirner, is true only by reason of the fact that limited existence is not the totality of value. It is not insofar as he is existence that man must take account of determinations; rather, he must take account of determinations because he is only a certain degree and kind of existence. In the course of an individual life, determinations are valuable only by reason of their influence, especially that mediating influence which permits the self to raise itself from determination to determination as by means of a ladder. In the course of social life, if communication through language and movements were the totality of human action, there would be nothing but robots. Robots only transmit, more or less well, an impulse they have received. At every moment value interrogates man, and depending on the response that man makes, the language and action which are applied to determinations promote either mutual hate, rivalry, the exasperation of egotistical ambitions, envy and competition, pillage and squandering, or the spiritual convergence which presupposes collaboration of wills and communion of souls.

Thus, beyond determinations and existences, it is value and value alone which is sufficient. This sufficiency cannot be exhausted by a definition. That would reduce sufficiency to determination. Sufficiency cannot be exclusively psychological. That would enclose it within the horizon of a limited existence. When sufficiency makes us concretely experience both the serenity of intimate coherence and the passion which the infinite brings forth when it creates, we have more than the

2. Dante, *Divine Comedy*, "Paradise," canto 33, verses 80–81.

abstract thought or the imagination of sufficiency; we attain sufficiency itself. Happiness is when we no longer need anything, when every determination is welcome though we lack nothing, when death is no longer anything more than one event for consciousness among others, when the self does not feel itself any more closely linked to this body which death will affect than to a garment or a vehicle. It can happen that value slips away from our grasp. When we ask happiness whether it is happiness, we do so because value has bidden us farewell. But the memory of that happy concrete experience, when determination has exercised its influence and existence has brought forth subjectivity, suffices at least to maintain in us the assurance that at the core of limited existence the *I* of unlimited value, i.e., God, can introduce himself.

During the minutes or hours of those tumultuous or peaceful experiences when value presents itself as the existential identity of God and the self, where spiritual assimilation replaces the analytic assimilation of determinations or the anthropomorphic degradation—it should be called "anthropotropic" degradation—of God to the self, *value reveals itself as personality*, in opposition to the impersonality of determination. It is here that the purely intellectualist conception of relation is dangerous and partial. When one makes relation not merely a truth but a detached fragment of the Absolute by forgetting that every truth is necessarily infected with the Absolute, one asks the self to abandon itself and to identify itself with truth. But from the outset what constitutes the value of the idea of relation is less that relation presents itself as something to be seen than that it does not sever an operation. One would empty every operation of its spirituality and liberty if one did not recognize in the relation the coinciding of an act of the Spirit and an act of the self. But this collaboration cannot reduce Spirit to self or vice versa. The value of the thought relation comes, in the self, not only from the obstacle which it allows the self to leap over, but from the superior existence it grants access to, in God, and from the infiniteness of creation, an infinity of which it is, so to speak, only the local point. If it could be otherwise, true knowledge would be suicide, diversion, or blindness, not a maturing. But from the outset the best sign of objectivity is the progress of systematization both in scope and in simplicity. And this progress would be a stranger to us if it were not accompanied by an intimate generation, by a *capitalization of consciousness*.

Since value is not suprapersonal except in the two senses where it intervenes to elevate human persons above their present nature and where it unites men to God by transcending their limits, value is inseparable from a communion which is opposed to communication as communication itself is opposed to determination. Having attached the word *transmission* to the transport of a determination, we keep the word *contagion* for that atmospheric propagation which is much more important for accord among men than is the superficial identity of discourse and acts. Since, on one hand, an atmospheric contagion must be without contours and without parts, but, on the other hand, two men whose existences come together in it must remain two, we admit that the passage from *communication to communication is an existential process which mediates the reversing of a predominance of mediation over immediation into the inverse predominance.* People can co-operate while scarcely loving one another. And they can love one another while scarcely cooperating. But both of these predominances presuppose that communication and communion are not suppressed by being opposed. If words did not convey any spiritual resonance, men could not understand one another. But how could the body and matter not intervene in love, since in experience determination is linked to value?

When one says that "science unites men," it must be noted that there are two senses in which this expression is true. In the lower sense, *to unite* signifies *identity of communication.* Ohm's law is international. But this identity can as easily mediate expressions of hate as of love. Artillerymen unite under the laws of chemistry and ballistics to bombard one another. In the higher sense, *to unite* signifies *identity of communion in the scientific mode of value, which is the love for useful truth without denominating the subjects for whom it will be so.* Nothing prevents two physicists from loving physics in the laboratory and, outside the laboratory, from subordinating the resultant determinations to passions. If one thinks that all science leads one to give preeminence to the identity of determinations, science will fail to make him appreciate the inexhaustible diversity of actual conditions in which men live, the opposition of interests and sentiments which make them feel compulsion. Likewise, science will fail to let him see the value which requires, beyond the identity of means and even beyond the cooperation of wills, an existential identification in mutual and profound love. Philosophy must maintain value as one and infinite above all modes which can specify it existentially and oppose themselves to one another. Otherwise there will be many more chances for science, essentially attached as it is to determinations whose oppressive influence on existence produces passions, to furnish human furors and fears with the means to be more cruel; and there will be more chances for science not to promote the happy and beneficent expansion of the spirit.

Since value is the interexistential relation *which unites persons,* not terms, it has no meaning except for persons. This is what current experience verifies. The value of bread and gold is permanent, because the desire to live by eating and by engaging in commerce is permanent. The value of a style is ephemeral, because souls give it only passing interest. No determination, considered in itself, has value. One will pay or will be paid for the same work depending on whether the value that men attach to the task is positive or negative. An economic theory of value will systematize some values in the extension of an idea which will have been inferred from them. But value will indefinitely furnish new facts from which an analysis will be able to infer new expressions. The coarser the theory, the more it will contribute to a misrepresenting and a degrading of the value of acts and souls. Nothing can be substituted for *intimate and singular* evaluation, which results for a given man from the encounter between the problems which his situation allows to happen to him and the interests or intentions which suggest to him his goal of value. This intimate orientation of everything is degraded objectively into the *circulation of merchandise and bodies* through streets and space. It is degraded existentially into a relatively indeterminate *trust,* without which little by little all determinations lose their worth. When money is depressed, it no longer changes hands, contracts are forgotten, treaties are without force, a neighbor inspires distrust, and ideas become weapons of war or means of swindling. Humanity necessarily oscillates between mutual hatred and the love of God. It is up to humanity either to demean itself by becoming more and more closed or to ennoble itself by opening itself to respect for and love of value.

5 / The Double *Cogito*

40. *The solidarity of determination and value*

Now THAT DESCRIPTION, greatly aided by obstacle, has dissociated the two parts of empirical content, namely, determination and value, which mirror for the *I* the duality of the *I*'s unity and sublimity, it is appropriate to return to their solidarity lest this division be transformed into pure exteriority. *Without value, determination would lack existence; without determination, value would lack variety* and thus could not be concretely experienceable. Further, value would *lack efficacy,* for nothing would show that it is more than a mere cipher.

For example, let us make value, the fullness of *I,* an object of theoretical knowledge, and let us empty it as far as possible of its content. If we do so, value will be reduced to the intuitiveness of empty space and time.[1] But this degradation will never reach such a limit that no turbulence, however weak, will disturb its purity. No one can represent pure nothingness. Indeed, can there be a space without positions, a time without instants? If Bergsonism were correct in holding that pure duration excluded all determinations and consequently all distinction between determinations, duration would be no more similar to time than to space. It would be contingency at the point where contingency dissolves into nonexistence.

1. This refers to Kant's account of space and time as empty forms of intuition.—Trans.

Thus one cannot sink to this lower limit. Experience will always *both bring together and oppose imagination and understanding.* Classical intellectualism has not been able to condemn imagination except on the condition of finding it in experience, where imagination is set over against understanding. But the opposition between them cannot exist without some kind of interiority, of the sort for which the word *infection,* if one adds that infection does not exclude definite divergencies, is most appropriate. Infection designates the universal relation between the multiplicity of representations and the unity of the concept, or, inversely, the relation between qualitative continuity and the dispersion produced by analysis.

Indeed, from either aspect value secretes determinations. From the point of view of imagination, determinations are interior to value and this "secretion" can be called an analysis. But it should be noted that sometimes this analysis reveals what was there before analysis produced it and sometimes it introduces what was not there before. Or, rather, analysis brings together in unequal parts a productivity which discloses and a productivity which creates. From the point of view of the understanding, on the contrary, determinations relatively cancel each other by being distinguished from each other, and they absolutely cancel value by making one overlook it. In principle, their multiplicity entails identity, since the objective one manifests itself in all of them. In fact, their multiplicity is synthetic in that their existence proceeds from value, which transcends them. Bradley has definitively shown that every judgment bears on the Absolute. The Absolute is value.

Inversely, the solidarity of value and determination causes determinations to channel value, reducing it to existences, limiting these existences, and retarding the expansion of the spirit, eventually leading it into passionate and destructive movements. Perception punctuates the love which attaches us to the fullness of actual and possible experience. Time forces us to segment that total familiarity with the content of experience which is the highest degree of knowing. Midway between pure materialization, which would be the condition of a compact universe of freestone, and pure dissolution, which would result from the complete vanishing of determinations, there is given an experience in which countless *categories* direct the dialectical operations by which the *I* subsequently unites determinations. Likewise, there are *concrete experiences* which make known all the atmospheric movements through which value creates by impregnating experience, by diffusing itself through contagion from one limited existence to another and by inspiring men. At the source of value, God is the fire of souls. He irradiates both the light which the determinations reflect and color, and the warmth which animates existence. But the more the self moves away from him, the more the light grows pale and the warmth decreases. Morality is the aspiration which aims beyond obscurity and coldness. Near the lower limit of consciousness, matter is the cold of night.

[XII] PUBLIC SELF AND INTIMATE SELF

BECAUSE OF THE OMNIPRESENCE OF THE *I*, what is true of the totality of experience is also true of each experience. Description must therefore be able to verify from the viewpoint of each self either the solidarity of determination and value or, since value becomes existence when it has a horizon, the solidarity of determination and existence.

41. *Detail and intimacy*

To get under way quickly, let us start with Amiel's remark: "Every landscape is a state of soul." First of all, in this phrase the identity affirmed by the verb *is* cannot be a dead identity. To return to existence is to marshal it. *Is* here signifies that the self specifies the *I*, the ideo-existential relation, by rotating from the discrimination without which there would be no houses, trees, or roads to adorn the landscape to an undivided impression which Amiel calls its sensibility. Thus there are two terms. But one of these terms is ideal. It is a detail. Its parts can be enumerated and counted. The other term is existential. It is an atmosphere in which all the details are mingled into an original totality without parts. When one speaks of it, one shows aspects of it. One could call it anguished, sad, somber, extraordinary, and so on. But all these allusions refer to the ensemble and not to any specific thing within the ensemble.

One must first observe, to get free of what is peculiar to

Amiel's example, that *one of these two terms, detail or atmosphere, can prevail over the other.* It is difficult for the non-poet to concretely experience the atmosphere attached to the view of a blackboard covered with mathematical expressions or to a graph showing the entrance of German products into France. The existence of such an atmosphere confirms the twofold fact that in the face of these expressions the self preserves the sentiment of existing and that one man loves whereas another detests the atmosphere of mathematical or economic speculations. It is no less true that in experiences of this kind it is ordinarily the detail which prevails over the intimacy, the "landscape" desiccated into topography which prevails over the untroubled "state of soul."

On the other hand, let us think about a storm, or autumn, or evening, or anything to whose moving influence we easily submit. There we are almost to the point where the landscape dissolves into a state of soul. The instability and vagueness of the determinations prevent the relative consolidation indispensable for perception. Compare the meager scientific importance of autumn with its artistic value! Autumn is an affective term, not a perceptual one. Autumn stands for the atmosphere of slow disintegration. The impoverishing of the colors of nature, the attenuation of the intensity of light, and a kind of incapacity in beings affecting not merely their ability to grow but even their ability to maintain themselves are only expressions of those concretely experienced languishings in which we recognize the approaches of death. Autumn is always someone's autumn. Similarly, there are no storms which are not storms of the heart.

We have just considered the cases in which the self, the relation of the detail and atmosphere, is drawn toward one or the other of its terms and is more passive than active toward their opposition. But, on the contrary, the self can determine whether it will tend toward one term or the other depending on what it expects from each. Value attracts the self toward detail when it inspires in it the need for intelligibility. This need, like every requirement of clarity and order, manifests the prevalence of discrimination over concrete experience. Number, or ordered multiplicity, expresses the convergence of distinction and order. The man who counts and measures either has little soul or suppresses what soul he has through provisional or professional asceticism.

Sometimes, on the contrary, one of those interior rebound-ings which express most strongly the relativity of the self will turn the self back from detail to atmosphere. Number is not enough to satisfy anyone. In that slight delirium which an astronomer or a physicist, suddenly ravished by the "poetry of science," concretely experiences in the face of astronomical numbers, one recognizes the existential conversion which re-discovers the atmospheric aura entailed by all determinations. Both the relative dependence of the self on its content and the dependence of detail and atmosphere on the self are verified in the movements which harmonize one's most secret volitions.

42. *Extraversion and introversion*

We call *extraversion* the emotional process by which the self passes from atmosphere to detail. *Introversion* refers to the opposite process. Insofar as the self grasps detail, it will be called *the perceptive and expressive self, the public self.* Atmosphere, on the contrary, constitutes intimacy, *the private self.*

Let us immediately note that *introversion,* a term borrowed from Jung, *is in no way introspection.* Introspection is a hybrid of consciousness of self and discrimination. As such, the term *introspection* is much more likely to discredit the sentiment of existence than to promote it. It discloses the habit of scien-tists and professors who cannot apprehend anything without thinking it and speaking about it, and without overlooking the difference between what has been concretely experienced and the expression they have coined and applied to it. If one calls the discovery which is creative of intimacy "introspection," it is too easy to apply categories to these determinations and thus link them together, for introspection culminates in the discrimination and location of determinations. And when this is done, one makes them fall into matter. That dialectic which consists in attenuating existence in such a way as to reduce it to the eternal absence of a mere hole will once again tri-umph. One will retrospectively denounce existence by calling it fog, cloudiness, and confusion. From the viewpoint of science, he who contemplates existence will seem to be the dupe of an illusion. From the viewpoint of ethics, he who joins himself to existence will be considered a sick man who is obstinately

Bergsonian when he should be a positivist and a Durkheimian. The technician will be regarded as the model of the normal man, the one to put the others into asylums. Excommunication will be called hospitalization.

One can better point out the opposition between introspection and introversion by defining introspection as a conversion from existence to determination, and introversion as a conversion from determination to existence. They face in opposite directions. Introspection is a mode of observation. But instead of looking for determinations outside the body, such as the moon or a flower, it looks for an organic detail such as the localization of an impression. On the contrary, to introvert is to adopt an attitude, wheresoever one is, by which one passes from a detailed view of a scene to the undivided sentiment of its totality. One does this by distancing oneself and closing one's eyes. Impressionism was that process which consisted in pushing discrimination, the breaking up of color, to the point where because of the limitation of our visual acuity we could no longer have anything but a nuanced sentiment.[2] This is *a dialectic through contrary excess*. But, here again, and this is generally the case when introversion stays too close to perception, impressionism restricts the atmosphere that it should concretely experience. The most poetic souls free themselves from the weight which draws the self back toward perception by dissolving perception in an intimacy in which many other factors join in confluence with excitations of the senses.

It is self-evident that at the moment when description passes from the unspecified self, considered in its universality, to the self having a specific kind of character, it will show that each of these emotional movements is easier for some men than for others. The opposition between introversion and extraversion corresponds fairly closely to that between the "sentimental dreamers" with large fields of consciousness, smitten by savage and solitary self-analysis, whose mean lies between Rousseau and Maine de Biran, and, on the other hand, the "sanguine," that is, those who are turned toward space and perception, who are industrious, practical, worldly, those for whom Bacon could be considered the model. Man should no

2. Le Senne is here playing off shades of color against shades of feelings.—Trans.

more be maimed by his soul than by his brain, eyes, or arms. There is no reason, then, for us to condemn here either the Baconian ideal or the ideal of someone like Sénancour.

Bacon has defined man as being able to do nothing other than draw near to and move away from things in space. It is true that the algebraist who unites and scatters symbols on paper, the experimenter who brings together or separates machines and products, the cattleman who breeds his animals, the physician who dissects, the painter and the chef who mix colors and foods respectively, do nothing more from the viewpoint of determination than handle the detail of experience. But no definition more naively presupposes the reduction of the ideo-existential relation, which is the essence of the self, to an ideal relation between determinations than Bacon's does. For if it is adopted one would no longer be able to understand how there is really a man and how he could separate things and bring them together again. Bacon, in fact, could not completely eliminate the memory of existence. However reduced intimacy may be, it persists so as to furnish the subject of action. For it is the essence of truth that, when relations are broken by a process of abstraction, each term preserves some remnant of the other, as a dog which has broken its leash still carries the leash collar around its neck.

The antithesis of the Baconian definition is a phrase in which Sénancour pushes the *cogito* to the extremity and seeks the commingling of existence and the infinite through the annihilation of all determinations:

> It is the property of a profound sensibility to receive a greater pleasure from its opinion of itself than from its particular enjoyments. The latter reveal their limits. But those enjoyments which the sentiment of an unlimited power promises are as immense as the sensibility itself is and they seem to point out to us the unknown world which we are always searching for.[3]

One could not more clearly express the opposition between the pleasures, which are merely localized determinations trailing a shred of value, and the sentiment of the interiority of God to the self, a sentiment which permits the self to base its anticipations on the promise of an infinity of determinations with the certitude that their nature is worth less than the boundless

3. E. P. de Sénancour. *Oberman* (Paris: Charles Bosse, 1913), p. 10.

perspective which they hint at. When value animates this perspective by making the now unimpeded and unrestricted self something concretely experienced, this perspective entails the joy of an existence indefinitely open to the future. When we obtain this perspective there is no longer any particular quality which matters to us.

Why would a man sacrifice one mode of value for another? The unity of value forbids this. Not only do determinations participate in the unity of value when they are true, and they are always true when viewed from the proper standpoint, but they take on a supplementary value when they mediate love and possession of value. *Though intellectualism very often turns away from emotional sympathy, emotional sympathy does not take place in such a way as to dissuade one from dialectical sympathy.* Intellectual ingenuity yields theoretical and practical means which transform obstacles into assistance and harmonize the assistance which determinations afford to the expansion of the self. Intimate confidence yields a spreading contagion of hope without which the utilization of theories and techniques would be without moral soul, and their study would soon be abandoned.

If, however, we insist here more on the value of introversion, we do so for these three reasons:

(1) Because of the connection between the self and corporeal determinations, extraversion is easier and more natural for us. Even those "sentimental dreamers," in whom the intimate sentiment of their own selves is most lively, ordinarily turn back upon their own existence only after having been turned outward. They turn back because they have concretely experienced painful shocks and lasting traumas arising from determinations. Neither effort nor grace is "natural" to us. Effort is not natural because it presupposes a relative negation of our nature by our will. Grace is not natural because it does not depend on us. As soon as we let ourselves go, perception takes hold of us and habit moves us. And when science adds to the indolence of common sense, which encloses reality in things, a training which learns to deal with the symbols of things, then it becomes extremely difficult to return to the self. Thus philosophy must, from generation to generation, lead the spirit by means of the same dialectics, though with different names, through that half circle which, extending as it does from the

Cartesian *cogito* to the Bergsonian "pulsion," is the very introduction to philosophy.

(2) Never has the temptation to reduce experience to determinations pressed more imperiously upon consciousness than
it does today. The nineteenth century bequeathed to the
twentieth century an idolatry of science and society which
would end up by annihilating the self in civilization if the very
disarray into which this idolatry hurls the self through the
multiplication of foreign and civil wars did not intervene to
restore the self to itself. Still, it is necessary that this disarray
not be the indefinitely reassertive source of impulsiveness. It
is the task of critical philosophy first of all to get rid of those
fictitious natures among which one is in danger of crushing the
person. It is the task of moral and religious philosophy, then, to
show that the happiness and goodness of man are not the
necessary products of an order of determinations but rather
presuppose in his intimate depths the reflective sentiment of
his own responsibility and the love of absolute and infinite
value. Explication by means of determination shows from below where the objective one is, but it moves within relativity.
Value animates us from above.

(3) Finally, one has to admit that philosophy is hindered by
the impossibility of thinking of value without determining it.
Philosophy indeed reveals its parentage, its real homogeneity
with the self. But in distinguishing allusive description from
reproductive description we have seen that this difficulty is not
insurmountable. If one uses determinations no longer as objects
to be viewed but as means of conversion to existence by reducing not their appeal but their influence, one promotes the re-
placement of extraversion with introversion. Extraversion is
turned toward movements in space, causal sequences, and
constructed wholes. In short, extraversion is enslaved to perception. Introversion, on the other hand, is that which alone
gives content to the words remorse and love.

If one wants this education to succeed, one must begin by
"thickening" existence. The determinist obeys the inclination of
his spirit when he thins out or extenuates what the self adds to
its perceptions. What difference does the soul make to a Baconian, since the soul is only an eye directing an arm! The self is
reduced, or practically reduced, to the condition of a motor. It
is like a worker with his machine who needs merely a glimmer

of consciousness to see the task to be done. Who would be surprised that an interior diminution of existence follows from such a theory? Every theory is also an ideal. By reducing consciousness to being merely the fringe of organic causality, epiphenomenalism has proclaimed the reduction of man to an automaton. If this *deminutio capitis* seems to us to threaten the value of humanity, we must react against it with every means which can confer on the spirit a stability comparable to that of determination. We must turn determination against itself. This reaction will require first of all a terminological consistency in multiplying the terms by which the description of our concrete experiences can rival in richness the description of objective determinations.

Unquestionably, in turning toward existence philosophy does not avoid that retrospection which defines the scientific observation of determinations. The existent is something past. It must have been realized if it can be proven. Since the existent specifies existence, existence must be contemporaneous with it. The concrete experience which is mixed in with existence, to be existential, is likewise retrospective. But this retrospection, by turning toward intimacy, already leads back to the expansion of value which normally animates existence when discouragement does not intervene to devalue it. Henceforth one can no longer question whether the liberty which is found in every self as a consequence of the immanence of the *I* is indispensable for converting every communication and every contagion into a moral thrust.

The only way to know value is to seek to be worthwhile. Value necessarily gives itself only to those who merit it by virtue of an uninterrupted preoccupation with interior striving. Nothing is easier than to be turned away from it. And the same dialectics which have served this wicked abandonment will also provide it with excuses. What can value be for one who delivers himself up to determination? The popularity of science results naturally from the fact that the ideas are conceived and the sensible objects are seen and touched. *Value is indivisible and intangible.* The negation of determination becomes absolute negation for the man for whom determination is everything. Determination is passed from hand to hand. It is a word, a number, a coin. It is the body of society. Value is concretely experienced in the depths of the soul, provided that the soul opens itself to it. In itself value is neither definable nor discernible.

If one is speaking rigorously, value is not even the object of an intuition, for an intuition can never apprehend anything but a given existence. For one who does not know being except as something determined, the word *value* cannot be anything but a *flatus vocis*.

And this must be the situation if morality has any sense. If it were possible to compare the moral part and the immoral part as one compares 3 and 4 in such a way as to take the larger, morality would merely be a calculus. But morality is not a calculus. First, a calculus presupposes situations sufficiently well-defined and stable to be put into equations. Second, a calculus results from an inventive effort which has set up these equations. Finally, a calculus can be just as helpful in a swindle as in an act of benefaction. If morality is interjected into preferring one rather than the other, it is because consciousness has opted for perspectives and not for determinations. In knowledge, what classical thought has almost exclusively retained is the known. But this is to restrict the self to some object instead of believing the learning which is concentrated in the possession of the known. *There is no knowledge which does not use the known to mediate a future which is future only by reason of its indetermination.* Insofar as morality is discovered only when it succeeds in enriching the future with that which can be joined to the past, it should be called, however paradoxical the expression may seem, the knowledge of the unknown. Only the unknown fills existence with its absence.

43. *The irreducibility of existence to determinations*

It is foreseeable that the distinction between the detail and the atmosphere of the self, between the determined self and intimacy, will provoke a dialectic which consists in *discrediting intimacy by making it a confusion of determinations*. We can content ourselves with responding to this reduction by saying that the description which sets these two terms in opposition merely succeeds in establishing both of them. *My experience is given to me at each instant as the mutual infection of distinct perceptions and ideas and an undivided continuity.* I see this book, I hear the ticking of that clock, I recall a face seen yesterday, I formulate a project. But it is impossible for me to scatter myself among these givens, for they bathe in an atmosphere. Where is reality? Sometimes it will be in these or other determinations whose influence on us we discover. It will be true henceforth to speak of a recently past atmosphere as confused and illusory. But it was not confused and illusory then. On the other hand, sometimes the determinations are the things which evaporate. My perceptions will be called hallucinations or dreams, memories will be no more than images, ideas, errors, projects, wishes. By what right does one immediately give preeminence to either perception or intimacy?

Further, these terms are merely limits. There are experiences of the self in which intimacy is almost absorbed into perceptions and distinct thoughts. But that fact guarantees neither that this extenuation of existence can be definitive nor especially that the determinations, of which existence is supposedly only a reflection, are anything other than fictions. The psychologist's self makes theories about itself. And when the psychologist has objectivized the determinations which seem to him to constitute the elements of the self, he denies his own proper existence by discrediting his consciousness. But his denial adds to his self and complicates it. It does not suppress it, for this denial does not give assurance that the determinations which he puts at the source of existence have the independence and objective reality which he attributes to them. Experience, on the contrary, teaches us another extremity of life where intimacy is so fluid and so living that no determination can either appear there or serve to explain it.

This is the case because experience is anterior to all the judgments about reality which can be made within it. If we think in order to find in thought the means of communicating with another, we look for reality in determination. But communication certainly does not condense all experience in itself. Mediation can only be grasped together with immediation. The scientist is professionally the social man, but he can only be so professionally by being intimately something else. If Peter and Paul were only regions of matter, there would be neither Peter nor Paul. Judgments about reality are opposed to a concrete experience of reality which intermingles the knowledge of existence with existence itself. Each time that the self collects itself, questions itself about what it is, it is its own existence that it rediscovers. It would be absorbed in its knowledge of existence if it did not dominate its knowledge, first by opposing its existence to its perceptions, and then by reversing the twofold retrospection through which the self revolves around these perceptions and thus setting in motion a prospection for value.

By entering into existence through influence we have seen the well-founded portion of the thesis which submits intimacy to a dependence on determinations. But, like every other thesis, this one is only relative. Not only does existence depend on determinations, whose bluntness verifies their actuality, but it also depends on memories whose object has been destroyed and on views of the future whose object does not yet exist. Further, existence depends on a fusion of characters which it in fact possesses, but which no determination itself possesses. Finally, must one always consider existence secondary to determination? It is here that value, bearing the infinite with it, intervenes to forbid such a belief. In all its forms, *invention manifests the prevalence of existence over determinations.* Invention is a gestation oriented by a presentiment for which prior determinations serve as means but from which new determinations emanate. One could subsequently ideally link the new determinations to the preceding ones. But this could only take place because an existential creation has emitted them into the space and time in which determinations separate and reunite.

44. *Oscillations of prevalence between the perceptual field and existence*

The complete truth is that it is impossible to speak as if existence must inevitably prevail over detail, or detail over existence. The self confirms here the rapport between the *I* and the content of experience. Insofar as the content of experience has a proper nature, it imposes it upon the *I*. Insofar as the *I* intervenes to distinguish natures and link them together, it imposes itself on them. At the outset we considered the *I* as exceeded by the matter of experience; the *I* was merely the reception of knowledge. In God, as the principle of value, the *I* is sovereign. But every crisis in experience threatens and restricts this divine hegemony. Likewise, human experience presents some phases—for example, suffering and knowledge—in which existence receives more from determinations than it gives them, and other phases where the nature and the connections of determinations are simply docile expressions not only of a master will but of a free flight of the spirit which determinations do no more than serve. Pity inclines one toward those weakened existences oppressed by determinations. But if the determinations result from the will of a conqueror, his existence dominates by ruling and multiplying at will the determinations whose brutality others concretely experience.

One can call the aspect of the relation between detail and existence, according to which detail prevails over existence, *affectedness*. To perceive is first of all to be affected. The self gives its passive attention to that which affects it insofar as the self is affected. On the contrary, one should call that aspect of the same relation, according to which detail emanates from existence, *adhesion*. By adhesion, a limited existence, in dealing with what depends on it, renders a determination existent. Adhesion entails active attention. But whether active or passive, this attention bears on the determinations. It is an *attention-to-things*. One must not confuse it with the *attention-to-existence* by which the self returns introversively to the sentiment of existing, which is so keen in the most dramatic or the most passionate phases of our lives but often so dull in the scientist that he becomes incapable of perceiving that "behaviorism" is nothing but a professional attitude, so much so that in the absence of joy sadness does not brusquely force him to admit that he exists since he suffers.

45. *The prevalence of existence over detail is liberty*

Liberty is not a state. It is an operation for which the word *liberation* would be a better designation if it did not have the disadvantage of recalling the lowliness of its origin instead of making evident its glory and efficacy. The transition from its humble origin to its glory and efficacy takes place in three moments:

(1) First, liberty is *independence*. The self, captivated by a determination, awakes when in the course of its experience it collides with another determination. The collision provokes a phase of interrogation concerning the value of this second determination. Then this determination becomes the object of a more or less severe negation, the object of a deadly attack. This negation not only diminishes the pressure of the determination on the self, enlarges the field of consciousness around the determination, and dislodges it from the center of the self, but it

mediates the existential conversion which inaugurates independence. The initial negation of existence by determination is compensated for by the new negation of determination by existence.

(2) To be independent is thus far merely the birth of liberty. One affirms his independence only under the pressure of obstacle or with the memory of a recent dependence. One finds here more hope than realization. To enjoy independence is sweet, but to have nothing but independence is miserable. The self has gotten rid of the distress, but it still has its poverty. Independence is often sullen. It is vindictive, it complains, it objects, it is envious. It is on the verge of imposing on another the oppression which it has suffered from. One has to be wary lest independence initiate a *redress* by which the self seeks a relative superiority or dominance over another self and begins a war of competition instead of leading to an *elevation* by which the self disengages itself from its infirmity in order to find, in the absolute love of value, the dynamism for its free flight.

So that independence may not go astray, and perhaps even degenerate in such a way as to become *hatred-for-missed-value*, liberty must replace the negation of the previously oppressive determination with an affirmation which makes the determination facilitate an action and become a means of being in sympathy with the other self. The second moment of liberty is *a seeking*, turned toward the past in discovery and toward the future in invention. Between a situation whose compulsion has been attenuated by independence, and God, who is the existential ideal of self and the goal of its aim, a groping upon which the self confers more and more of its available powers progressively frees intentions. And the subsequent confluence of these intentions foreshadows a creation.

(3) Up to this point liberty depends more on the will than on the soaring free flight of the spirit. One could say that independence, through determination, mediates the passage from lowliness to confidence, and that seeking, through limited existence, mediates the passage from determination to value. But where there is mediation, there is as yet only willing. *The free flight of the spirit distinguishes itself from the will in that the power of the self in free flight is not specified by a definite intention.* The free flight of the spirit moves the self by a single thrust to its peak of existence. The direction of free flight is aimed at value, and this direction subordinates every thought

direction to itself. Psychology has indeed exaggerated the importance of the will. *There must be a hindrance breaking the continuity of the free flight of the spirit in order for the self to point the energy that it receives from the body at the interrupting obstacle and thus to begin to will.* The will is identical to existence at its point of origin, but it coincides with a determination at its terminus. From being will, it becomes volition. It is an atmosphere which precipitates itself into a localization. The self finds there the objective expression of its own power, the verification of its own existence and liberty. But, strictly speaking, existence cannot divide itself in two, cannot become an object for itself except by reason of the locatedness of the point where it applies its action. However, existence surpasses this locatedness by its knowledge. I go to take a walk, but I want to open the door which is stuck. I am thirsty, but I want to find the beverage I need to quench my thirst. I want something, but only because I am aiming at happiness. Through an intention, the self wants some specific thing. Through a goal, it seeks itself.

Seeking is *the existential mediation through which the self makes use of the will to stimulate its own free flight.* Seeking begins with the effort which turns from past oppression toward future creation. But the effort is performed with a view to making effort unnecessary. The objective contradiction of determinations and the intimate conflict of emotional energies, if the effort is judicious and ratified by grace, necessarily lose themselves in an inspiration where merit is no longer distinguished from value. When seeking, from being feeble, becomes triumphant, then liberty becomes *creation.* Intimately, liberty can no longer be distinguished from the happiness of being united to creative value, to infinite love. Objectively, liberty manifests to the eyes and hearts of all, through the determinations which it is lavish with and through their influence, the generosity of the source whence they so copiously flow.

The "rational liberty" of classical philosophy is simply the ideal expression of creation. It either betrays or involves creation, depending on whether the philosopher subtracts or adds the sentiment of what existence adds to the idea. If the determinism of the idea is substituted for the self, if determination suppresses indeterminateness, then existence, the adoration of value, is ossified in objectivity. Truth, however, is not designed to be substituted for the spirit. If, on the contrary, the idea is the suggestion of an act of opening through which the spirit succeeds in entering upon a future which not only will be better but which was unforeseeable both in principle and in fact except in its broad outlines, then this rational liberty becomes the ideo-existential liberty, of which the Spinozist conception of the intellectual love of God and the Bergsonian conception of the identification of the self with creative duration are simply two facets. *Liberty is the revelation of value*, to others by invention and in one's own intimacy by the experience of ease and abundance.

These three moments, which have to be distinguished in order to be recognized, fit together in diverse ways in the intimacy of their relation. Thus the self can tend unequally toward one or another of them, since introversion is the return from a succession of distinct moments to an eternally present actuality. The first aspect of liberty's claim to independence is accentuated in *negative individualism*. It is a defensive process. But it is easy for defense to become aggression. Liberty here becomes polemical. It repels, refuses, and keeps at a distance. Sometimes negative individualism is the refuge of easily hurt sensibilities. It is then a kind of shame, but a rather peevish shame. At other times it is the resentment of an immense ambition in connection with which no determination can be anything but negative and something to get rid of. But liberty of negative individualism always manifests, under the pressure of compulsion or by an emotional taste, the weakness of a self which is either too sensitive to its objective situation or too occupied with itself. If every volition is simultaneously extorted from us by some more or less proximate compulsion and yet expresses the gratuitousness with which we will it, then negative individualism manifests more the willed will than the willing will.

Whereas negative individualism is much nearer to distrust, to the concrete experience of unhappiness, is more preoccupied with matter and entails belief in the postulate of man-who-is-only-man, the second attitude, which we will call *the taste for imagined initiative,* is much nearer to art. It is a pleasure for us to enter through a *sympathy of experimenting* into processes which free us from our situation to let us taste other ways of living. The novel is written to satisfy a need which inspires self-renewal. But the self here undertakes new experiences only in such a way that it can easily lay them aside if or when they demand effort and risk from it, as one would separate from casual loves. Philosophy resembles literature insofar as philosophy is curious about the diversity of dialectics and emotional processes, which are just so many arts through which we can "grasp life." But philosophy and literature would be mere diversions, and would vanish like puffs of smoke whose interplay imitates reality, if the imperious demand of value did not intervene and breathe into them the seriousness of absolute existence.

These two modes of liberty, then, cannot claim any other significance than that of correcting each other. The first leads man back to the situation against which he has to struggle; it protects him from an evasion in the direction of a too facile and somewhat cowardly contemplation. The second promotes the enlargement of consciousness, the subtlety of sympathy which prevents us from seeing enemies behind every stone. But their moral vocation is to lose themselves in *an existential synthesis* which will simultaneously inspire both the gestation of works and the maturity of the self. The *I* cannot go beyond itself, but the self necessarily always does so, whether it contracts itself through the loss of what it had acquired, or whether it surpasses the limits which constantly encircle it through the conquest of new determinations and the growth of its intimate tension. In expanding its own liberty, the self expands the liberty of the *I*. *To experience is to contribute to making experience.* Experience contracts or expands with us. Our human horizon measures the progress which has been made from animal to man. The obstacles which define this horizon are merely provocations which our liberty must convert into sources for the free flight of the spirit.

It is one and the same liberty which triumphs in the intelligence of the scientist, in the passion of the moralist and in the courage of the hero, in the admiration of the artist and in the adoration of the saint. *Liberty's supreme end is to mediate between the transcendence of God with reference to the self and his immanence in the self.* If the moral history of souls were subject to limits, at the lower extremity the ideo-existential relation of the *I* would lose itself in pure exteriority. God would be exclusively transcendent, and the self's willed consent would cancel both itself and the self's very existence. At its higher extremity, interiority alone would remain, the immanence of God in the self would be perfect, and we would no longer know what it is to will. In the interval, when liberty fulfills itself, it brings together God and the self in the love of value.

It is impossible to understand this if one encloses oneself in determinations. When isolated, determinations disperse into contingency. When systematized, determinations bind themselves and us in a necessity. But each time that existence does not abdicate, at least as much as it might, to determination, it opens itself to the undetermined, which resolves itself into value or into nothingness, depending on the morality of the self.

Each and every one of our decisions verifies the impossibility of accounting for them solely by considering motives. First, the decided-on part is never the absolute terminus of the decision, for this terminus is never more for us than the foretaste of an appeal or the hope of an influence. The basic error of determinism is in enclosing the act between the situation which provoked it and the movement by which we responded to the situation in such a way as to link them objectively, as they would be linked by causality if the self en route to deciding would not alternately will to sink itself into the situation or to disengage from it, to oscillate in the interval between bondage and unimpeded mobility. Finally, to use the language we have introduced, if the intention is ideally the terminus of the goal, the goal is existentially the terminus of the intention. We live by reason of having, but in order to be. Or, better, every intention is transcended by a goal for which intentions are only adaptations to our successive situations. Beyond the last thinkable intention the goal opens on the void to find God. "One does not live to eat" in the sense in which "one eats to live." There is no consciousness—and to this extent, at least, every consciousness is moral—that doubts that utility is for value and not vice versa, as the remedy is for health and health is for happiness.

What definitively count in a decision are the beliefs about value. Poorly defined perspectives, fear of the unknown, a taste for risk and adventure are added to all determinations, which are the points of application for them, in order to orient the determinations. If comparison and measure were enough to dictate a decision, determinism would be defensible. The appreciation of issues, which are known only by knowing where they come from, has no meaning for determinism. But to decide is to think that the act which we bring forth will introduce value, rather than nothingness.

46. *Perception, expression, and emanation*

Influence has shown us the solidarity of determination and value, in the direction going from determination to value. Their connection must also show itself in another direction. This is the condition for the self, which intimacy leads back to itself, to be able to enter into communication with other selves. The self cannot in fact be limited without concretely experiencing its own insufficiency. And the existential unity of God must manifest at one and the same time his interiority with reference to every particular consciousness by conferring on the self a certain assessed value, and his infinity by making the self feel the definitive inadequation of limited existence to infinite existence.

This inadequation necessarily leads the self to admit the existence of other finite consciousnesses of which and to which determination, inasmuch as it is negative, manifests their existence and their limitation at the same time as it manifests to the self its own proper existence. Thereafter, *determination no longer presents itself to the self merely as expressing the self to itself but also as furnishing the self with the means of communicating with another self.* Whereas communion is the immediacy of two existences, communication is intersubjective mediation. Insofar as the other self escapes from all localization and insofar as one can and even must doubt whether the other exists, the *given* must be called *impersonal.* This is the case with physical determinations. At a higher stage, the given is *personal but anonymous,* like a bank note which presupposes an issuer, but one lost in professional anonymity. At a still higher level, the given is *namable,* as for example a book whose author is known. Thus a telegram, which reveals something of an impersonal given insofar as its paper is made of cellulose, and something of a personal but anonymous given insofar as it manifests the activities of the telegraph employees, also reveals its signer by name. Through the belief which transforms determinations into means of communication, the object into intersubjective rapport, the determined self becomes public self. *Detail is opposed to atmosphere as the social is to the intimate.*

Since every relation unites identity with distinction, communication allows both the union and the separation of persons, as is shown already in the term *other* by which we signify both that someone is the same as we are and that he is different from us. The telephone permits me to keep up with my friend, but it transforms my voice for him and does not let him see my face. Likewise, every determination, insofar as it is identical both for another and for myself, permits us to agree about it. But insofar as it presents itself differently to our distinct existences, conditioned as they are by differently situated and composed bodies, it limits our accord. And, further, neither the identity nor the differences can be recognized apart from one another.

Let us suppose now that a less crude, less incomplete, mode of communication, e.g., a television telephone permitting vision at a distance, would be established between the other and the self. Those perceptual indices, like a finer intonation or a facial wrinkle, which mediate the passage from perception to sympathy would be multiplied. Then imperceptibly the now transparent communication would lose itself in communion. The obstacle, after having been a restraint, would become an opening.

One must not expect that this communication, which intermingles two intimacies in an immediacy without which the word sympathy would be meaningless, can terminate in suppressing their distinction. The *I*, the ideo-existential unity of every relation, prohibits pure identity, whether existential or ideal, just as surely as it does pure duality. Immediacy by virtue of value cannot be exclusive. *Communication can only relatively close off existences to one another because their duality must still maintain the sense of their communion.*

Thus it follows from the solidarity between determination and value that every existential revolution within the self must have its echo in the social plane of perception and mobility. After one makes the distinction between affectedness and adhesion, three levels of this repercussion can be recognized. When there is a prevalence of affectedness over adhesion, when the self is more passive than active, the manifestation does not leave the level of *perception*. Perception is that determination for which the search ends in discovery. Automatism, which is a form of the appeal of one determination for another, entails adhesion. But adhesion intervenes here to make perception an act of the self. The self is constrained and provoked. Its situation gets the better of its intention. But still the self cannot have a perception unless it acts to perceive. One could say that the self's activity here is the activity of a slave, but it is still an activity. Perception weighs upon existence, drags it down, holds us on a leash. It makes us feel our condition as finite selves to such a degree that we often renounce our essence as spirits and discredit value. But perception belies these counsels of discouragement insofar as our adhesion is indispensable for its occurrence. Thus perception is already social. *To perceive is to go toward a subsequent rendezvous, to look for a means of communicating with another self.* Hobbes located perception in the encounter of two *conatus*. There must be not only an external cause and an energy issued from the body of the perceiver but also the perceiver's act. The more this perception is elevated, the more this act spreads itself out. At the lower level, perception is a concentrated, almost instinctive contraction. At the higher level, it is an operation whose movements leave some time and thought between them.

By multiplying the occasions for being united by the identities of perceptual descriptions, e.g., a rendezvous, a coin, an emblem, a uniform, a password, a ritual, or a religious creed, perception makes society possible. But as perception invites only a brief and impoverished participation in intimacy, only a curtailed and mechanized process, the need for perception which opens our senses to the influence of excitations must be extended into the need for expression. One can put *expression* on the plane where affectedness and adhesion are in equilibrium. The consideration of the conditions which determine the possibility of our communicating with another self grows with our concern to have it come to know our intimacy. By itself, perception merely prepares for a practical collaboration. But expression looks for emotional sympathy. In each of us the alternation of the need to express oneself and the need to recollect oneself, the alternation of fear of and love of solitude, reveals the relation between determination and existence and verifies that this relation is really life itself. The two limits of this alternation are cynicism, by which one makes determination disturb or brutalize—one might well say "choke"—the intimacy of the other, and shame, by which one protects his own intimacy against the hostility of determinations.

Expression does not wait for others to make a number of efforts to understand us. It invites them, presupposing as it does more weakness than strength on our part. In expression, value is strained into forms which force it to weaken itself and to render itself commonplace. Doubtlessly, the description of social relations must recognize their unbounded diversity. The word, which logicians reduce to merely a sign, is an outline, an order, an image, and a cry. All of these are aspects of expression which manifest themselves here. But expression is still always *a compromise between the adaptation of value to determination and the orientation of determination by value.* Expression very strongly manifests the weight of communication upon communion.

Just as perception is almost completely within expression, *emanation* is almost completely beyond it. Emanation is that generosity by which an intimate gestation which permits as much mystery as it does distinct operations brings forth a work whose secret congruence with the needs of others and with value assures its beneficence. Expression only manifests what is proper to and distinct in the self. *Emanation reveals in the self's action the eruption of a value which transcends the self.* Instead of continuing a course, instead of following a direction, emanation revolutionizes determination and manifests in the course of history the duality of the Absolute and inertia, the duality of creation and nonsense.

[XIII] THE RELATION BETWEEN GOD AND THE SELF

AFTER HAVING SHOWN that the obstacle provokes, on the one hand, the disjunction between determination and value, and, on the other hand, the diffraction of the *I* into the self of determination and the self of value or God, we have begun to study the existential relation between the self and God, beginning with the self. We will now investigate this relation at its higher levels.

47. *The threefold interiority of God to the self*

We would not be able to ascend by reason of this relation to higher levels if the study of the self did not compel us to find God. He is recognized here in three ways:

(1) First, *he must sustain, insofar as they are positive, the determinations which structure the self.* If one were to push this structure to its ideal source, determination would be im-

personalized. At the extreme, determination would be pure nature. The objective one would appear as its primary reason and, with subjective existence now forgotten, this objective one would become God-world. One cannot go all the way to this extreme. The objective one serves to explicate determinations, but it can do so only hypothetically. God and the self gain by not becoming things. But it does not follow that determination has no need for God, for if the objective one, or the interiority of every relation with reference to its terms, is the foundation of all deduction and induction, this foundation does not provide a reason for existence. In the obstacle which eventually manifests the rebellion of the structure of the self against its liberty, determination is not only conceived as possible but is concretely experienced as existing. As such, it entails not the objective one as the principle of all validity, but a one superior to the duality between definite determination and limited existence, superior to the duality between object and subject. It entails the one of value, or God, of whom the objective one is merely the ideal expression.

(2) God is thus found not only at the source of our nature; *he is also at the source of our existence.* If the self were not intimately existence, it would only be an arbitrarily isolated portion of the object. Existence, which is a passing and partial section of value, is equivalent to the incarnation of God in us.[4] There is no need to insist on this idea, which is really Descartes's *cogito, provided that one unflaggingly retains existence's indivisibility.* It is true that the *cogito* is complex. One can count its five moments with the rosary of five mediations: *"Dubito, ergo cogito; cogito, ergo sum; sum, ergo Deus est; Deus est, ergo res sunt; res sunt, ergo multi sunt."* It is also true that one can indefinitely discuss whether the *cogito* is intuition or reasoning, bicentric or monocentric, psychological or metaphysical. Whatever position one takes he cannot avoid either treating these five moments as a series or setting them in opposition to one another as aspects which have the property of being grasped only through one another in the concrete experience of expansive existence. It was necessary for Descartes to speak, and one speaks in time. If one wants to mediate his unique intimacy for others, he must distinguish its facets. If one forgets this, he

4. "Section" here has the force of a slice of tissue available for laboratory examination.—Trans.

will do what Kant did. Kant started out by separating the ontological argument from all of its existential infection in the *Meditations*, and then denounced the *Meditations* for their inability to yield existence.

On the contrary, Descartes's constant concern was to contract the steps of the discourse expressing the *cogito* in order to return to the unique act which constituted it, an act whose efflorescence is philosophy itself. In the incompatibility of two determinations, whose relative contradiction prevents absolute solidity, the self concretely experiences that existence which, though limited insofar as determinations impose their nature and their opposition on it, is absolute insofar as existence is the absolutely primary and infinite condition for all existents even though it itself is subject to gradations. Thus the *cogito* can be rightly called either human or divine. But if it can be distinguished into my weakness and divine infinity, it is because this duality entails the unity of their connection, the *I*. *The cogito is a double cogito*, and it cannot be double unless the connection can be distinguished from its existential terms. But we will not say that the *cogito* is triple, for this connection cannot be separated from its terms except in idea. And it is as existence that the *cogito* consists in recognizing itself.

(3) Not only is God indispensable for conferring existence upon determinations, since even the most impoverished order entails value, and not only does he sustain the existence whereby the self opposes itself to the determinations which it distinguishes in itself or which emanate from it, but God must intervene to *confer upon the self the value whereby this limited existence can enlarge its limits.* If one wished to reduce consciousness to knowledge and knowledge to the past, he could easily deny God. Nothing presents itself in experience, insofar as it is determined, which resembles either God or value. It is the condition of every self, at each instant, that it can advance only by looking behind itself and beneath itself. But if a dog only knows the world of a dog, we who are men know quite well that the dog's experience does not contain the totality of experience and that in our experience there are givens which the dog can neither discriminate nor concretely experience. By avowing through each of our acts the value which incessantly invites us to shatter the limits of our experience, we imply that human experience is only a strictly limited fragment of universal experience and that positivism is not authorized to limit

the scope of all real experience to the postulates of perception and science. *Explication by means of the lower, the objective one, is never more than one of the means by which a movement of existence toward the higher actualizes itself.* This is what one expresses when one places God at the source of value, for the love of value stimulates every effort of consciousness. God is not divine except where he creates, and he creates wherever someone loves value.

Intelligence and value. By making the *cogito* an existential conversion from determinations to intimacy, one does not betray Descartes's attachment to intelligence. Strictly speaking, intelligence is in principle neither good nor bad. Objectively defined, *intelligence is the relation of the self to determinations.* But the necessary solidarity between determinations and value has as its consequence that intellectual discrimination and linking, namely, perception and judgment, alternately intervene, opportunely or otherwise, in the moral life of the spirit. Though analytical intelligence, which pulverizes, undoes, and dissolves, is dangerous, it becomes beneficial when the critique either prepares for the discernment of what is worth preserving for a proximate construction or delivers one from the despotism of the determination. The term *edification* is a beautiful word, for it refers to the work of an architect whose buildings make one cherish the master plan. But to construct something the architect needs materials. Intelligence cheats when, instead of collaborating in the more or less difficult maturation of a work, it takes short cuts to obtain a cheap imitation of the work, which is of use only to a swindler. But if one were to conclude from this that intelligence is something bad, he would be forgetting that there is no single given, or method, or process of experience which is not likewise capable of leading one into error. There are indices of truth and value, but there is no criterion for them which releases one from having to put forth effort to obtain them. Errors in knowledge and action are not worthless insofar as they prevent the self from confusing itself with determinations. And by leading it back to the sentiment of its own liberty and responsibility, error makes the self rediscover the *cogito* and, with the *cogito*, the interiority of God to nature, to existence, and to the value of the self.

Self-sufficiency of the self. If the interiority of God to the self were simple, God would not allow the self to distinguish itself from him. But experience, by revealing in due course the opposition between particular consciousnesses and by showing which of their actions betray value, simultaneously precludes both materialistic and pantheistic monism. A twofold opposition places the self at the intersection of determination and existence and leaves the self always to choose between the temptation to passively subordinate existence to determination and the duty which submits determinations to the expansion of existence by and toward value. From this vantage point *the self specifies the I as the relation between detail and atmosphere,* the relation between the perception and action directed toward determinations and the intimacy condemned either to decay or to invent. This relational unity, which is still nothing but that of the *I,* is no more distinguishable, except nominally, from its ideo-existential matter than the *I* is distinguishable from the content of experience. But this relational unity suffices to assure the self an authenticity destined to be humiliated by its automatism or to be confirmed by its authority. Insofar as this relation unity manifests its liberty through love and creation, *it is a self-sufficiency which expresses itself on the ideal plane as an autonomy.* But the incessantly renewed internal opposition which is indispensable for this unity to be the unity between an ideal and an existential relation prevents it from ever being a thing without consciousness or a purely illusory consciousness. This relational unity is originarily living. It is exhausted neither by the concept of itself nor by the sentiment of itself. It can consent either to matter or to God. Or, rather, it will always bring together these consents, one of which expresses its impotence and the other its power. This *irrefragible ambiguity* is what everyone calls the self. It is an eternal seeking. This relational unity, within the scope of its powers, is responsible both for itself and for events. One falsifies its essence as relational unity when one replaces it either by determinism or by the caprice of things, as a materialism of necessity or chance does, or by the inclusive all-powerfulness of God, as a pantheism of order or duration does. *This is why the philosopher must indefatigably maintain the idea of human responsibility.*

48. *The theandric connection*

Let us now begin to describe the double *cogito.*
What essentially constitutes the double *cogito* is that *the*

two existential terms that it opposes and unites, namely, God, whom the self concretely experiences alternately in his will as obstacle and in his grace as value, *and the self,* which restricts the concrete experience of value by reason of the determinations of its own nature, *can only be considered and can only exist by virtue of their connection.* As in every relation, this relation provides for unity and distinction. *Unity* manifests this relation's eternity through the impossibility of conceiving one of the two terms without the other. Without God, the self could have neither a nature nor an existence nor a vocation. If one reduces God to the Absolute by denying that the self has any power to apprehend him, the self devoid of both truth and value is abandoned to itself and delivered over to the contingency of phenomena. It does not exist and nothing exists for it. For in the affirmation of any being whatsoever there is involved a faith in a real principle which is not only unitary in its own right but which inheres in the positivity of what we grasp. By a kind of backlash, if one denies the self, then the Absolute can no longer be called God, for our existence no longer verifies his creative activity. He is no longer either powerful or good.

To allow for *the distinction* implied by it, the theandric relation allows for all the modes of exteriority, from antagonism to juxtaposition, without, however, fully abrogating the bond between God and the self. God will be relatively other than the self, and he must be so if infinity is his essence. And the self may ignore almost everything about God if determinations cast their relative opacity between God and the self. The theandric connection will therefore always be *en route to being established and to being dissolved.* And, depending on these oscillations, time will come and go for us, passing from the dispersing succession, which, if perfect, would explode our experience into instants having neither content nor connection, to pure and complete eternity, which would reassemble the entirety of multiplicity into the unity of an atmospheric intuition. Midway between these limits, experience brings them together in a present which is at once vanishing and eternal, in an instant which is neither exhaustively empty nor completely full.

It follows from this that the theandric connection is always *both given and ideal.* From every point of view it can be expressed and closely examined by means of more or less determined relations having both an existential aspect and an ideal aspect. This is what makes both philosophy and theology possible. But this theandric connection infinitely transcends both philosophy and theology. As a consequence, this term indicates an ideal, of which the determined relations are merely translations or adaptations to a particular situation.

The value of these expressions will depend on the liberty of the two existential terms which this connection unites. At each instant, insofar as the double *cogito* is union, *it is the convergence of a double act of liberty:* the act of God emitting value and making us emanate from him, and the act of the self confirming the existence of God by associating itself with his creation. The divided *I* binds itself back together here.

Among the classical thinkers, Condillac is certainly the one who has perceived most clearly that the self and God cannot be considered independently of their relation to each other. His doctrine provided the intellectual mediation for Rousseau to convert, as *The Profession of Faith of the Vicar of Savoy* shows, his affective spontaneity into participation in God. But Condillac's partiality for analysis unfortunately prevented him from recognizing the existential aspect of experience and consequently prevented him from describing what the "infusion" of value into our existence makes possible by way of creative liberty. He thinks that he cannot know anything about God's act of creating. Indeed, man could not know creativity in God except by concretely experiencing it himself, and Condillac is turned away from this concrete experience since he has reduced man to the condition of a statue supposedly passive with reference to determinations. He has failed to apperceive that the self would not know the passivity of its existence with regard to any given unless, conversely, it could concretely experience the emanation whereby existence reveals its hegemony over some other things by emitting them or modifying them. This Condillacian ideology weighed far too long upon the spirit of Biran. Not only did it excessively delay Biran's discovery of the notion of the three lives, but it prevented him from finding at the very interior of human life, i.e., at the interior of "the primitive fact of the intimate sense," the relation between animal life and divine life.

If this were the place to show *how the principal philosophies have defined themselves by starting from the double cogito* and retaining only one aspect of it, we would have to classify them according to whether they intellectualized it or intuitionized it. *Intellectual realism* isolates the theandric connection from its existential terms. It becomes pure, objectivized idea. But one forgets that the objectivized idea is either routine or powerful, depending on whether it serves as a negative or a positive inclination for the living spirit. *Subjectivist idealism* reduces the theandric connection to being nothing but a human event. This is the insufficiency which is generally condemned by the adversaries of idealism. Idealism becomes *absolute* when the idea is related exclusively to absolute existence. But from the outset this abstraction, by eliminating what can be called the humanity of God, reduces God to the condition of pure, impersonal Self, in short, to the *I*. And as this Self becomes a beyond with reference to all the determinations of our existence, idealism soon loses itself in an *ideal-realist agnosticism* which no longer stresses anything except the transcendence of the Absolute. From Rousseau to Bergson, the intuitionists have returned to the immediacy of God to the self. One demands from intuition the metaphysical reality which had been expected from the idea. But for want of stressing the connection between mediation and immediacy in our life, one ordinarily risks either, as Rousseau does, divinizing every human emotion, or, on the contrary, as Bergson does, dissolving the self in a duration in which one can no longer see how obstacle can appear and how an interruption of continuity which either materializes or conceptualizes the spirit can emerge from it. By maintaining the *I* at the intersection of determination and value, of the self and God, and generally maintaining the *I* at the center of all ideo-existential relations, one allows for the conflict, then the compensation, and finally the confluence of the givens which philosophies divide up among themselves.

Verification. Even before it is inserted into the materiality of givens, a dialectic already has value as an intellectual experience. Let us first consider the theandric relation in itself to see what happens when one ruptures it. Ultimately, such a rupture entails the annihilation of God for man; for if there is no longer any connection between him and us, we cannot know him. If we do not know him, we would not be able to name him or to seek him. But this is contrary to what experience teaches. This annihilation of God for man would be equivalent to the annihilation of God. For whatever we think about God, he is not something intrinsically indifferent to the true and the good. A God without efficacy and goodness would not be God.

Even the gods of Lucretius have found a way of making themselves known to Lucretius. One does not escape the difficulty by means of the hypothesis of a revelation. That would be merely playing with words unless the external revelation is necessary to mediate the internal revelation by which the self, in supposing that its limitations are suppressed, finds in itself infinite existence as the source of its own existence.

Man is at the lower end of this theandric relation. He gains nothing by suppressing God; rather, he loses everything. For if one removes from man this attraction toward the higher, an attraction which is never tyrannical because it is indeterminate, his life no longer has value either now or in the future. When human existence and intimacy can no longer appear as the incarnation of an absolute value, since every absolute principle is ruled out for man, then human existence either has to appear as an absurd and incomprehensible phenomenon or it must be explained by the subhuman. But how does causal or teleological explication, which can only link determinations to determinations, give an account of the ideo-existential relation which constitutes the consciousness of these determinations? *The effort to reduce existence to intelligibility ends up in a mystery.* One must indeed eschew the objectivist conception of man, for it is false.

This falseness does not prevent the man who tries to explain himself as an object from imperceptibly weakening and losing the sentiment of his own liberty, which is identical to the sentiment of his own existence. Through psychophysical parallelism, the self opposes itself to its body as one series of determinations to another, as a subject now become a second object. When one explains man by the subhuman, the parallelism is soon replaced by materialism. The mental series is no longer anything other than the reflection of the cerebral series. Thereafter the way is clear for pure mechanism. Life itself, insofar as it is the effort to organize determinations and to expand existence, loses its meaning. And there is now no other difference between life and death than that between a machine in operation and a machine in pieces.

It would be interesting to describe the resistance thrown up by the instinct of self-conservation to this degradation. But far from the instinct of self-conservation being equivalent to confidence in God, it is nothing but the quasi-animal and always mediocre recourse of a living entity completely subject to compulsion. Even when efficacious, i.e., when reflex and habit suffice, this instinct cannot replace prudence and invention. Man cannot organize, create, and prepare for distant dangers with only a bare minimum of consciousness. Nor will he help another and disinterestedly love value by reason of an egotistical instinct of self-conservation. Instinct is impotent against a critique which dissolves all the reasons for being devoted to something. Instinct cannot impede the multiple effects of a toxic atmosphere of discouragement, just as it cannot produce the effects of a vivifying atmosphere of confidence. Instinct is quite similar to causality, which derives a localized effect from a localized cause. On the contrary, value symbolizes itself through diffuse or scattered actions, as a wave of air produces diverse actions, here reanimating a half-asphyxiated animal, there rusting iron or making butter rancid, and so on.

No dialectic remains purely intellectual. The people do not know the philosophers, but the philosophers' influence impregnates the people. In the course of being used, every dialectic will receive an emotional existence for which philosophy is responsible. If it is intellectually true that God and self are annihilated by the rupture of their connection, God vanishing into absence and self discrediting itself to the point of extinction, this intellectual crisis is necessarily a moral crisis. By introducing the relative duality of God and man which gives meaning to transcendence without making God an irrational monster and man an abandoned animal, and by introducing their relative unity which always assures a certain degree of immanence of God in us without authorizing the divinization of all human acts, the double *cogito* is the metaphysics of morality. Value, which is the soul of truth, is obtained only through truth. But it spiritualizes truth.

If, on the contrary, man is not and can never be anything but man, his volitions, which are manifested either in affirmations or in actions, are the supreme ends of experience. The volitions decree the true and manufacture the just. In point of fact, the volitions will not always be bad, but if they are not it will be by luck and not by right. He who feels himself borne by his character toward goodness will be tender and charitable. He whose nature disposes him to hatred and egotism will follow his passions. Both of them will say and do what they wish without being able to find any reason for doing what they do other than that they prefer it. Experience will be the reign of one's pleasure. The Absolute will have been hurled down from heaven to earth and shattered. From the generalization of this caprice, all that could follow would be the avarice or greediness in each man and competition among all men. How could society and the State substitute themselves for an Absolute which is at one and the same time capable of transcending them and of giving itself to the intimacy of every soul? Society can be vile and corruptive. Most of the time it is nothing but the expression of a mean of ever expanding human prejudice. The State can be despotic and degrading. Both society and the State scarcely disguise the caprice of human wills which are capable of betraying value for the profit of the lowest ambitions.

The contempt of man for man which results from the intimate habit of thinking about and treating him as an object, a thing, a depersonalized and devitalized piece of matter can generate a discrediting of value, a cynicism about sentiments now reduced to their physiological determination, and a hatred of moral grandeur in which one now sees nothing but necessity or chance, calculation or good luck. Likewise, it can generate a substitution of utilitarian interest which shuttles from determination to determination in place of the disinterestedness which is the goal of value. This contempt thus manifests a diffuse and intimate decadence against which the scientist is impotent because, like an atmosphere, this decadence is not localized and it sweeps the scientist himself along in its influence.

If the scientist does not see for himself that science, by indiscriminately applying the postulates of exclusive determinism, contributes to spiritual decadence, it is first of all because, at the core of his existence, he concretely experiences the love of value in the love of scientific research, and because he is elevated by science above the materialism of its objective postulates. And, finally, he does not see this because he constructs for himself an ideal substitute for God, namely, the idea of a universal and systematic nature of which one can indeed say that it is the face of God. But if one passes from the given disorder of the phenomena to the affirmation of an order of things, it is because one has surreptitiously introduced value, under the guise of order, into the principle of determinations. If order were entirely given, we would not have the experience of the obstacle, nor would we have to reduce the obstacle and develop science. Order is organized only if value inspires man.

Again, order is not the only mode of value. Science is dangerous at the point where the scientist, sacrificing his sympathy with existence to perception of and thought about determinations, condemns or merely misunderstands the other modes of value. Just as the love of truth is intimately more profound than the knowledge of it, so too are promptness to sacrifice and heroism, admiration for beauty, respect for holiness and the effort to inspire oneself by its example—in short, all the forms of the love of God, where the double *cogito* reintegrates itself, are independent of the intellectual or practical means which science can put at their disposal. By turning toward perception and the intellectual schemas which it ascribes to what is perceived, science turns away from emotional sympathy. This can cause the scientist, when he is irritated by sentiments with which he has no sympathy, to take an exclusively polemical and militant attitude. Abstract intellectualism necessarily becomes brutal precisely because it is abstract. But intelligence is not designed to discredit sympathy, since it itself is nothing but the dialectical form of sympathy.

Two critical consequences follow from the double cogito.

(1) The first consequence is that every hypothesis, every affirmation, every thought, and every philosophy of man necessarily manifests its own insufficiency. Divine insofar as it is valuable, every philosophy is human by reason of its negativity. The aspects of this negativity are innumerable. We replace the uniqueness of each soul and each event with *a generality*. Every identity is a myopia, every relation masks a "between-two," and every formulated equation replaces a situation which involves the infinite with a framework of intellectual or practical technique. Every existence is mixed, but we substitute for existence the purity of a concept, of a limit. But a knowledge pressed further on always reveals isotopes which are hidden in the indistinctiveness of an average. From something concrete we make something abstract. What we perceive and think gets its value from the situation in which we apprehend it. At a distance from this situation, every expression loses its meaning and value. From something real we make something ideal. Everywhere we replace the multifaceted interdependence of the terms which we define with some false absolutes which never have anything but a fictitious ideality.

(2) It does not follow from the foregoing that our experiences are without value. But this value, by reason of its limi-

tations, is only a mode of value. We replace value with values, the conflict among which shows our impotence. Certainly, value can only be given to us absolutely. It never refers to something other than itself. But *the absoluteness of value is not equivalent to absolute value.* This inadequation is the very soul of our search. Objective progress, which is judged by the quantitative comparison of determinations, is nothing but the ideal symbol of the intimate and limitless appropriation of God by subordinated consciousness. And just as the scientific spirit consists in successively denying all the results obtained, not to suppress them but to improve them by integrating them into a more ample and more simple science, so the value of consciousness consists in a secret expansion, expressing itself both by an enlargement of scope and weight and by a purification which ends up in the most uncomplicated simplicity. Knowledge becomes progressively more and more simple. But this simplicity becomes more and more fertile.

From the first of these two observations it follows that a critical spirit must accompany all our reflections. First of all, a *transcendental critique* should discover the limits of knowledge imposed on every finite consciousness insofar as it is finite. More concretely, an *anthropological critique* will discern the determinations which imprison our knowing as a consequence of our peculiar human structure. At a higher level, an *ethological critique* will recognize the manner in which a given character restricts and refracts a man's knowledge of the universe if he yields to this character of his. Finally, a *historical critique* will discover in the concrete situation to which a thought or a deed has responded the reasons for its determination. But *extrinsicness never explains anything but human impotence.* To the extent that the insufficiency of each determination would be taken as a reason for discrediting it absolutely, value would be betrayed. Following from the second observation, the soul of knowledge and life is *hope without motives for hope.* When the self is weak, it seeks reasons for security. When confidence and love inspire the self, they create their own mediations for success. The most intimate expression of the theandric connection is wisdom which ignores neither the determination of man nor the divinity of value, wisdom which reconciles a prudence bearing upon things and ideas with a faith sympathizing with the spirit when determinations hide the theandric connection. The intimate core of everything is spiritual, but we are always in the process of being born to the spirit. "If the dawn heralds the sun," Boutroux has written, "it is because it emanates from the sun."

49. *God-without-us and God-with-us*

If the self is condemned to decay in proportion to the forgetfulness which obfuscates the interiority of God in the self, the idea of God correlatively impairs his spirituality when it removes him from his connection with us.

Suppose we were to understand the relation between determination and value in a sense which would lead to pure value if one were to forget the solidarity that one should maintain between these terms. The *I* as God must be posited as the principle of this value to confer on it unity and infinity, i.e., coherence and empirical efficacy. But at that extremity where value would become exclusive, can the *I* still be called God? One has to deny this. Value which did not manifest itself through determinations would, for want of creatures, no longer be creative. And, in an inverse sense, value which did not receive influence from determinations and was incapable of being nuanced in atmospheres would be identical with nothing. What would poesy be if it could neither inspire poems nor translate them into emotions? What would philosophy be if systems did not express it and if souls were not nourished by it? What would charity be if it gave nothing and if its gifts awakened no love? Value which does not create does not exist.

Someone will undoubtedly answer that *this nothingness of God would be the best expression for the incomparability of the infinite and the finite.* The absolute would lose its essence as absolute if it were infected with any experience. To this response one must grant that the duality of the absolute and phenomena is irreducible, that this duality must be respected. This is the duality expressed by that aspect of every relation (ideal as $y = x^n$, existential as sympathy, ideo-existential as the influence of a legal pleading) whereby duality distinguishes at the same time as it brings together. But the fact that every relation is a duplicity does not mean that it is only a duplicity.[5]

5. Le Senne uses *duplicité* here without its usual connotations of deceit. Duplicity here merely stresses the discreteness of the terms of a relation in contrast with the simplicity of the relation taken as a totality.—Trans.

Rather, it means that it must also be a unity. God is Absolute in that he is beyond what we are, to the point that his existence can always seem to us to be uncertain, and it *necessarily seems so to us* when we yield to passion or to discouragement. But it is likewise necessary that, if truth and value are accessible to us, the Absolute be God.

Although the Absolute is absolutely other than phenomena, it is still the Absolute *of* these phenomena. If we cut this connection, the Absolute is exiled to one knows not where and the phenomena no longer originate from it. And, consequently, this principle of everything would become the principle of nothing. But whence comes the credibility which the Absolute proposes to us except from experience, and indeed from our own experience? We can be mistaken about the relation of the phenomena to the absolute by taking the true for the false, the illusory for the real, and so on. But we could not do so if we did not presuppose that the Absolute makes the value of some phenomena greater or different than that of others by mingling itself into them. The idea of an absolute mediates the emotional conversion by which we concretely experience, if one can speak thus, the "categoricity" of existence, apart from the limits that existence undergoes in us. More bluntly, the distinction between the absolute and the relative derives its meaning from our disappointments. This distinction is made to bring us to recognize our disappointments and to spare us from other disappointments. On the other hand, the union of the absolute and the relative is the value of the relative.

When the Absolute presents itself as the source of value for us, it should be called God, since this recognition acknowledges that he is assimilable by our spirit, is good, and is creator. Further, the idea of God has value only by reason of the influence that it exerts on our intimacy. The self can regard the idea of God as an invention of other men or an invention of its own, as the celestial reflection of a terrestrial glimmering. Indeed, if one stays on the ideal plane, which is the plane on which one determination *appeals to* another, the ontological argument can engender only the *idea* of the divine existence. This idea is no different from other determinations. Each determination, insofar as it is given, is simply an object. But each can be the occasion either for spreading over things the atmosphere of negation which expresses the peculiar lowliness of the self, or for making the determination the means to reattain the Absolute as a universal principle of order and love. When the artist in the enchantment of a perception sees the goodness of a universal Soul which animates everything with its breath, or when the artist in admiring beauty concretely experiences a certain gratitude toward the spiritual principle which gave him that beauty, he performs the same conversion which the ontological argument allows the philosopher to perform.

If the existential proof of the existence of God rests on our being animated by the love of value, if the presence in us of this sentiment, however it might be nuanced, is recognized in that it excludes doubt so long as it lasts, there is no need to depart from experience in order to know the Absolute. Further, love of value, the existence of God, creation by him, and human morality exist only when they form a unity. *God is God-with-us or there is no God.* God is more than given, created existence, more than the world. God exists insofar as he creates. But whereas a limited existence necessarily expresses its limitation by creating only things and ideas, i.e., determinations, God necessarily manifests that the value of existence is concentrated in him by making limited existences emanate from him. And these limited existences become conscious through that which value adds to determinations. These determinations will persist in order to allow the limited consciousnesses both to be distinct and to collaborate by establishing among them both communication and separation.

The idea of God-without-us can therefore be nothing but a fiction-limit. *Like every fiction-limit, the expression God-without-us gets its meaning from the orientation of value which is applied there to make this idea either a mediation of reconciliation or an occasion for despair.* If in a period of distress we go by means of abstract thought to the extreme of exteriority between God and us, we conceive of God as withdrawing into the solitude of his own intimacy. We conceive of God as for himself, as each of us is for himself when he turns from extraversion to introversion. The self's will can attach either of two vectors of value to this conception. At the moment when our despair, by pushing God-for-himself to God-without-us, would end in our own condemnation (what does it mean to deny God other than to push discouragement to its ultimate), the self would have to renounce existence. So long as the self persists in existence, it is because God still somehow sustains it. And, consequently, he is not yet a God-without-the-self.

But another outcome is possible, that of good despair, which is the development going from a "hopeless" effort toward a restoration. In this case, the idea of God-without-us is that which mediates our ultimate confidence, in the face of the sadness of existence, in a power which we believe that we lack but which we still think is capable of coming to assist us. When this confidence institutes a stimulation which makes us pass from conceiving the idea of God to communion with his inspiration, it is because God is already with us.

Let us suppose, then, that the idea of God impregnates our confidence more and more; then God-without-us, who had presented himself immediately as the negative pole of our life, returns to stand before us as our positive pole. We will call God-without-us, God without gaps, a union of souls so purely total that they could no longer be recognized as individuals. But it is true to say of every ideal, whether determined or existential, that *it is merely a program, whose value rests in the expansion which it serves by its mediation.* We can certainly make an ideal merely an artistic object, the imagination of which releases us from the effort to realize it and surpass it. Or, on the contrary, we can make the ideal an occasion to confront and deepen the gap between what we are and produce and what we should be and create. In its two parts, but in different degrees, the ideal of God-without-us dissolves into the experience of God-with-us. It becomes clear to us that the idea of God-without-us was nothing other than a determination pushed to the extreme. *God-without-us is the transcendental myth which is to existence what the transcendental myth of the world or of nature is to determination.*

More simply, the union of God with us admits more or less of three states: (*a*) the affirmation of the possibility of God, which is already implicit in the denial of his existence; (*b*) the affirmation of his existence, which is immediately belied if one does not seek a more intimate participation in his power; and, finally, (*c*) the action which converts this affirmation into a search for value. At none of these stages does one encounter God-without-us. Apart from these stages, the problem is not explicitly posed. But as value is always somehow felt and sought by us, this problem is implicitly resolved in favor of God-with-us, as against the hypothesis of God-without-us.

Transcendentism stretched to its farthest point reduces this union to a contact between God and us comparable to the creative finger of God on the ceiling of the Sistine Chapel. But this contact cannot be suppressed. For to affirm or to imply that God is a stranger to us is possible only through the immediacy which gives content to the idea and name of God. To be known as a stranger is still to be known. All knowledge refers to a concrete experience. The whole problem of God is enclosed between the dialectic of Karl Barth and that of Spinoza, without it being possible to go to the extreme either of transcendentism or of immanentism. At their extremities these two dialectics coincide, since absolute transcendentism is equivalent to atheism and absolute pantheism is equivalent to acosmism. Thus God is, and necessarily must be, with us. But we can either seek to extend our union with him or we can act so as to restrict that union.

50. *Infinite and finite God*

The solidarity of determination and value which is, in the content of experience, a trace of the double *cogito,* entails the consequence that God is both finite and infinite. The description of experience requires us to admit this. There is value. But value must be both infinite and assimilable by us. Insofar as he is the principle of value, God must be infinite. But *there is no value except the value in experience,* and indeed value has no meaning except in connection with that which cancels it, namely, materialized determination and the criminal self. It is precisely because value is not alone that philosophy must preserve love for it. Similarly, it is those things such as evil and vice that tend to deny God which make us feel the need for his existence. Undoubtedly it is easy, in the tranquillity of theoretical knowledge, to deny evil and fault, to presuppose their complete dissipation in order to make the sun shine on every part of experience. Unfortunately, this dab of the sponge does not suppress the sadness caused by the perfidy of treason or the exaltation of hatred, the exploitation of nobility or labor by swindling, or the pathogenic bacilli. One must therefore account for the finite, not only as finite but as rebellious, hostile, resistant, and impermeable to value.

Here the acknowledgment of the double *cogito* brings a light which, like every other light, draws its richness from the opacities clarified by it. Insofar as God is value he must diffract himself into limited existences, since a value which creates nothing would be valueless. The divine free flight sustains and holds together the thrust of these limited existences. But *the liberty* which these limited existences possess, from the single fact that God makes them emanate and distinguishes them from himself, *would be annihilated along with their existence* if he did not accept the determinations which give nuances to their existence by their influence and which limit this existence by their negativity.

It immediately follows that in God and in us this free flight must be infected with the will. Just as at each instant we will a certain end by reason of some obstacle, so God must will a certain world by reason of our initiatives. Through his relation with this world, he must be finite. Indeed, there must be value, coming from God, which assures and incessantly renews the order of determinations. This is a condition for a world which expresses, through the compatibility of its parts and its *relative* solidity, the divine unity which elevates the objective one to the plane of perfection, and which makes both a science and a society possible. But it is also a condition for a world which reveals by its defects, which make one want a better order, the limitation of the subordinated consciousness. God, who wills the world, could not will it without submitting to the finitude arising from it.

But *this consent,* a model for the consent we must give to this very world from the outset, *does not have any pejorative character for God.* For just as need is either indigence or generosity depending on whether it desires to receive or to give, so this consent permits this ambiguity to be either the resignation of impotence or the condescension of power. Every will is willed insofar as determination imposes itself on it, and is willing insofar as it imposes itself on determination. In us, by comparison with God, our volitions are more willed than willing, and they are only willing by reason of concern for value. In God, by comparison with us, his willings are more willing than willed, and they are only willed by reason of God's love for our initiative.

Divine finitude and human thought. God is therefore finite only by reason of and for the sake of our limitation. It is this finitude of God which makes truth possible. The world is a mobile order of determinations, relatively necessary and contingent, *which is not experience but is in experience,* by comparison with which our affirmations can be spoken of as true or false. Insofar as this world determines the conditions of our union with one another, the determinations which constitute the world form science. Insofar as these determinations are models whose emotional influence on us orients us toward God, they form theology.

If, indeed, science and theology are identical in that they substitute thought about determinations for the concrete experience of spiritual existence, their assimilation is legitimate only if one considers the content of the determination *apart from its relation to the self.* For once science and theology are related to the self, *they oppose each other as condition and model.* I can say that it is one and the same determination that conditions the act of the painter who copies it and that is his model. But I do not take the same intimate attitudes when I consider the determination on the one hand as a condition and on the other as a spectacle to be reproduced.

Let us give a summary description of these attitudes. In the first case, I suppose that I am other than the painter, watching him paint and ready to remove everything which would prevent him from seeing the determination because I believe that he could not reproduce it if it did not affect him. The determination is for him *a condition of possibility.* No consideration of value is mixed into my thought except that a definite security is indispensable for every enterprise. As condition, the determination is a *permissive mediation,* coming from below. If, on the contrary, I propose this determination to the painter as a model, it is because, without having yet determined whether all the conditions which would permit it to be reproduced are given, I put myself in his place to experience concretely whether it is worth the effort to try it, whether it would be desirable that this determination be saved from destruction. As model, the determination is an imprint of value. It is an *informing mediation,* coming from above.

From this summary comparison, it follows that the scientist looks within determination for the means of being affected by the world, whereas the theologian looks within determination for a means of being inspired by God. The scientist comes close to the theologian not when he utilizes the knowledge furnished by past science but when he utilizes by imitation the model of famous theories. Both the scientist and the theologian, if they let themselves be fascinated by determinations, will treat as absolutes those givens whose value for science is to serve research and application and whose value for theology is to lead souls to spiritual confidence. All science and all theology are divine insofar as they presuppose a relation to the absolute which must provide them with their truth and value. They are human insofar as they must adapt themselves to human limitations, as the infinite becomes finite to determine us.

What is true of all knowledge of perception and ideas is necessarily true of philosophy. All philosophy is a compromise between the philosopher and the existential unity of God. Philosophy is true insofar as it participates in the Spirit. It is a mere ornament insofar as it manifests the insufficiency found in every determination or finite existence. This is the case with philosophy as with every task and every action. They deserve esteem only *if the self raises itself to stand before God* and overcomes *the inertia of matter and passion,* while *value lowers itself to meet this effort in such a way that it moves away from pure indetermination,* consolidates itself in a new work, and inspires a fruitful searching. Dualism is true to the existential origins of being; monism is true to the convergence of their initiatives when this convergence succeeds in coming about. Convergence is always to be renewed. Compassion is the best existential symbol of this union. An oppressed consciousness aspires to salvation. Its effort rises toward a generous consciousness which sympathizes with its emotion simply in order to descend toward it through its concern.

51. *Perfection and infinity*

To reach God, the self must balance the mediation of perceptions and ideas with the immediacy of value in order to avoid the two opposite dangers of evasion and resignation. Thus God must be thought of as the existential principle of the world and lived as the soul of our existence, and his transcendence with respect to our limits must initially be opposed to his immanence with respect to our lives. Consequently, God-with-us, that is, God, must always present himself to us under a duality of aspects, the ideas of which would be concretely experienced by us as contradictory if we treated them rigidly and apart from their relation. The first of these contradictions, that which is generative of the aspiration which molds experience, is *the antinomy of divine perfection and infinity.*

The essence of God, insofar as he is an object of thought, is perfection. The essence of every idea and every perception symbolizes him. *Order is an outline of perfection. It is perfection considered at its lower level.* Though order is the condition for the possibility of both science and society, it is only a minimum condition, for this order, i.e., the exclusion of incompatibility, can be merely rudimentary. Science looks for and finds coherence. But this can be the coherence of just a few givens obtained by abstraction, a coherence which eliminates complexity and forgets value. The planetary ellipse is nothing but a rough view of the circulation of the star whose orbit it describes and whose center of gravity, through the totaling of all the actions which affect its mass, delineates a historical, unforeseeable curve, ultimately undefinable by reason of its connection with the infinite. Likewise, when the immorality of those who are responsible for and beneficiaries of a political regime has led to its ruin, the army intervenes to put an end to anarchy and to "reestablish order." But this order is an order of bodies in the street. For conscious beings, order can be either degrading or vivifying.

In its higher form, perfection becomes beauty. Order was that which had to appear so that life could enjoy the security which makes life possible. *Order is that which must exist, from the viewpoint of necessity.* But an indefinite variety of existences is compatible with it. In beauty, perfection manifests the prevalence of existence over determination. Determination here not only becomes as supple as is necessary for the spirit, but it no longer even draws attention to itself. When we "see" someone's joy on his face, we no longer see his features. When we admire the beauty of the body, that body is no longer merely biological. *Beauty is what ought to exist, from the viewpoint of value.*

Thus, on the level of determinations, beauty is the best expression of God. God must exist for value to exist. Without God, value would be nothing but an existential possibility. Like beauty, God must be and can only be loved for himself. Likewise, beauty elicits contemplation rather than notions of utility which refer indefinitely to something else. If value is not to be self-contradictory, it must be unique and must surpass all generality. Beauty, like love, confers on that which it illumines the property of not being replaceable by anything else. Its singularity localizes it, but also expresses infinity. If God were not unique, two values would be at odds in experience, and the evil issuing from their conflict would be radical. A moment of joy given by beauty belies this hypothesis. From perception, in which most men are imprisoned, beauty speaks to the soul. If God were nothing but a determination, he would be hypothetical. But the hypothetical does not stand on its own. By elevating determination to the absolute through the love it inspires in us, beauty initiates us into the joy of a contemplation which is self-sufficient. This contemplation can only be self-sufficient by reason of the transcendence of value which embraces it as the sun embraces a church window.

The experience of beauty *offers description three aspects,* aspects which cannot fail to be found there. Its content is *an order of determinations,* like the golden mean in the rectangle of a beautiful window. The relation here becomes structure. But it is not dead, for beauty is not merely a perception. It is not even a merely understood perception. It is a loved perception. This love inspires in us a circulation which makes us bounce from one part of the contemplated order to another. Symmetry calls for a certain form and it is there. And it refers us back to where we came from. When faced with a beautiful human body, we no longer distinguish between its life, which successively moves its parts, and our admiration, since its lines merge into one another by calling for one another. In a beautiful picture a color presents itself where another color makes us want it to be. Object and subject are merged. The objective essence of beauty is to lead us. To repeat the word with which Aloysius Bertrand has depicted the tulip lover, we would "thin out" before beauty to the point of starvation if the beauty perceptible by man were absolutely absolute.

Academicism has misunderstood the second character of beauty, namely, that it must not only lead but also captivate. In itself, determination is never sufficient. It must make itself be desired by existence. It must *get hold of intimacy.* One can show that this desire, like every tendency, brings together intention and goal, that it needs nourishment, but also that it goes infinitely beyond that which nourishes it.

When the impatience of the near at hand prevails over the aspiration toward the unknown, art becomes more formal than spiritual. Titian's *Profane Love* strips beauty, while his *Sacred Love* clothes it in order to increase the seeking for it beyond every revelation of it. All artistic love is both profane and sacred. When a pagan passion makes us desire to possess determination, perfection makes us love it by requiring us to bring it to completion. The relaxed air of the statues of Polyclitus invites us to attune ourselves to that liberation which, at the most intimate point of life, the love of value thrusts upon structure. But there is no violence in this thrust. Beauty would be little more than a sustained order if it did not involve an inexhaustible flexibility which raises beauty to the same level as the highest heroism. This flexibility is *grace*.

Let us move on now to the most ardent works which have inspired Christian art. One could show that the greatness of the works of Michelangelo proceeds from the fact that they manifest *the superabundance of the soul over everything which emanates from it*. At the lowest level of our fate, the *Slaves* of the Louvre makes us sympathize with the oppressed consciousness at the moment when determination becomes matter so as to stifle consciousness. But even here one has a presentiment of a resistance offered by courage, which is simply value and is called courage when it is attached to a subject. At the highest level of our power, *Moses* expresses the force of a soul disturbed by the menaces which surround it but which intimate infinity elevates above all menaces and beyond its own specific action. For no other artist does the negativity of determination arouse so profound a pessimism, nor does beauty have a more tragic fate. But for no other artist does faith in the Spirit more deliberately convert sadness and agony into love of the infinite.

Between these limits, let us consider in its generality the beauty of the most noble object which art can direct itself to, namely, the human body. The harmony of the body's proportions can arouse admiration. But this harmony is less moving than is the hint of life awakened in us by the directions and the possibilities which its incipient movements introduce all around it. A halo of relations bathes the human beauty with value. The body of a man is capable of more movements and especially of more spiritual expressions than is that of any animal. At each instant it renews the aspects which it offers of itself; its acts open perspectives which immediately close because other perspectives succeed them.

This existential halo of incipient relations refers to every aspect of experience and makes the human body a radiant universality of suggestion. The most animal parts of the body— that scarcely attenuated jaw, those nails which can still scratch —recall the long history which was indispensable for the organism to reach this point of harmony and suppleness, and they

manifest that there is still some brutality in us. The birthmarks
evoke the memory of the mother who has nurtured this body.
The body's malformations and blemishes manifest the hostility
of matter, whereas the beauty of a form and the elegance of
a curve testify to the prevalence of the spirit over matter. Its
sexual characteristics force one to recall the relation which
united man and woman in a solidarity of such depth that it
confirms the presence of love at the origin of creation. In
presaging the children who will be born of their union, the
sexual characteristics subordinate the past to the future. These
are some of the mediations which, by revealing the grace of life
to the one who admires it and by associating him with life by
means of an already active sympathy, keep him from treating
the body as a cask in which consciousness is, as it were, enclosed and sealed in. Rather, these mediations manifest the local
expression of an existence capable of conquering all of nature
step by step, because existence is nothing but a point of application of the Spirit who gives light and warmth to the entirety of
experience.

Beauty is not only harmony and grace; it is also *charm*.
Beauty not only expresses an order among things and the suppleness of a human intimacy; it also implies the presentiment
of the infinite. Charm, a word which extends the mysterious
efficacy of witchcraft down to us, is in its highest sense the
artistic aspect of divine grace. Its sign, which is indubitable as
are all signs which spring from the absolute, is that power of
convincing and persuading which dissolves the intellectual and
affective resistances of man. In its lower form, the charming
gets lost in the gracious. An animal can be gracious, but not
charming. In its higher form, charm reveals at the heart of
beauty the transcendence of the Infinite. Charm gives, or more
often promises, that which tragic pessimism makes one concretely experience as a lack. This happens, for example, when
a despair of love dissolves into delight when it encounters a
consenting smile. But one indeed has to acknowledge that at
this point art changes into religion. According to the movement
indicated by the stranger of Mantinée, sensible beauty mediates
the thrust of the soul toward the idea taken as model. But an
idea is still only an infinity of a certain kind; and the idea of
ideas, the idea of the Good, has the defect of sacrificing God's
infinity to his perfection.

This is because perfection, if considered alone and apart

from its relation to infinity, necessarily leads to bringing God down into the world. By attributing perfection to God at the summit of the hierarchy of determined perfections, one signifies that there is no structure which has not proceeded from him. His perfection requires that there be nothing existent, *in whatever positivity this existence possesses*, which is foreign to him. For he would be imperfect if he lacked whatever this foreign existence might be. But this apotheosis of determination in God cannot suffice. If the perfect is positive in that the compatibility of parts now becomes the reciprocity of an intimate appeal, it is still negative in that it closes off the future. *The perfect is the past which has died in its own achievement.* Value requires more because God is not exhausted by what he has created. Perfection is infinity channeled by determination; infinity is perfection surpassed by indeterminateness. In God these two facets alternately prevail. The past taken apart from the future would be fossilized, dead, irrevocable. And we know well, through that experience which we have of eternity in the midst of actuality, that the present must always be the relation of determination to indeterminateness. Divine infinity cannot therefore be reduced to boundlessness except by losing thereby both liberty and intimacy.

The mutual distrust between art and religion is the expression within our experience of the conflict between perfection and infinity in God. By separating itself from religious inspiration, art does not render the world lovable to us except in such a way as to make us aware of the fragility of the enjoyment of the world which it gives us. Art cannot thus separate itself without provoking in the believer the iconoclastic tendency to destroy everything sensible, a tendency which religion must guard against if the love of God is not to degenerate into hatred for the world and men and thus give rise to their destruction. From the infinite, one can easily derive the absolute negation of the finite. But if one ought to call the Absolute God, it is precisely so that the idea of the infinite not influence us by suggesting destruction to us, but rather influence us by inspiring creation in us. When art and religion converge, art receives from religion a profundity and force which it could not grasp except from the goal of the infinite. Religion finds in the testimony given by beauty to the sovereignty of the spirit over things the concretely experienced verification of the most definite finality which is accessible to us.

The opposition between perfection and infinity is prolonged *within religion itself.* Religion receives its life from the antagonism between two contradictory movements. Christianity has oscillated between the *dialectics of security,* which protect against the vertigo of indeterminateness by pointing out within the order of determinations verifications of the existence of God, and the *dialectics of stimulation,* which increase our participation in the Infinite by utilizing the repugnance and the horror aroused in every man by the anguish of annihilation. Both kinds of dialectics, establishing which elements of union and separation the existential relation between God and the self must bring together, cooperate alternately or together in the progression of existence toward and with God. God, insofar as he is superior to the opposition between determination and indeterminateness, between the ideal and the existential, must at one and the same time be thought of as perfect and loved as infinite. It would be dangerous for one of these processes to dissociate itself from the other. Exclusive quietism, by attenuating the dissatisfaction of the particular consciousness, would end in a deceitful divinization of the self. On the other hand, an exclusive Jansenism would lead the self to despair if the witness of the past, by offering to our admiration and sensitivity examples of perfection whose charm makes them persuasive, did not help to reassure us that at the root of what we call value there is not the emptiness of nothingness but the inexhaustibleness of divine goodness. Just as perfection is found in things but the infinite must always transcend them, so God is everywhere but is in no particular place. Consciousness is an abyss which is hollow at the same time as it is a world which constructs itself.

Will one object to these considerations, saying that *they presuppose the reality of the infinite* and that the infinite is nothing but an expression for the mental power to surpass every finite thing? The truth of this observation, taken from Locke, is that indeed the infinite cannot be treated as an object. There is no more an infinite object than there is an infinite number. But if we conceive of the opposition between the finite and the infinite and if this opposition is referred to the power of the Spirit, the *I,* it is because the *I* is composed of two aspects, the subject and God. And if the finite and the infinite are grasped only through their mutual negation, it is because these two aspects, which are existential since they are not objective, define the theandric relation. Strictly, God is neither essence nor existence. He exists only by surpassing at each instant and from every point of view everything which he is. If the infinite number expresses him from the point of view of quantity, it is insofar as this infinite number does not exist. But man is so easily fascinated by determination that he never ceases applying to God negations which could only belong to finite objects. God indefinitely renders essence thinkable and existence lovable by uniting them, since the essence cannot come to be thought except through an existence thinking it, and the existence cannot come to be lovable except through value and through the determinations which furnish it and give it color. But if experience also presents us with ruptures in the ideal relation, it is because God does not reduce himself to the *I*.

52. *The impossibility of confusing God with the* I *or with the self*

In looking for a term for the unity of experience, we have cited the impossibility of identifying the *I* with God. The sequence of description, by requiring us to recognize value as over against determinations, has confirmed this indication. The *I* is in God, as it is within the self. But God could not reduce himself to the *I* unless he absorbed both the self and the *I*. This is what would happen at the limit of God-without-us. The self would drown in God and consequently the double *cogito* would be reduced to the divine *cogito*. But this limit is precisely what is excluded by the double *cogito*. The description of experience forces us to recognize this fact because experience does not contain only value and love for value. Rather, it unquestionably also contains both obstacle, which is everywhere opposed by reason of determination to the reign of value, and evil, which is the intimate cowardice of the self when it responds cowardly to the conflict of determinations.

Pantheism, therefore, has the partialness of a limit. It cannot reduce the plurality of individual consciousnesses, error, and human will to the indistinctness of God except by making value disappear in an undifferentiated world. God is more than the principle of Being. He is the principle of value. Being, in relation with non-being, is simply one aspect of value. This relation between being and non-being cannot be overlooked. It is concretely experienced daily when we hesitate between the need to possess and the love for adventure, between the desire for the here at hand and the desire for the beyond.

God-with-us *maintains himself between the two limits of indifference*. If he were at the lower limit, he would be reduced to the *I*, to the pure *I*, the unity of knowledge without either action or influence. With the reservation that it excludes absolute contradiction, or, more precisely, excludes that massive solidity and pure exteriority which would be its limits if it were a thing and not experience, the pure *I* is indifferent to the empirical content presented to it. It permits lying and crime, cruelty and treachery, war and envy, as well as the most noble sentiments and acts. A glance at experience is the most formidable temptation to moral consciousness. So many aspects of history belie morality and value that consciousness cannot fail to ask itself whether morality is not merely a word for children, a bookish concept, or a disguise adopted by impotent people who flatter themselves. When the honest man frees himself from this faintheartedness, it is because he has set the pure *I*, whose knowledge is the more pure the less it concerns itself with the *importance* of what it knows, in opposition to God, whose existence and infinity he affirms by avowing that the value toward which he directs himself is not reduced to absolute nothingness. For if the Spirit, insofar as one opposes it to determinations, is not a thing, it is likewise true that nothing exists except through it.

One can call this lower limit *the indifference of universal tolerance*. It permits everything by inertia, by refusing to separate the best from the worst. Fatigue brings us to this indifference when it forces on us a tired consent or an accomplice's resignation by depriving us of the energy to refuse and of the dignity coming from effort. This indifference presents itself in various, even opposite, forms. It is found just as much in the despair of "What's the use!" as in the passivity of "Whatever God wants!" With the former we avow our weakness without leaving room for outside help. With the latter we rely on the principle of value, but without offering it our effort. The former sacrifices disinterestedness to the justification of laziness, while the latter sacrifices disinterestedness to disinterest.

In opposition to this almost total debility, the higher limit is *the indifference of infinite sovereignty*. One can conceive a power such that no event could disturb its hegemony. We experience such a power in artistic transformation. The worst torments, the most frightening convulsions, even ennui, as in the novels inspired by the realism of the ordinary, become agreeable things for consciousness. Nero is more interesting in art than is Marcus Aurelius. He moves us more. But this emotion is no longer linked to danger. God-without-us would be this *supreme artificer,* for whom the worst catastrophes of existence would be nothing but an artistic diversion. The spectators at a tragedy know well that the suffering of the actor is not proportionate to his cries. By its sovereign indifference, likewise, the Absolute would remain outside our sorrows, for if they were merely artistic our sorrows would be simulated sorrows.

Reality transcends any of the functions of the spirit. And artistic indifference does not grasp the importance of reality any more than does theoretical indifference. Divine liberty, and consequently our liberty, which can exist only as a participation, does not reduce itself to the liberty of indifference. The concrete experience of and the threat of suffering lead us back to the sentiment of value, even if our love for God is too weak to do so. God's compassion descends into the midst of our distress to bring us the idea of duty and, while preserving our power to assent, the grace to love duty, a grace which already makes duty shine forth as the dawn of salvation.

We thus rediscover two kinds of evidence, both coercive and assumptive, which no concrete experience can do more than reinforce, namely, the evidence of obstacle and of value. Impediments bring on sufferings which no consciousness can honestly deny. It is insufficient to say that morality is supposed to sanction these sufferings. If they were sanctioned, they would lose their existence as sufferings, the very nature of which is to invincibly arouse repugnance. If a stoic were to achieve a strength of will and a believer a power of love which would make suffering vanish before their glance, they still could not deny that others are tortured by suffering. In the absence of the actual sentiment of suffering, the thought of the evil would lead them to the evidence of the obstacle.

The evidence of the obstacle is inseparable from the evidence of value. The first act of the infant chewing with its lips on its mother's breast and the last act of the drowning man struggling to keep himself afloat manifest an effort not only toward an end but, by means of this end, toward the appropriation of value which is existence itself. The skeptic, who denies value, defends the value of skepticism. At its lower limit, the need for value inspires the driving power of repugnance, fear of evil, rejection of the unknown, and concern for protection and defense. At its higher limit, the need for value inspires the driving power of attraction, desire for the good, joy in adventure, generosity, and charity.

God and self. After having admitted the distinction between God and the *I*, will one reject the distinction between God and the self? It might seem to be possible to make immanent, to psychologize, every description which we have just made. We do not go beyond ourselves when we have the experience of a conflict between tendencies, some of which we call good and some bad by reason of their convergence or their conflict with others.

If such a humanism were to consist exclusively in recognizing that everything determined which is in experience bears our mark, there would be no reason to object to it. What one cannot admit is that this determination is all there is to our experiences. For what is important for us is not what our experiences are. What is important is the truth and the value of these experiences. Truth, which is the projection of value onto the plane of determination, and value in general have no sense if one makes them, to use the term of the Cartesian Malebranche, who has set forth this idea in the clearest light, "modifications of our spirit."

It is, therefore, not the judgment which we bring to bear on what exists which gives it legitimacy; it is the congruity of this judgment with the Absolute. When science unifies under one and the same law many processes of one and the same spirit or of many spirits, this accord has value only if it is not merely conventional. Would one base science on a transcendental structure of the human self? The transcendental structure of the human self would explain the determined characteristics of science, but not the applicability of such a formalism to matter or its value as reality, which is in relation to absolute existence. With much more reason science cannot be reduced exclusively to the decision of a human will. If knowledge and virtue manifest nothing but the decree of one or many men, that decree would not establish the truth of knowledge and virtue but rather their falseness. Pure voluntarism has never sufficed to account for value.

After having seen that value presupposes a more than human principle, at once transcendent to and immanent in man, will one deny that value needs God to convey it? If value must necessarily express the Absolute and if, further, value is necessarily accessible to us, since it would be equally illusory if it were only of our own making or if it were absolutely foreign to us, it must either be determination or existence. Since value defines itself in opposition to determination, it is as existence that it must be accessible to us. Since it unites the Absolute and us without any mediation, value presupposes a homogeneity between God and us, i.e., personality. To the degree that value reigns, the *I* is God.

If Bradley seems to refuse to grant personality to the Absolute so as to admit nothing in it but its unity, it is because he remains on the plane of theoretical knowledge where God only intervenes to confer existence upon something objective. But personality already germinates in that gift which is the first gift of value. It is not sufficient for truth that truth be merely theoretically possible. If truth makes some human consciousness concretely experience its influence, it becomes value. At the very core of the act by which Bradley embarks on his thinking, there resides a faith that the unity dominating the collection of appearances and the unity inspiring Bradley as a man are one and the same unity. This is why he cannot call the deity infrapersonal. What is not impersonal is personal. And if Bradley prefers to qualify the deity as suprapersonal, this is to avoid having determinations introduce their negativity into God. Our analysis agrees with this caution, since our analysis makes God the source of pure value. But it is still the case that the suprapersonality cannot be less than personality and that consequently God is personal, i.e., capable of uniting himself spiritually with every finite consciousness, except that he does not submit to their defects against his will.

The religious experience of prayer confirms the relation between God, infinite in himself and finite in his connection with each of us, and the self, perceiving and thinking about the finite but participating in the infinite. At the outset, the self says to God, "You and I," an insolent attitude which makes the two persons two finite persons. This is so because you and I are still more like objects or negations than like existences. Objects are in space, separated one from the other, rather than in the spirit. Objects stock the unhappiness of consciousness, as is reflected with such pathos in Gabriel Marcel's *Metaphysical Journal.* This is because grace is still almost completely absent from prayer. But prayer is not made for the sake of the prayer. It is not designed to pay for favors with words, as is the case with flattery. No determination has any religious value except by reason of its existential influence.

As soon as prayer mediates grace, the duality of the you and the I yields to the communion of divine existence with human existence. As soon as and insofar as they flow together, there is no longer either finite God or finite self. There is the *I* now become love, in which prayer consummates itself and cancels itself. *It is only through this union, strictly, that God exists, for he is where he creates; and it is only through this union that we ourselves exist, for we exist only insofar as value raises us above nature and the body.* This union is not a confusion, for God distinguishes himself from us by surpassing us through his infinity. And if our body, transfigured and freed from its inertia and opacity, persists in our existence without being distinctly thought, it nonetheless specifies that existence. Immediately, by again becoming obstacle, our body drives us back to disjunctive consciousness.

53. *The insufficiency of humanism*

Though we have described experience by recognizing the solidarity of determination and value in the ideo-existential unity of the theandric relation, in which determination grounds the communication and value grounds the communion between God and self, philosophy is not authorized to reduce itself to humanism. *Man is always at the meeting point of a situation which encloses him and an attraction toward value.* This attraction brings together the recollection of past morality and the presentiment of a better experience. But this attraction has to be nourished and strengthened by the influence of our volitions and the cooperation of experience as a whole. If we consider nothing but the limits which determine the human self, then humanism is deposed. If we consider nothing but the universal unity included in value, pantheism annihilates man in God. In our times, the more familiar of these two abstractions is humanism. Thus its insufficiency is what now needs to be stressed.

Against individual humanism. It would be more worthwhile to profess antihumanism than humanism, for moral effort begins with a negation which delivers one from everything which is all too human. Further, humanism presupposes that the concept of man has a definite comprehension. Antihumanism is simply the negation of humanism. Humanism, indeed, has meaning only if it is possible to fix humanity within an *invariable* nature. One can do this abstractly, fictitiously, by considering humanity from the outside, like a lily or a snake. But this immobilization is merely a caricature of the liberty which animates man. This immobilization usefully allows one to recognize man's limits, but it leaves out consideration of how man utilizes what those limits allow for. The more man raises himself, the more cerebral plasticity bends itself to the initiatives of consciousness in such a way that, if one decided to define man by what he is at a certain instant, his initial success over one of the determinations which serve to define him would set him apart from humanity. There is nothing more precious, for example, than characterology if it points out to a man his strengths and weaknesses. Nothing is more deadly than characterology if it serves to restrict an individual consciousness to its determinations.

If our weakness, which could be absolute only if we were mere things, does not force us to espouse exclusive humanism, which we call pure humanism, neither does obligation recommend such a position to us. For if one understands by man not the definition of a nature but the name of the self which animates that nature, it is illegitimate to make this self, insofar as it is man, the exclusive, unique end of an ethical goal. Unquestionably, the spirit in us, but non-localizably so, is never a means. If there is any tradition which philosophy must defend and which French philosophy in particular has always defended, it is the affirmation of the absolute value of the person. But it is here that humanism lends itself to a dangerous confusion, and thus it is proven that no doctrine is sufficient for morality unless value is added to it. *The value which the person receives is the value he looks for and deserves.* If the self, at the moment when it claims to be absolute value, makes this claim the basis for yielding to caprice, for refusing to be honest and to put forth effort, for betraying the future of the spirit, in short, for conferring on itself the divinity which it refuses to God, it still verifies that liberty entails something absolute, but it does so in order to make liberty the initiative for destruction and corruption. By repeating to man that he is merely man, by suppressing the stimulating variety which should oppose the ideal of a superior self to the natural self, by refusing to rise with the infinite God beyond every determined realization, exclusive humanism weakens the strength of morality. And this weakening is verified not only in the debasement of the moral life but also in the vitiation of all the processes of the spirit. For if there must be a sentiment of what value expects of men in order for there to be heroes, there must also be such a sentiment to sustain the intellectual and affective ambitions of great scientists and artistic geniuses, the disinterestedness of statesmen and great public servants, the devotion of the most charitable souls, and even the noble dreams of childhood. When a man dies, one single thing counts: Has he loved or betrayed value?

Value is cunning. It often insinuates itself where one has little interest in it. If humanism can be defended, it is because when it is reproached by value for glorifying man insofar as he is man, it transforms itself into an ideal. What one calls man is no longer what he is but what he ought to be. This conversion calls for two observations. The first is that at this moment the idea of the ideal man is no longer anything but a mediation by which one invokes value. If this ideal manifested only the one who expresses it, it would be discredited as a dream. It would become a means for subjecting others to one's own will. It would be an act of tyranny. Further, this idea of ideal man is little more than a word. Ideal man has to be sought for and made to live. One looks for an undetermined value to intervene and support it. If there were adequation or identity between the idea which one has of man now and of what he will be, this identity would be realized from now on and ethics would be identical with morality. As this indeterminateness is value only on condition that it is absolute, infinite, and assimilable to every spirit, it is God who is, in disguise, reestablished at the source of philosophy.

Thus the fact is that the term *humanism* deserts the goal it should serve. It is essential for all education of self and others to begin by expressly noting the gulf between what is and what ought to be. Pure humanism always falls into a naturalism which consists in letting oneself either be supported or be carried away. Sometimes one lets himself be transported by natu-

ral forces or what one calls social forces in such a way as not
to recognize therein the self-sacrifice or cowardice of others.
One will draw from them as much pleasure as possible. Sometimes one gives oneself over to the most brutal spontaneity. A
paganism of nature or race misunderstands the essence of
moral effort, which consists in hoping for the grace of value
only if we have already done everything we can to pass from a
nature to a supernature. Thus it is preferable not to give nature
and supernature the same name.

One need not fear that the idea of God would be oppressive.
By identifying God with the principle of value, one frees the
idea of God from whatever negation is entailed by a determination. What God gives in the love of value is liberty. He progressively delivers me from obstacle. Obstacle was a hindrance
which now becomes the objective mediation whereby the self
raises itself from inferiority to triumph, from an attitude in
which negation prevailed to a free flight in which obstacle no
longer intervenes except as a supplementary propulsive fac-
tor. Humanism, when it is understood in a larger philosophy,
has the usefulness of leading man back to examine the situation
from which his effort starts and of preventing his ambition
from wandering off into illusion. Humanism is transcended at
the point where the immanence of God in the self no longer
permits the opposition of God and self as though they were
separated members of a ruptured relation. This presupposes
that humanism enters as a dialectic within an emotional process
which allows humanism to appear when it is appropriate but
which is not limited to humanism. Taken alone, it was humanism which divinized the Caesars. One democratizes the Pan-
theon in vain, for that changes nothing of its nature.

Against social humanism. By multiplying its application,
social humanism simply multiplies humanism's danger. The
term *social humanism* designates the doctrinal postulate which
consists in *proposing to men as the goal of their life an ideal of
an exclusively human, juridically defined order which is insti-
tuted by subordinating the soul to formal intelligence.* The law
—one does not know whether to call it theoretical or normative,
indicative or imperative—would be the universal instrument for
communication between the competent man, who is abstractly
considered as having no interest other than truth and justice,
and the incompetent man, from whom one demands obedience

by assuring him that he would understand what the law required if he were competent. The law is the natural limit of an intellectualism which does not distinguish between the *infinitely complex ideas,* which should indeed be thought of as molders of experience, and the *abstract determinations* which are offered to the limited perception and thought of man.

It is sufficient to extend the critique of individual humanism, made in the name of experience, to show the varied and numerous dangers of this social ideal. One should remember that every ideal, whether it is defined as a program or is existential as in the phrase "the Republic under the Empire," is merely a determination or a limited presentiment. Consequently, value infinitely surpasses it. An ideal can mediate the entrance into value, but it can also degrade value into passion. A war of ideals is more formidable than a war of interests, for it presupposes on the part of belligerents a more intimate involvement of the self. Also, value in itself should not be determined or specified. Value's destiny is not to provoke war. It gives itself, even in war, only to love, to those who fight to protect the weak and to safeguard liberty. *Man holds his head above society.* He is affected by value and he must yield to value. He would be required to reject God himself, if God were to distinguish himself from value, for man must give himself over to nothing but value. This is why social humanism, by replacing value with an ideal order of determinations, entails a psychology which is not merely false but is dangerous for man.

We will mention here only three ideas, as samples, of the entire critique which could be made of social humanism from the standpoint of value.

(1) The doctrine of social humanism gets its prestige from the tendency of the human spirit toward systematization, a tendency which projects itself, i.e., expresses itself and specifies itself, in the idea of the "unity of society," or, more simply, of "society." Like every objective expression, this idea is indifferent to value. Unity binds men together just as much when they are fighting one another as when they do business or when they love one another. But unquestionably the first of these modes of connection is the most limited.

War and human love are existential relations of a bipersonal mode which it is often difficult to distinguish between, for there are both fraternal enemies and inimical brothers. Man and woman oppose one another, to speak summarily, as the ideal opposes the existential. From this opposition, as many misunderstandings as solidarities follow as consequences.

Likewise, it is necessary to specify unity. Thus one slides from the idea of society to that of juridical order sanctioned by the State. Does it follow that this order is good? To a certain point, yes, for order is in itself value. But it can be minimal, for finite order is necessarily inadequate to infinite value. There is an indefinite variety of orders. Many are more detestable than lovable. Not only do men feel themselves to be oppressed by some orders, but these orders weaken in them the desire to produce and be creative. To judge orders one must interject a sentiment of value *clarified by the study of its effects and, further, inspired by love for the infinite.* In every respect, what matters in order, and this is so for every determination, is not its content but its influence.

A human order cannot be perfect. Every code is halfway between compulsion and beauty. It is neither the work of consciousness reduced to impulsiveness, nor the work of glorious spirits writing the rules for a terrestrial Paradise. At the higher level, which is the existential ideal of anarchists, there would be no need to regulate divinized souls. At the lower level, instinct would release one from reflection and will. The code oscillates, with experience, from the brutality of military tribunals, which are dominated by compulsion, to the ideality of juridical academies, which are temples of purity. But these oscillations are enclosed within rather narrow limits. One can, for example, take a step or two in the direction of fitting punishment to the individual, but that will not go far because a society cannot spend much time and money on the institution and application of its laws.

The law, which defines the lines along which men will interact with one another, will necessarily be mediocre. It will be as impoverished as words are, which can only express the common element in personal sentiments, or as financial statements are in comparison with the emotions which develop on the basis of these statements. Society is made of prejudiced means. It expresses value in its own fashion, but always in a debased form. And the exaggeration of political preoccupations, by strengthening the idolatry of the concept and the hypertrophy of the will, involves the degradation of the spiritual richness of souls.

(2) This essential insufficiency of law increases even fur-

ther when it is presented more insistently as the exclusive object of our moral preoccupations. It is true of every activity that one strengthens it at the outset by assuring its priority over other activities, but that beyond a certain point every effort to accentuate it weakens it because it can draw its energy and value only from the force of other activities and from the force of the entire soul. The surest way to weaken the State is to extend it beyond its capacity to rule. If one wants the law to become a formality without power, one has only to universalize it. The more the law extends beyond condemning evident moral violations like armed robbery and counterfeiting, the more it will reveal the arbitrariness of the human wills which established it. The prestige which the law gets from value will vanish and it will then appear as nothing but the means whereby some men assure their domination over others.

Thus if one grounds the law on the objective one, in imitation of science, *the validity* which law draws from its foundation will no longer suffice to confer *value*, and consequently existence, on it. Law receives its power to impose itself not from the public arena but from the secret depths of souls. Law is worth what men evaluate it as. Far from being sufficient to direct them, law emanates from men. Law can only subsist if there are men who are ready to sacrifice their lives so that law has a sanction, and if others approve of and help these men. By reducing human morality to its juridical expressions, one betrays both the force of law and the future of souls. For if these souls are envious, cowardly, and trifling, the law promotes the decadence of society. If they are noble, more ready to give than to receive, the law will serve their mutual well-being and the free flight of the entire people.

(3) Finally, one should note that he who relies on the law without a rather severe demand forcing him to do so ordinarily engages in a conversion of consciousness which shows his weakness rather than his energy. Just as science, which is a means for changing obstacles into aids, offers us the fictitious ideal of a world in which we would only have to let ourselves be carried along and in which work would be replaced by a painless harvesting, so law offers itself as the facile means for replacing our own seeking and effort with exploiting the labor of others. It is not at all a question of condemning the human need for happiness but rather of acting in such a way that it does not

lead to the intimate degradation which takes away from man the joy of creating and leaves him nothing but revenge, pleasure, and waste. He who cannot be anything but a tourist has lost his life.

After the foregoing descriptions, it goes without saying that by refusing, contrary to social humanism, to give preeminence to justice to the detriment of love, our intention is not to give preeminence to love to the detriment of justice. The twofold effect of obstacle is that it requires one to acknowledge determination and that it prevents one from confusing the self with God. Man is not capable, at whatever level he might be, of anything more than human love. And human love can be nothing more than a lowly participation in absolute and infinite love. A man can love only a few men and can love them only a little. The juridical law, if it stays on the level of communication and cooperation, renders communication and cooperation possible among souls who do not know one another. The law thus has a legitimate function. If someone doubts this, we can call his attention to the experience which makes law emerge from anarchy. Like everything else, religion can do no more than infuse the love of value. It cannot substitute itself for value. By returning to his situation man necessarily returns to objective and ideal functions.

Generally, the description of the transcendental processes of the spirit must recognize *the irreducible opposition between ideal processes,* of which pure science is the extreme case, *and existential processes,* of which pure religion is the highest example. The former consists in taking determination as a necessity given in connection with existence which, at the extreme, would be annulled in the face of determination by being mingled with determination in order to confer substantiality on it. Religion, on the other hand, turns toward God, who, as infinite existence or pure value, is reached through the annihilation of all phenomena and who is knowable exclusively through the mystical union of spirit with Spirit. Man, a wholly finite consciousness whose life consists in submitting to obstacle so as to make it the means for an increasing participation in God, is and always will be situated at the center of the ideo-existential relation of these two processes. None of the *occurrences* in experience are to be suppressed. All are to be spiritualized. Each occurrence must be both ratified and canceled.

54. *Activity and passivity*

The twofold opposition between determination and value and between the self and God introduces a clarity into the quite important opposition between passivity and activity. It allows us to distinguish three degrees here.

(1) We will call *passivity of passion*, or, more simply, *passion*, the coercion of existence by determination. This coercion is more than the pure inertia of matter. Purely inert matter would exclude all affectedness by being independent of all consciousness. But since experience is possible only through consciousness, purely inert matter is nothing but an asymptotic limit like the objective one. Short of the limit of inert matter, passion overwhelms the self and the self yields. This is immoral consent, excusable insofar as it is forced but cowardly insofar as it is given. It has different nuances depending on the relation of determination and existence. Emotional description has to distinguish, among its modes, reflex and instinct, association and reasoning, habit and impulse, assimilation and the spirit of contradiction, all of which are still passions insofar as the self does not subordinate them to the goal of value.

(2) To these passions is opposed the *activity of determination*. This is technique subordinated to intelligence. It is the ingenuity by which we strive for the union of our existence with value by means of propitious determinations and rectifications. It is the activity of determination which specifies our merit. The activity of determination depends entirely on the self, but the success of the activity does not depend exclusively on the self, for this activity does not go beyond what one can expect of a limited being. This activity lacks that secret cooperation which the subconscious and the unknown—these are merely names for the beyond as it is related either to us or to determination— either give or refuse to the most scientific concoctions and to the most informed intelligence. The influence of this secret cooperation is called *flair, divination, spirit of finesse, intuition,* or *inspiration* when it is added to technique and to that activity whose success it assures.

(3) One must therefore admit, beyond the activity of determination, an unforeseeable irruption of value which is on the one hand a receptivity or, if one wishes, a passivity insofar as

the self cannot produce it, and on the other hand an *activity of value* insofar as God and the self act together to add it to the activity of determination. Because of its worth, we will call it the activity of value. As God must be its ultimate source, one can call it *grace*. It is to grace that the scientist, the strategist, and the inventor owe the *idea* without which everything that they are able to make disposition of would be at loose ends and the true could not be distinguished from the false. Beauty owes its *charm* to grace. Prayer owes to grace the *fervor* which makes its granting possible. The anxious mother owes to grace the *healing* of her child. The restless intelligence owes to grace the *book* which will illuminate it. Through grace, the limitation is no longer an impotence. It is now nothing more than the object without which light would be lost in invisibility.

This is where it is most strikingly established that value does not come from us. Our sole moral resource is to grope and seek. We march toward value like a soldier toward the cannon. Either we reach it or we will be lost. The technique to which value refuses itself is merely a ludicrous gesticulation. Art without value is merely a business, and the most useless business of all. What remains of Delille or of Sardou? The physician administers medicine, the military commander applies the studies learned at war school, the philosopher reasons formally. Their activity is nothing but a waste if healing, victory, and truth respectively are refused them by God. Religion becomes a caricature of itself if the formalities and the ritual are not vehicles for love and charity. And those who do not belong to religion by faith ask themselves what aberration has taken hold of the people they see praying. If you stop up your ears while looking at the most moving singer, you could not help but laugh.

By reason of the inertia of matter this empty activity could sustain itself for some time. There is always some time left for us to reflect. The songs of a ceremonial, which the unanimity of hearts no longer animates, will delay the collapse of an institution. But, imperceptibly, *an interior depression*, comparable to that by which lands undermined by water gradually sink, will reduce the intensity of existence's value. It would be easy to trace in the history of a social or individual decadence the symptoms which show, outside the structures, that existence has gone. The artilleryman shows his power by destroying a place. God does not have to destroy. All God has to do is withhold himself from men and peoples who do not submit the pursuit of their interests to the disinterested love of value. Exchange pays for one determination with another. The subordination of the relation of persons to the relation of things is a form of commerce. Human love and the glory of divine existence are two generosities which meet each other, two free gifts which now become one ardor.

6 / The Dialectics of Separation

[XIV] POPULAR AND SCIENTIFIC DIALECTICS

55. *How can the self be separate from God?*

A LINE ON A MAP is simply the sign for the itinerary of a journey which takes place not on the map but in the soul of the traveler. Similarly, the theandric connection which reflection objectifies as a guide is real only by reason of the life of the relation-soul, in which are concretely experienced both the union and the separation of God and the self. It must be emphasized that both the union and the separation *are not states but operations.*

With reference to union, there are no difficulties. Union is pursued when the expansiveness of value increases the self's participation in God and, if one can speak thus, increases their "intimization." We concretely experience this dilation of the self in happiness when a future of new and auspicious perspectives is opened up before us by value. Joy is always partially a deliverance. But it is also enrichment. If we turn back from the future to the past, the past is presented to us in the form of an enlarged field of contemplation. With more possessions we obtain more security and more capabilities. Security and capabilities minister to our liberty.

The separation between God and the self is a more delicate matter, if it is true that God sustains our very existence. It would seem either that God separates himself from the self and the self is thus annihilated, or that the self exists and there is

[230]

no separation. Like every alternative, this one projects the relation-soul of the double *cogito* from the domain of existence
onto the plane of determinations. The plane of determinations
transforms an operation in its very operational character into
surfaces which can overlap or be juxtaposed. The separation
between God and the self is not a relation of localized positions. This separation is the deepening of a cleavage. In fact,
every concrete relation necessarily manifests the divine infinity
by means of the infinity of its own content. A definition of
the relation which would isolate the relation from its connection with every experience would substitute an intellectual phantom for the relation. With reference to this infinite model, all
thought relations which get abstract universality from the
operation that isolates them from their surroundings are like
sprigs or fibers which themselves get their ideal nature by being
discriminated.

These are the fibers which separation breaks one by one. The
union between God and the self comes about through the at-
tentiveness which a limited existence accords to all its thoughts
and impressions. When this grasp which the self has on determinations weakens, disarray and panic take the place of the
divine life. As the rupture deepens, our ignorance increases
and our horizon becomes proportionately restricted. But our
ignorance never becomes absolute, nor does our subconscious
degenerate into unconsciousness. To be ignorant is to know
that one does not know. One thinks even while sleeping. Separation is relative, a matter of degree. It falls from level to level,
from degree of intensity to degree of intensity.

Even if the opposition between the relative and the absolute
simply expresses the opposition between determination and existence, or even if it is in the absolute itself that relativity is born
through dehiscence, there must be some absolute aspect of separation over against the relative aspect. *In fact, separation is
relative by reason of the order of its degrees, but is absolute in
its meaning.* The sole absolute contradiction is that of movements in contrary directions on the same line. Likewise, if
each degree of the self's existence is a measure of its union
with God, there is nevertheless at each instant a complete opposition between the sense of the spiritual or material movement which increases or decreases this union and the contrary
sense. Morality or immorality begin here absolutely.

The first effect of the rupturing turn is necessarily the inauguration of the materialization of existence. As soon as I no longer sympathize with the sentiment of a smile or the intention of a word, these become merely a reflex or a noise. *Determinations can be treated by the self either as things or as revelations.* They become things if I refuse to look for God at their source. Two steps can be succinctly recognized in this devaluation. First, value in its infinitely many modes will be reduced to order. One will deny God by naturalizing him. Then, as the experience of disorder forces itself on us by every obstacle, one will eventually deny the very order of obstacles. The anarchy of determinations will deliver the self over to spatial disarray and temporal caprice. The sovereignty of the spirit will have been betrayed for a more than Epicurean incoherence of elements.

Every intimate movement of falling is expressed analytically by *an explosion of dialectics,* as a sorrow is expressed by cries, groans, and violent movements. For one who is interested in the description of consciousness for no other reason than its human importance and its spiritual value, there can be no more precious application of this description than in the recognition of the dialectics which produce sadness in consciousness, whether consciousness ponders its distress or whether it thoughtlessly neglects it. The only way we can be in a position to free ourselves from a dialectic of emotions is to recognize it in reflection. Undoubtedly, this recognition is not enough. To be a slave and to know it is still to be a slave. But the knowledge whereby one feels himself and thinks of himself as a slave prepares for the detecting of the other dialectics which conspire with the first to oppress him. Insensibly the self will raise itself from intellectual knowledge to emotional power. We are now going to begin an inventory of the dialectics of separation, with, however, no intention of being exhaustive.

A

56. *Popular dialectics of separation*

We will start with some dialectics with which common sense is familiar and for which literature furnishes as many examples as one might wish.

(1) *The dialectic of naturalization.* This dialectic is the operation whereby the self, ignoring the spirit which performs this operation in the depths of its own being, thinks of itself as and professes that it is a fragment of nature or of matter.

It is easy to specify the steps by which this dialectic changes into a mental diminution on which no discussion can any longer make an impression. We commonly have concrete experience of our weakness. Perception imposes on us an impersonal given which we differentiate, depending on whether or not the given was foreseeable, into necessity and contingency. Further, the limitation of human consciousness constrains us most of the time to treat one another as objects. It is easier to think about a man than to sympathize with him. By reason of the convergence of these factors we are led to substitute the self's body for the self. The prevalence of the sentiment of existence over the perception of the organism, which furnishes existence with its point of application, presupposes, in fact, that a sufficiently strong energy raises the self from perception to intention and from intention to goal. When this energy weakens through the chilling impact of knowledge on sensibility, the subject falls back to the realm of perception where he becomes the witness of an object which he considers to be independent and about which he thinks almost exclusively.

There is no need to suppose that language is at the source of this weakening of energy. But language does enter in to record it, to ratify it, and finally to advise it. One says that "Peter has been crushed, buried" instead of speaking of "the body of Peter." If the intellectualism of the intelligible finally leads us to forget that which intimacy and value add to determination, the way is clear for us to pass on to an objectivism, either naive or disguised, materialist or intellectualized, according to which the self is nothing but a piece of nature. Once the accent is unreservedly put on the object, one will treat intimacy, whenever one does refer to it, as an impurity which reality must be cleansed of by the requirements of both truth and ethics.

Besides, what if this purification could be pushed to the ultimate! Such a dialectical suicide, by exterminating our consciousness, would also exterminate suffering. But even if one can stretch a relation to the point where its terms seem disjoined, one cannot absolutely separate its terms. The self is and cannot be other than the relation of detail and intimacy. Shreds of subjective idealism hang all over the object to which one claims to reduce the self in such a way that they add to the supposed inanity of our existence the misfortune of its con-

crete experience. The self is now consigned to being nothing
other than that which suffers from thinking that it is nothing.

The result of the operation abides and persists. Intimacy becomes the myth of a nature defined by the negation of all the
characteristics of the spirit. We suffer, hope, and love. But
nature is "impassive." It "hears neither our cries nor our sighs."
We foresee, but it blindly follows "its regular path." We look
for value, but it posits determination as a metaphysically inex-
plicable fact. "Nature's springtime does not feel our admiration."
The self creates for itself two hostile things out of two aspects
of obstacle, i.e., the ideal nature of determination and the existential prop which gives obstacle the power to affect us. From
these the self sometimes fashions the brutality of a merciless
law. At other times it fashions the opacity of the unknowable.
Nature brings together in itself the indifference of necessity and
the scandal of randomness. And, in an inverse proportion, the
self strips itself of creative power, reduces itself to that which
judges, and then reduces this role of judging to the status of a
mere witness. It accomplishes this reduction of itself by expect-
ing nothing more of itself than to be a place traversed and filled
by nature.

Reversal from being against to being for. This unhappy
state, like all the others, consists in falsely presupposing the
uselessness of the spirit. *There is nothing but the spirit with its
dialectics and its processes.* These dialectics and processes are
what give rise to the "formations" from which we derive nature.
And when we suffer from them we are simply the victims of the
idolatry of our hallucinations and passions. Morality, which converts these hallucinations and passions into instruments of liberty, is consequently the source of truth as well as of happiness.
But, if it does not have error and unhappiness as a counterpart,
it could neither define nor experience itself.

To perform the conversion which releases one from slavery
to determination into faith in the value of existence, one must
first reveal and *enlarge the duality between being and being
known* in order to avoid reducing knowledge to nothing. Then,
following the direction opened up by idealism, one must show
what role expectancy and intimate action play in vision, i.e.,
one must back away from abstraction, which can only isolate
determination from intimacy by isolating intimacy from determination. Then, by leading consciousness, through sympathy,

to the experiences of invention which manifest its prevalence over determination, one must reestablish this ruptured connection by showing that determination cannot be understood except through the spirit from which it emanates. To do this is to rediscover value at the source of existence itself, and, consequently, at the source of determination.

This is what establishes the fact that determinism is not affirmed in philosophy by reason of its own force but by reason of the adherence and love of the determinist. Description has to look for a situation, structure, and goal which converge in determinism. It will find at the same time what the service is which the determinist renders to value. Still, no determinist can believe, without discrediting his own naturalism, that the affirmation of determinism expresses nothing but the arbitrary will of the man who affirms it. The determinist presupposes, then, that the self which proclaims the truth of determinism participates in a transcendent reality. He presupposes that determinism is more than a fact, for to limit it to being a fact would be to liken it to a dream, which does not cease being a dream simply because it is systematic. He therefore locates the principle of determinism in a value whose source must be absolute, infinite, and spiritual in order for man, who adds the affirmation of determinism to determinism and who distinguishes himself from it contingently by the errors which betray order, to be able to comply with a knowledge whose furtive appearing verifies the irreducibility of spirit to nature.

A most fertile way to suggest this dialectical and emotional reversal is to *meditate on concretely experienced contradiction.* Insofar as determinations oppose one another, contradiction excludes determinism, since determinism entails the perfect systematization of determinations, a world without flaws. Insofar as the self concretely experiences its weakness by suffering from not being able to resolve a conflict, it finds itself. For if the self were merely an inert space, $2 + 2 = 5$ could be juxtaposed to it without bothering its indifference. Printing $2 + 2 = 5$ would not bother the paper; it accepts anything. Insofar as this suffering involves an unexceptionable aspiration to an existence without suffering, the self discovers the presentiment of value. Finally, insofar as it recognizes its impotence as spirit, the self discovers the idea of the all-powerful Spirit, which is the sole existence from which it can expect salvation, for every other finite spirit must be, like itself, half slave.

(2) *The dialectic of seclusion.* We will say only a few words about the dialectic by which the self encloses itself in determination as in a vein of stone. Every determination is a mediation toward another determination or a communication with another self. But in obstacle the contingency of this transition is suspended. Determination appears here as negative. It denies the prevalence of existence. Existence has only to transform this relative negation into absolute negation to feel itself definitively stymied by this obstacle, and has only to generalize this attitude to cover all determinations to feel itself walled in. An abstraction, breaking all ideal relations and all the influences which could reunite one determination to others, whether to other existent things or to other existences, can be so brutal that the self transforms the reason for a delay into a cause for a halt from which there is no appeal. On the transcendental plane, Kantian formalism encloses the human knowing self within an immovable structure. On the psychological plane, man groans from his solitude, which is thought of as preventing both knowledge of another self and mutual love.

The best remedy for this frequent and always pathetic form of unhappiness consists in bringing to light the difference between isolation and the sentiment of solitude. Isolation is the condition of a being which has no other being near it. This is an objective property which further presupposes an abstraction from the relation between the one and the many. Someone is isolated. On the contrary, one *concretely experiences* solitude, and one can only experience it through the dialectic which, after having affirmed the union between the self and another, ascertains the other's absence. The self knows this other to a certain degree and wishes to know him better. An obstacle intervenes and it then sacrifices dialectically the positivity of what it knows of the other to the negativity of what it does not know about the other. In fact, the skeptic himself, who claims not to know the other because he does not know him completely, acts daily, and often with joy, in foreseeing the acts of his neighbors and in sympathizing with them. But he pays more attention to his failures than to his successes. Negation is the paradoxical bias whereby a man, in the stance of theoretical knowledge, condemns that which he does not at all doubt in the course of spontaneous knowledge.

(3) *The dialectic of grief.* Never is the dialectic of separation more serious than in the process whereby we conclude

from the perceived dissolution of a cadaver that the self is annihilated. Likewise, the task of philosophy is never more difficult than when it confronts a cadaver, for at that point the problem of death arises in its manifold totality. This is not the place to broach the problem of death, but one can say that human reflection has not yet been applied to this problem with the requisite perseverance and confidence. There is no more depressing experience than the spectacle of the death of a beloved person. And too easily this depression, which is simply the sentiment of the incommensurability of the infinite to the finite, becomes the origin of a definitive trauma. So often it leads to the conviction that there is no problem of death because death is not subject to more than one interpretation.

But one can believe, on the contrary, that there must be an experience in which the negativity of determinations necessarily so concentrates its influence that the self concretely experiences both the decaying of the object and the radical impotence of limited existence to maintain itself as existence apart from infinite existence. That is, one can believe that there must be a negative pole to which God presents himself as a positive pole. One can believe that there must be some situation in which, as the hero testifies, the option in favor of value can disengage itself from all compromise with the specific interest of the man who chooses. If a man, when confronted by death, discredits human existence by reducing it to the status of an illusion, he confers upon the givens of perception and on our natural dialectics an absolute reality and truth. This is to ontologize determination. However, not only is it the vocation of existence to prevail over determination, but existence can do so only by an act of faith in absolute value as the principle of everything which experience offers or can offer. It is this act of faith which death requires of us. This act of faith is mixed in with that which we renew in the various moments of our existence when we affirm with effort and trust that matter is designed to stimulate and serve the expansion of the Spirit, in God and in us. "Necessity suffocates the self," Kierkegaard wrote. Death opens the window.

B

57. *The degradation of the self into coenesthesia*

There is *knowledge* of man, and it is inseparable from the goal of value. It is therefore philosophy itself. But one can try to substitute here a *science* of man by prolonging the naturalization of the self we have seen begun in common thought. As a sample of these scientific dialectics, we will consider here only the process whereby, explicitly or implicitly, so many "psychologists" rid themselves of the self and its liberty *by reducing it to its coenesthesia.*

This reduction takes place in two moments: The first moment is *an existential retrospection* that distends and freezes existence, which is turned toward the future when the love of value animates it, so that there is nothing to investigate except a complicated spectacle whose content excludes initiative. The second moment is a dialectic of *scientific explication through analysis and composition* which reduces existence to being merely the jumbled reflection of organic, localized determinations.

Retrospection is the attitude which determination imposes on consciousness when consciousness sets out to delimit existence. Existence cannot be determined and defined without thereby becoming something past. When preoccupation with constructing a psychology on the model of physics takes hold of the psychologist, he finds himself in the paradoxical situation of having to apply to existence those procedures which help the physicist specify determination. Like the physicist, he uses retrospection, and thus adulterates existence as retrospection is bound to do. When existence is inspired by value, it is prospective. It tends toward tomorrow, explores the void of the future, and begins to create. One cannot apply retrospection to existence without depriving existence of its initiative, or, if one prefers, one converts an initiative of emission into an initiative of reflection. But when one filters existence through the theoretical self, one strips existence from the so-called real self in order to observe it. The appropriate name for that existence which one wants to be well-defined is *sensation.* But since one has to distinguish existence from sensory sensations, one calls existence *common sensation,* or coenesthesia.

The originality of that sensibility devoid of determination, which we have called atmospheric, necessarily vanishes in the face of a scrutiny which tries to make it depend on determinations. Without perceiving that the meagerness of the result is a consequence of the erroneous construction of the enterprise, the psychologist can only condemn, as an illusory confusion, the jumble into which he has wandered. His particular mode of thought is scientific explication. This mode of thought never consists in starting from the determined and going to its influence, but rather consists in enclosing itself in determination to circulate there among the elements and their composites. He has to try to resolve existence into conditions, and he looks beyond what existence offers for an organism and brain. He then treats coenesthesia as simply the synthesis or complicated replica of this organism and brain. Introspection ends up as observation and psychology is annihilated. Psychology is now merely a chapter of physics. Or it would be such a chapter if the very functional complexity of the brain did not manifest the prevalence of unitive existence over its structure, and if the self were not to be found precisely where it surpasses structural or nonstructural limits in order to form new relationships whose influence on the past and especially on the body is unforeseeable in virtue of the body alone.

The necessary consequence of these two processes is that coenesthesia is merely something fabricated and passive. It is such, in fact, insofar as existence undergoes the influence of determinations and the more so as the relation between determination and existence establishes the prevalence of the former over the latter, as happens in the case of those subjects whom psychiatrists study. Here, as everywhere, science shows that it springs from the humbling of consciousness by obstacle. Take the case of a man who does not know how to regulate social and corporeal determinations because he is locked within himself and struggles with himself. His physician will adopt the minimum objective, namely, to readapt the patient to his surroundings. He reduces the influence of the determinations he can handle on the existence of the patient.

But even supposing that one defines the ill consciousness as an originality which does not succeed in blending into the social forms, such a consciousness still presupposes the reality, if not the value, of coenesthesia, since coenesthesia is capable of introducing disorder into the public life of the individual. To the effects which the organic functions would produce without it, there are now added those which result from their concourse in and through this coenesthesia. One can distinguish between that which yields the physical theory concerning visual images and the effects which this image produces through the intermediary of a human consciousness. One cannot so distinguish between the effects of organic activity and those of coenesthesia. Coenesthesia is an obstinate and therefore positive fact.

In the socially normal man, coenesthesia gives way to self-sufficiency, and the more moral he is, the more this is the case. It has already been shown that the *I* indiscriminately allows for either the prevalence of the content of experience over its unity, i.e., knowledge, or the inverse prevalence, i.e., action. The reduced *I* is the transcendental apperception. The higher, sovereign *I* is God. Similarly, even if the self has to submit to the influence of determinations, it can and does impose its authority on them.

In this glory of self-sufficiency which is expressed on the intellectual plane by the affirmation of autonomy of which reason is the symbol, intimacy should no longer be called coenesthesia, for it is invention. The reign of medicine and psychiatry has had the serious consequence of reducing life to its functions of repair and maintenance. Mediocrity here is taken as an ideal. Equilibrium is taken as the totality of value. But with reference to invention, repairing is secondary. By offering duty as the mediation between what is quantified [1] and love, morality promotes the conversion of coenesthesia to creation. It is foolish to struggle with medical means against tuberculosis if morality and religion do not inspire in men a horror for alcohol as well as for all degrading poisons. It is absurd to ask an army for security if one does not promote any of the sentiments which prevent a people from sacrificing its birthright to avarice or to pleasure. When value sustains existence, coenesthesia is changed into synergy. In this aspect, it is impossible to confine coenesthesia either within the limits of the body or in matter. Memories, ideas, possibilities, and hypotheses introduce non-being here in a hundred forms. The action of the ensemble of these memories, ideas, possibilities, and hypotheses on these individual contributions modifies them, orients them, and adds intentions which they cannot explain. One can explain only the determined by the determined. It is not the body which makes the spirit, but the spirit which makes the body.

That this creation is not an emanation *ex nihilo* follows immediately from the fact that the self is not God. Thus it will always be possible to find some aspect of negativity whereby the self is reduced to determination. Determinism is always true

1. Le Senne's word here is *grandeur.*—Trans.

of our impotences. But since impotence has absolutely no meaning except in relation to potency, it would be a betrayal of the reality of the self to transform the limitations of its originality into reasons for totally rejecting its originality. That cannot happen. The selfsame scientist, at the very moment when he takes himself or another self as object, pursues an existential destiny with reference to which his analyses and their results are simply means.

Naturalization and object. All dialectics which consist in degrading determination from being a plea for sympathy into an element of an impersonal given end up preventing the communion of the self with the other, whether animal, man, or God. Such dialectics therefore introduce intimate separation. They obstruct spiritual convergence. It does not follow, though, that these dialectics rupture the relation between God and the self. As has been said, not only must communion be sought at a lower level so long as existence continues, but the self, in reducing itself to nature, still falls under divine authority, though now in another manner. At each instant in our relations with men we treat others both as objects which we think about and in whose regard we employ laws to orient them to our ends, and as subjects whom we love and whose expansion we want to assist. Likewise, the man who progressively materializes himself through dialectics of naturalization, who converts his creative and beneficent initiative into sterile or destructive passivity, becomes an object in the world which is presented outwardly to God and to others as a nature to be treated technically. The mutual refusal of sympathy culminates in war. War is that relation in which the other is perceived more than loved.

58. *Reappraisal*

The dialectics of naturalization, which tend to reduce the self to the body and to kill the body, have as their necessary counterpart the dialectics of deliverance, which make use of the negation found in determination to liberate the spirit both from slavery to categories and from servitude to perception. But since it is not the case that by a reverse shock the liberation of the spirit dissolves categories and perception, it is appropriate not to condemn unreservedly those dialectics which lead to the study of and esteem for determinations, since determinations are those things which intervene to define the situation whereby God incarnates himself in the self.

Here we come to *the value of obstacle*. If obstacle necessarily, though in a changed condition, lives on within our experience, it is not only in the negative sense that limited consciousness can do no better. It is also in the positive sense that obstacle is the indispensable condition for *any intellectual dialectic to become a real process*. By thrusting itself upon us, it protects us from falling into inertia. By imposing its presence on the free flight of our spirit, it mediates the conversion which leads us from the ideality of an abstract philosophy to the seriousness of lived action. Any philosophy can be the consequence of an evasion which replaces moral life with its conceptual phantom and love of value with the idea of value. Thus it would become an aesthetic. Obstacle is the concrete test of our sincerity. *The essence of an activity loved in view of the value which it appropriates is that the self does not engage in it to receive profit from it but rather to devote itself to it.* It is to be hoped that men do not have to sacrifice themselves. But when they love they are ready to do so, knowing that the bitterness of their sacrifice will be dissolved in the joy in which love will inundate them. Prior to obstacle, value is merely an idea, an ideal, almost a pretext to avoid seeking value. In the face of obstacle, the self gives expression to its profound choice. *If it is ready to risk, to give, to suffer loss for value, it is engaged.* And what was hitherto only a theoretical object on the surface of the public self, an exhortation to others and a sublimation, becomes first in the heart of the intimate self, and soon in its expanded and manifest free flight *that experience in which experience creates itself.*

This is because every dialectic, taken apart from others, is a fiction. Even if consciousness gives itself over to a dialectic, it will soon wander into an emotional path. Every error consists in erring. Every dialectic is an odyssey, always pushed away from Ithaca. By halting this wandering, obstacle obliges the self to modify a particular dialectic with others, and these others by still others, to the point that their union objectively assures the order which permits action and subjectively assures the convergence of directions and forces without which this union could not arise and develop. In those souls and at those moments in which ideas and existences merge in value, in which the will and duty cancel each other and find completion in love and creation, one rediscovers at the core of actuality the radiation of creative Goodness. Salvation is beloved and generous activity. By reason of the balancing of dialectics and processes, creative Goodness is a poising, an equilibrium, a mean. By reason of the confluence of the energies which these dialectics and processes refract, it is ardor.

7 / The Principal Phases of Human Experience

59. *The three phases*

IF EVERY DESCRIPTION brings together ascertainment and evaluation, then the relation between God and the self, inferred by the *I* from the experience of determination and value, necessarily presents itself as the principle of a division between diverse phases of experience. Experience confers existential verification on this division. The opposition between obstacle, which manifests to every self *the prevalence of determination over existence,* and expansion, which on the contrary makes one concretely experience *the triumph of existence over determination,* is expressed for everyone in the opposition between two phases which we call *compulsion* and *inspiration.* If these two phases were absolutely foreign to each other, experience would be split from top to bottom, and such a condition would exclude the *I.* The relation-soul, of which these phases are the existential modes, must therefore reunite these phases by means of a connection. The essence of this connection is the preservation of the relation-soul's aspect of being the thought relation, the objective mediation, the transition between the self's destitution and the existential identification of God and the soul through value. One can call that phase, whose ideal expression is the thought duality of object and subject, either *cold knowledge* or existence-which-is-nothing-but-existence. Affectivity expresses the relation of the self to its content. Within the scope of compulsion, this is an affectivity marked by a negative sign, an affectivity of repulsion, of repugnance. Cold knowledge guards against the self's impulsiveness. But there is still, in the soul which is weakened and scattered among the objects of perception by cold knowledge, either a nostalgia for the half-ideal, half-lived spontaneity which preceded the emergence of obstacle, or the desire for an inspiration in the course of which mediation disappears within immediacy and belief and credibility merge in the passion of a conviction with no looking back to the past and with no impatience for the future.

A

60. *Compulsion*

From the standpoint of determinations, compulsion presents itself as the oppression of the self by a situation which is both confining and menacing. When the self can bring two terms into opposition, for example, a mass pressing against an arm which is pushing it away, in such a way as to convert the brutal stalemate [*l'arrêt*] into a theoretical conflict, it has started to intellectualize compulsion. There is no more compulsion, only an attenuated memory of it. Ethics, whose essence is commandment, presupposes that the pressure of determinations has been weakened and that the self has recovered the semiautonomy of the will. *Compulsion is found prior to this attenuation.* The worker whose arm is actually caught in a gear cannot consider his arm and the machine simply as two objects distinct from himself whose conflict he can gaze on as an uninvolved spectator. Compulsion has suffering as its inner core. In common with suffering it has the essence of being insupportable, of not permitting a reduction which would turn it into nothing but a perception, a name, or an idea. Suffering cannot become a fortunate warning or a good suffering until it has ceased being compulsion.

One can even say that compulsion precedes the distinction between physical and moral pain. Pain, like pleasure, is physical by reason of a localization which makes it the halo of some determination. Pain is a "titillation," unquestionably disagreeable or agreeable depending on whether it is constant or intermittent and on its intensity. Physical pain presupposes discrimination, is the object of perception, and calls for a local remedy. Moral pain likewise shows the influence of an idea. A mother, crushed by the news that the ship on which she believes her son has sailed has been totally lost, revives on learning that he missed its sailing. Prior to the scientific or ethical determination of intelligence, brute suffering is not thought about. It cries out. Brute suffering is an existence, *the atmosphere of a lacerating,* differently nuanced depending on whether accident colors it with disappointment, or obstruction colors it with fury, or conflict colors it with disarray. The determinations within which existence is set produce compulsion.

The *description of compulsion* assigns the following characteristics to it. The more imperious they are the easier they are to recognize:

(1) The first characteristic is *impulsiveness.* Compulsion makes it very difficult for the self to control by its will the energies which compulsion sets in motion. The reflexes of destruction, hostility, panic, and flight are practical manifestations of compulsion. Compulsion delivers the self over to a passivity toward its nature. It quashes higher motions in favor of lower motions, the more spiritual motions in favor of the more organic ones, love in favor of fear. Obstacle acts here like a shock provoking an explosion, when nothing but the "state of affairs" determines whether it channels or scatters the liberated energy. At the peak of its intensity compulsion produces actions whose ordinary characteristic is to run directly counter to help from another. It diminishes the assessment of the self's value. And if the sharpness of suffering and restlessness did not enrage the self's feelings and did not heighten its power to spread its feelings to others, one would think that man was reduced to the blind causality of an organism.

(2) The second characteristic of compulsion is that the self, in its communication with others, *gains in atmospheric efficacy what it loses in intellectual and practical efficacy.* A cry, which is an intense form of prayer, conveys an emotional contagion which makes panic the most formidable of the epidemics of negation. When compulsion takes hold of a people, it causes intellectual quarrels to disappear, welds individuals into a group, and makes them desire a chief. But all this takes place for the sake of acts of defense, battle, and destruction. Compulsion leads the self back to its body. The self barricades itself in its body. And destruction shows others the prevalence

of self-love over love. The Erostratus complex is the reduction of negation as means to negation as end. When a tendency has a hold on someone to such an abnormally exclusive extent that everything that happens hurts him, that tendency holds him in a state of compulsion. And destruction manifests in one who destroys a hatred-for-missed-value. For such a man, destruction serves to reflect his power more effectively than creation could. Indeed, he is incapable of creation. For it is unquestionable that destruction, which replaces a here and now localized determination with a void, establishes itself with a distinctiveness unmatched by the creator's mark upon his creation, for creation is the more spiritual the more it consists in the atmosphere of value with which it impregnates men and things.

(3) By shrinking the self's horizon, *compulsion contracts the self's intentions.* The essence of the lavalike atmosphere of compulsion is that one faces it day by day without large thoughts or long-range projects. One no longer cares for anything but to stay alive. The psychology of the will has almost always reduced the will to those easy volitions in which the connivance of external conditions permits us at our whim to do this or that, as for example to open or close an electric switch. On a billiard table, every ball can roll just as easily in any direction. As elaborated in theoretic leisure, the psychology of man consists in thinking "flat." But this isotropism, manifesting as it does the intention which moves thought toward purity, is partial and false when compared to our experience of willing. We would not have to will unless some obstacle intervened to interrupt our free flight. The more serious the obstacle, the more is volition extorted from us. To will is always therefore to pay. When compulsion presses upon us, we sell our kingdom for a horse. How can one hope that men's will at the onset of a war will dominate the storm? Each can think only about protecting himself from the rumbling menaces. And it is a divinization of the political leaders to attribute to them more responsibility than is attributed to the population as a whole.

(4) One of the most important effects of compulsion is, through the restriction of clear consciousness, *to remove from consciousness all power of analyzing the postulates of the present action.* It is out of the ordinary for scientists to interrupt a scientific study to ask themselves whether science does or does not produce happiness for men. Nor is it usual that

in a general meeting the administrators of an industrial complex interrupt their annual report to ask whether it is appropriate to devote their lives to the pursuit of profit. Still, they could do so. For if it is true that there must be some compulsion so that science and industry can exist, compulsion is nevertheless at some distance, in the wings. When compulsion becomes imminent, the possibility of such reflection becomes an impossibility. The soldier, faced with a threatening enemy, can no longer ask whether war, or this particular war, is unjust. In opposition to cold knowledge, compulsion has the characteristic, which it shares with inspiration, of being an existential sufficiency. But it is oriented toward negation instead of toward creation.

(5) The most noble function of analysis is to multiply the determinations which permit us to communicate more and more intimately with someone else. By restricting analysis, compulsion *reduces sympathy*. Instead of sympathy's intervening as the means of spiritual assimilation with a complex and precious intimacy, as the means of an ennoblement, it is now nothing but, for want of subtlety in perception, the exchange of a practical impulse. It follows, then, that instead of elevating the given as far as possible from the realm of the impersonal toward the realm of what is personal [*vers le nominatif*], compulsion sets everything in opposition to us. The sign of this condition is a contempt for both our own human dignity and that of others.

While inspiration is greater than the will, pure compulsion precedes the reign of the will and is thus essentially negation. Intimately, compulsion is the negation of self in suffering. When it reacts to what is outside, it is the negation of those determinations which oppress the self. Compulsion precipitates and abridges our sentiment of time by multiplying events, by preventing us from uniting them, by reducing the present as far as possible to the instantaneous. At its lower limit, compulsion establishes the atomicity of time which makes each instant the negation of other instants, whereas at its higher limit, where consciousness becomes coextensive with the entirety of experience, the instant becomes a point in eternity. Compulsion makes determination more negative than positive. Affirmation is directed by it *against* other selves and things. Rendering acceptance impossible, demanding that man both depreciate the other and reprove himself, being the source of murders and suicides, suffering acknowledges that value is absolute. But it does so to acknowledge that it itself is deprived of value. As value invincibly attracts one who opens himself by turning away from strife, so suffering invincibly represses whomever it afflicts, to the extent that, in compulsion, value concentrates itself in the acts of the hero who converts energy for flight into energy for defense, more for others than for himself, and leads the unleashed forces back to the control of the will. It is no mere chance that has often led Durkheim to justify his social objectivism with examples drawn from a crowd. In compulsion, every society becomes a crowd, either chaotic or military. Either disorder or discipline converts the self here into something material.

In cold knowledge, a *cause* is the recollection of an obstacle to which compulsion gives weight. A cause gets its three characteristics from compulsion, namely, the characteristic of being independent of the self, then that of being isolated from the collection of things from which it is usually indiscernible, and finally that of presenting itself as having the power in its own right to produce the effect. If, in fact, the cause were under the control of the self and expressed the self's power, far from being a cause which would have to be noticed and whose effect would have to be submitted to, it would not even be a means, for means always impose their own duration. The cause would be swallowed up in the free flight of the spirit. Thus the cause has meaning only as the objective, determined counterpart of the self's impotence. It is impossible to make the cause completely foreign to us, for in a perfectly or even partially systematized world, the cause could not be distinguished from actions which are formed in it. How would one break up their solidarity? If the solidarity splits here or there, it is because reality is not a thing, a block, but a relation which allows for disjunctions and liaisons. By its negativity, determination when submitted to as cause expresses the limitation of the self; but by reason of its positivity, determination is open to the appeal of value. However, just as in compulsion the self has the sad concrete experience of its weakness, so it must interpret this appeal as an absolute necessity. Thus it separates causation from the radiation of the Spirit in order to make causation a property of matter.

Malebranche gave preeminence to the positive rather than to the negative aspect of causality by concentrating causality in God. But this idea, if taken alone, risks making God the center of a nature. Further, this idea destroys and dissolves the cause, for cause always presupposes a frustrated expectation, a brusque deviation, a variation of vitality, some rupture in inertia. Spontaneity and inspiration do not know cause. In the depths of spontaneity, causality is utilized without being recognized. In inspiration, causality is subordinated to the self's free flight. Cause only appears at that point where compulsion, by attenuating its pressure, allows the self to reach theoretical knowledge. But the characteristics which theoretical knowledge retains from compulsion reveal its historical origin. Science labors at a distance from eruptions, but it is only understood in their wake. Science makes men free, but these men are not born free.

It is description's task to recognize the consequences of compulsion and suffering in the self. The traumas of compulsion leave behind complexes whose influence will be good or bad depending on the use which the self makes of them. Suffering will be open to a revivification which will be to the revocation of the situation of compulsion what atmosphere is to detail. In the course of this revivification, suffering will be attenuated and modified in such a way that it can eventually become the source of artistic or religious emotions. But through this transfiguration, which makes it lovable to consciousness, suffering will lose its essence, which is to prevent one from consenting to it.

A more developed description is possible only in connection with the consideration of characters.[1] Between the extravert of weak emotivity, in whom the sentiment of existence dissipates at almost every moment into thought about determinations, and the introvert of profound affectivity, whose sentiments as a consequence of a strong congenital or acquired inactivity cannot be diverted into action and which get entangled in intimate rumination, there are interspersed so many degrees and modes of sensibility that suffering necessarily always and in various ways oscillates between the scarcely felt incompatibility between two determinations and that constriction of the soul in extreme compulsion which

1. Le Senne is here referring to the study of characterology.—Trans.

leaves open scarcely any possibility but suicide. From one extreme to the other, suffering can depress or exalt, turn into egotism or change to love, serve prudence or unleash fury, suggest irony or inflame indignation, convince one of the perverseness of man or lead back to God, inspire courage or deepen cowardice. The outcome depends on what the self and value decide. When religion fulfills its mission it converts suffering from negative and destructive energy into the source of love and beneficence.

B

61. *Cold knowledge*

Compulsion does not allow one to conceive of ennui, which is disaffection with regard to all determinations. Ennui is a consequence of security. In fact, compulsion crystallizes determinations at this point so that every atmosphere appears to be torn up by them. How could the most insipid of experiences be foreshadowed in the most searing of concrete experiences? But the fact is that in compulsion any harbor which offers us calm waters attracts us as the locus of definitive salvation. In such a case it seems that it is enough for existence just to exist. Few joys are more prized than the influence exercised on us by the termination of a danger, convalescence, the healing of an infant, or an armistice.

The recollection of compulsion and its constraints contains the reflection of these releases from compulsion in such a way that the majority of men are more sensitive to the advantage of escaping an evil than to that of attaining a good. Bentham observed that the good itself provokes more effort if the question is of preventing its loss rather than of acquiring it. Workers who would not strike to get an additional dollar an hour would do so in order not to lose twenty-five cents. Determination makes its weight felt in action as in knowledge. Most men's lives are one long act of distrust, haunted by anxiety for security and impeded by impulsions arising from accidents. Rare are those whose action is inspired not by impulses animated by fear but by impulses animated by love for value. Most men live drawn up into an attitude of defense, which expresses itself in negative sentiments, judgments, and acts. Realism draws its strength from that intimate weakness of the soul which ends up esteeming the blows it gets and adoring the hand that delivers them.

When the restrictions are relaxed, when by a fortunate reaction or another's concern the self has left the tumult which the disorder of determinations stirred up in it, the phase of mediation into which it enters has as its essence these two characteristics: (*a*) the characteristic of placing, so to speak, *on an equal footing, on the same level, the perceiving self and the intimate self,* the object and the subject; and (*b*) the characteristic of transporting, after suitable adaptation, *onto the plane of abstract intelligence* the givens of lived experience and then "categorizing" them.

These two characteristics are discovered during the existential conversion which inaugurates this phase. The conversion begins when the self, while believing it is remaining faithful to its unitary and atmospheric experience—which, however tortured it may be, always keeps it at the center of existence—replaces it with the sheerly conceptual duality of object and subject. This is an extraordinary conversion. Here the object ceases to be a lived object, since it loses its original nature of being obstacle, and the subject becomes another object, forgetting its own vulnerability and initiative. One could not more radically distort experience. But theoretical knowledge can now begin. Tarrying appears when lived experience cools. "I am seated here, before the fire, in my robe." [2] Is it mere jesting to say that this is the most important phrase in the *Meditations*? The phrase supposes a man removed from danger and ready to distribute the givens of existence among two substances.

Tarrying permits the easy but rootless rotation from the determinations of the public self to the existence of the intimate self. "That exists" has as its counterpart "I exist." In compulsion, the self is, as it were, projected outside of value, knocked hither and thither by determinations. In inspiration, the self is identified with value. In the interval between almost pure materiality, in which the soul is scarcely more than the impotent reflection of things, and almost pure spirituality, in which things are grounded in the passion of the soul, intel-

2. Descartes, *Meditations touchant la première philosophie, Oeuvres,* ed. Charles Adam and Paul Tannery (Paris, 1896), Meditation I, IX, 13–18.

lectual activity defines a middle region in which the play of signs and images replaces danger and enthusiasm. These two movements seem to reduce each other, to balance each other, to neutralize each other. In compulsion, the self is almost completely passive, affected, a slave of the object. In inspiration, the self is almost exhaustively active, triumphant. It absorbs the object. In the intermediary state of tranquillity, the subject is, by virtue of science, simply the reflection of things, and, in art, things are nothing but images of the self.

That philosophy has most often described only this middle phase follows directly from the fact that theoretical knowledge is enclosed within this phase. Theoretical knowledge must maintain itself at equal distances from unfavorable temperatures. It must quasi-officially distrust extreme experiences. Since the process whereby the spirit penetrates into cold knowledge replaces the existential unity of experience with the duality of two thoughts, a duality which once again objectivizes the subject and separates the self from the *I* so as to make the self a pure determination, it is natural for philosophy to manifest the tendency to replace the relation-soul with the ideal connection of two intelligible determinations. In sum, for Descartes the same system of relations constitutes, on the one hand, the intelligible structure of matter and, on the other hand, the mathematical physics freeing itself in the human spirit from the scattering effect of confusion. The relation of the object to the subject, or, to use Cartesian language, of the formal to the objective, is converted here into an identity which is such that one is surprised to find that it has been gone beyond. Knowledge here is a one-to-one correspondence. But the paradox is that knowledge makes the knower as well as the known an object.

This transformation is equivalent to a *depersonalization*. There is now nothing but determinations alternately qualified as subjectivities and objectivities. One admires the fact that matter and spirit correspond to each other, while forgetting that this correspondence is procured too facilely by means of the identity of the dialectic which has distinguished and opposed and determined them. Every determination is transferable, transmissible. A determination can pass from spirit to spirit, from hand to hand. It can be given and received. An idea is carried over from one discourse to another. A thing is transported from place to place. Intimacy, on the contrary, is inalienable. Intimacy is what we rediscover in its source when, appropriating to ourselves through imagination other determinations than those which are now ours and grounding them in a continuous thrust, we concretely experience that incommunicable contact with the absolute existence which is the *I* of the self. Cold knowledge diverts us from eternal and living actuality. In place of the sentiment of existence, which is searing in compulsion and passionate in inspiration, cold knowledge substitutes the petty emotion which accompanies the judgment "I exist." But this I now has little more to it than the universality of "anyone whatsoever" in the frigidity of a knowledge of slight interest to it. And this existence is little more than a word. The self is no longer thought of except as an arithmetical unity interchangeable with every other self. It is merely another name for objective unity, like a token or identification papers. Everything is prepared to become matter for an industrial technique.

This juxtaposition of determination without hostility and an observer without psychology is the phase in which we ordinarily spend the greatest part of our existence. The principal sign of this is *the intellectualization of perception.* Perception and idea have some common characteristics. These are characteristics of determination. But when determination is perceived and not merely thought, it is because we feel ourselves still stopped by it, excluded from it, repulsed, in the presence of an exterior object, as Hermite vividly expressed it to Stieltjes [3] when he wrote him that in his analyses he had the feeling of working on material things. But the more a thing is known, taken apart, and put back together by the spirit, made into an idea or an image, the more it is stripped of its hostility and exteriority. The phase of cold knowledge, then, is that phase of either trivial or important reflection which strings together useless bits of knowledge as readily as it constructs theories and techniques. In its imitating function, intellectualism sketches the plan for an order or the sequence of a story from which violence and love are excluded for the benefit of science and law. Intellectualism is established as much in the periods or places in which fatigue has dulled the passions as in those periods and places in which mediocrity has replaced noble and ambitious calculations with petty ones.

3. Hermite and Stieltjes were mathematicians.—Trans.

This intellectualization reduces the object to relations and the subject to the action-depending-on-relations, i.e., to the will. In the meeting of the intelligible with the willing, *technicity* [*technicité*] arises. Technicity becomes the ideal of consciousness instead of remaining its servant. One aims to adapt men reciprocally to as impoverished an intimacy as possible and also to machine tools, laws, and theories. Technique serves both these ends. On the one hand, the self receives from technique the perceptions whose concatenation constitutes the periodicity of organic and social life. The self will move from one food to another, from one sleep, one source of income, or one newspaper to another. Consciousness will form for itself the ideal of a world so exactly regulated that the self would merely have to receive favorable perceptions and produce easy volitions. This is the perceptual self. Value is no longer encountered except under the degenerate form of competency. The attenuation of affectivity in the course of a life which can be neither dramatic nor lyric will at the same time exclude the disorders of passion and the ambitions whereby a man goes beyond the concern for proximate and egotistical interests. On its own side, the intimate self gets its share of the artistic technique which debases beauty to the least common denominator so that beauty is procured without effort or pain. The self converts suffering and heroism into harmless diversions and sources of emotions. Luxury is found in the encounter of these two techniques. Consciousness believes that it has diverted itself here from the sentiment of the infinite.

The degradation of philosophy into positivism is the intellectual equivalent of *the degradation of the spirit into civilization* considered apart from the intimate value of souls. The positivity of value is reduced to that of determinations. Attention-to-existence is eclipsed by attention-to-things. The only reality one believes in is that which one sees or touches. Sentiment is transformed into abstract thought and corporeal actions in such a way that the spiritual energy of the soul is now reduced to the material energy of intellectual and practical mobility. Man undergoes a kind of centrifugation. His limbs supply the movement and the brain supplies their motor connections. But this cannot happen without the industrialized affectivity leaving behind itself an unclear power whose eruptions are dreaded.

Throughout the course of existence-which-is-only-existence there persists at least a dull apprehension of the stirrings of affectivity. Such an existence defends itself against affectivity with science, cynicism, sarcasm, or irony, all of which have the common trait of going back toward determinations. But as one cannot go back toward determinations without going from God to the natural and limited self, this return reveals the profound sadness that existence-which-is-only-existence conceals. This is the sadness of machines, the sadness of the worker, the sadness of formalities without soul, the sadness of art reduced to diversion. The distrust directed toward metaphysics and mysticism is not enough to suppress altogether the powers it does not appreciate.

The phase of cold knowledge is *more favorable to communication among persons than to their communion.* It is intellectual, but it is spiritual only in the smallest possible degree. Cold knowledge is directed toward determination. Determination allows men to communicate but presupposes their separation. Cold knowledge facilitates those social contacts which are of the order of conversation and traffic. Standing between war, where determinations present themselves to the belligerents as obstacles, and love, which grounds determinations in the union of hearts, existence-which-is-only-existence is a kind of commerce. It sustains itself in the drawing room, in the market place, in the street. The State, which is the system of mediations according to which the members of a society harmonize their thought relations, is on a kind of plateau. But this plateau is descended from when the spontaneity of consciousnesses calls into question the postulates of its existence, and it is ascended from when souls, independently of all social connections, unite with one another in love. The animal and the criminal are both below the State. The free man, the saint, and the genius are above the State. Woman, whose existential profundity is essentially antijuridical, is both below and above it. The State is at every moment the compromise between necessities which presuppose human imperfection and ideals which are the ideal projections of value.

Attitudes of the self toward determination. The whole development leading from compulsion to inspiration may be summed up in the story of determination. In its initial moment, in *obstacle*, determination presents itself as an almost unanalyzed unity whose essence is to exclude the self from itself. As soon as it is named and recognized as the cause of compulsion, it begins to be an idea. But insofar as compulsion remains, it is because determination is still *an oppressive determination*. The intimate self responds to it with repugnance. And the impulsive movements whereby it seeks to free itself from this determination manifest both the brutality of the object and the suffering of the subject. One could consider the passage from obstacle to *objection* as the mitigation of brutality and suffering. Objection is distinguished from obstacle by its intellectual character. It calls forth nothing more than a refutation.

Objection prepares for the intellectualization of determination, and this is a mediative form of its spiritualization. To go from the crushed self, which admits to being in the position of an absolutely unknowable thing in itself, to the self's glory, which presupposes that the spirit has made the determinations intimate, one must pass through the mediation of cold knowledge. First, the determination, made more intelligible through analysis, presents itself as an idea, a formal system. Now it is no longer merely an *object*. It no longer blocks the self as an obstacle does. Rather, determination offers itself to the self as a spectacle. And, if it reminds one of its origin, it does so insofar as it is still felt to be independent of the self. At this stage *determination* has become *ostensive*. It offers itself to verification and analysis. The self's attitude changes from repugnance to investigation. Investigation is essentially a matter of looking. All fears and all passions are reduced now to curiosity and ingeniousness. Imperceptibly, the self becomes disinterested in value. Value is found there only under the intellectualized and minimal form of the lack of contradiction, which is the permission to link together, as opposed to harmony, which is the enjoyment of the most intimate and easy unification. Scientific systematization is confined between the order which starts it and the order which is supposed to perfect it.

The passage from cold knowledge to inspiration requires the animation of intimacy. Intimacy is expressed on the plane of determinations by replacing the formal idea with the relation. The unquestionable superiority of an intellectualism of relation over an intellectualism of idea lies in the fact that in giving mobility to the idea it renders it homogeneous to the spirit. Undoubtedly, no definite relation can be the spirit itself, for the spirit is infinite relation. But the outline of an operation is already close to the operation itself. And, further, to be distinguished within the spirit, a relational operation need not oppose itself to the spirit. The idea is an object. The relation imperceptibly ceases to be an object to the degree that it becomes intricate and animated.

At this moment, *determination* changes from being ostensive to being *propulsive*. It contributes to the advancement of the spirit. The more it changes from an intellectual dialectic into an emotional process the more it becomes indistinguishable from the total passion of the self, which is now participating more and more in value. The infection of dialectical operations, if value assists it, is inspiration itself. Intellectualism remains true, but it is no longer that simplified and debased intellectualism which claims to reduce divine intelligence, impregnated as it is with the infinite, to the poor, schematic movements of human intelligence. If a meeting between human and divine intelligence is possible, it is because a judiciously used dialectic, which is abstract from our viewpoint, can be inserted into an ensemble whose echoing can extend indefinitely in experience.

The psychophysiological parallelism. It is appropriate to underline the influence of the spectator attitude on the theories which are the expressions of this attitude. One finds at once the duality of the thought object and subject in the psychophysiological parallelism according to which objective psychology defines the relation between body and spirit. By observation one constructs a series of corporeal events, and by an introspection which imitates observation one constructs another series of mental events. Then one establishes a one-to-one correspondence between them. One can admit that this schema allows for certain useful systematizations here and there, though this utility has been more often asserted than verified. But that this intellectual and practical success has any philosophical value is something which must always be challenged. The parallelism effects the reduction to determinations. And this is precisely the act of science. But this taking sides has such grave consequences and so brutally falsifies experience that it cannot be accepted without criticism.

First of all, this partiality is dangerous in that it cannot lead to two series of determinations without entailing the prevalence of the organic series over the other. By nature, definite, rigid, resistant determinations are matter itself. Matter, then, must be found in the mental series as well as in the organic. Everything which opposes intimacy to determinations, namely, intimacy's essence of being absolute, its atmospheric continuity, its incommunicability, eventually its initiative, and above all its homogeneity with value, has been volatilized by discrimination, which replaces intimacy with a series of determinations. If one further observes that science explains the lower series, the bodily series, by building from the simple to the multiple, i.e., by going from the bottom upward, then the lower series, that of the body, has to be the reason for the higher series, the series of the spirit. How then will this parallelism remain an exclusively technical postulate? To replace the spirit with what it is not amounts to denying it. Parallelism imperceptibly turns into epiphenomenalism, just as the influence of positivism is not distinguished from that of materialism.

Thus it is important to expose the peculiarity and, when it is forgotten, the partiality of the phase, of the mental attitude, and of the dialectic which leads to parallelism. Our experience is not definable by means of the ideal relation between two series of determinations, as can be done with the frames of a film and their image on a screen. Our experience is constituted by the relation of existence to determinations. And existence is the infinite which one can never do more than merely begin to plumb. Every human act is an original mode of existence. Description can do no more than catch some expressions of existence and take note of some of its attitudes. If the parallelist scheme is appropriate to certain expressions and attitudes of existence, it is appropriate only to the most impoverished ones, those which most minimize the spirit's liberty, those which happen to be most imitative and apish. Art provides us with the symbol of victories, where organic or extraorganic determination is nothing more than the docile instrument and even the supple and indistinguishable content of the spirit. When the spirit elevates itself to its most exalted experiences, of which art furnishes merely the model, the whole of reality bends and submits to its hegemony. But how will the scientist account for precisely those phases in which cold knowledge is impossible? To know through the senses, to see, is to place oneself outside of what one sees.

Yet science cannot deny what its essence and its postulates prevent it from reaching without becoming fictitious and vain. It is not enough for knowledge to be faithful to its postulates. It must also ruminate on reality. What value requires us to seek is not *knowledge*, but *important knowledge*, and important knowledge cannot succeed in its enterprise except by multiplying the determined schemes with which it tries to embrace the infinite. Among those schemes which allow us to express rather than to exhaust man's activity, the strategic schema of Meynert has the advantage of approaching man's activity from that aspect whereby the *I* becomes self by distinguishing itself from others. Matter enters into action, as the sun and the climate do in human geography, not to predetermine man's action, as parallelism would have it, but to determine permitting conditions, conditions which close off or at least obstruct some routes while at the same time opening other routes for him. All the same, Hannibal was able to cross the Alps with his army. Whenever a man makes the consideration of his relations with others predominate over the search for value, he remains on this level. The spirit, in such cases, is a strategy. When the spirit succeeds in raising itself above these military preoccupations, and instead of contenting itself with denying and fighting against the obstacles which others put in its way it turns them around in order to try to unite them to itself in one and the same convergence of souls, then the relation between body and spirit is abolished in the triumph of the spirit, for now there are no distinct determinations. The victory of intimacy over perception turns one from the idolatrous worship of determinations toward identification with God the creator, from appearances toward the enjoyment of the absolute, from weakness or violence toward generosity, from seeing toward passion and love. Spiritualism is true by reason of the value we get in our sentiments, thoughts, and acts. In the face of spiritualism, positivism is nothing but a professional postulate.

The two atmospheres of cold knowledge. It is appropriate, therefore, to stress the insufficiency of the phase of cold knowledge and the impossibility of understanding it other than through its relation to other phases. This phase is inserted between compulsion and inspiration as, in Spinoza's objective projection of it, knowledge through common notions is inserted between imagination and intuition. It is of the essence of a mediation, even an existential one, to have no *raison d'être* except through the terms which it mediates. Those terms are already manifested by the reflections they project onto an existence which is satisfied with being existence, reflections which make clear the mediocrity of such an existence. These reflections appear either as a twilight or a dawn, depending on whether the recollection of compulsion or the presentiment of inspiration embraces existence in its atmosphere.

In fact, there is no man so professionalized, no man with a soul so cramped in a structure of postulates or rules, of conventions or habits, who does not at some time question himself about the value of what he does. This questioning is an artistic disturbance which the will provokes to extract itself from the seduction of appearances or to incite itself to invention. Man here awakens from being fascinated by something and, in rediscovering himself as man, he rediscovers the problem of his value and the problem of value itself.

Depending on whether one assigns a negative or a positive value to them, science and art express either man's unhappiness as caused by obstacle or the spirit's superiority as seen in its disengaging the idea from perception or in its transfiguring perception into a lovable image. Existence is never completely indifferent. *It is alternately dismayed and illuminated.* Sometimes existence is subjected to a reechoing of past or distant catastrophes, as is expressed by the phrase *suave mari magno*,[4] a phrase whose sweetness is peculiarly attenuated by sorrow. Sometimes existence gathers up the "echoes" of a joy to which the philosopher is necessarily a stranger insofar as he stays in the phase of cold knowledge. To the extent that it is the philosophy of determination, intellectualist objectivism is the philosophy of indifference. But absolute indifference is impossible for a man, and however weak his affectivity might be, it will color his objectivism with a tint of value, a love of order, or a preference for what is open.[5] The idea in a philosophy is an operation in the spirit of the philosopher. To the degree

4. This phrase is from Lucretius. It has the sense of how fortunate is one who is secure from the turmoil which still swirls on.—Trans.

5. Le Senne's term is *l'ouverture.* He uses it here in opposition to the closing-off brought about by determinations when they are treated as definitively set over against the spirit.—Trans.

that through this operation he mediates value, since he can receive it, he derives some joy from it. But this idea is in danger of being merely aesthetic unless intellectual dialectics involve intimacy in their movement.

One can see this point in the case of the most important classical idea, the idea of substance. Let us consider it as it operates in our experience. For a living consciousness, the affirmation of the reality of an absolute substance is nothing but an intellectual mediation whereby the self succeeds in raising itself from a phase of distress in which it feels itself to be entirely too human to a phase of confidence in which the participation in the Absolute makes it more than human. Likewise, in the ontology of Louis Lavelle, the idea of the being which is one, univocal, and universal gets its value from the fact that it allows the self to rediscover at the heart and source of its subjectivity the Act whose adequate idea of being guarantees absolute value. Thus the Act intervenes at the center of theoretical knowledge to assure the transition from a sentiment arising from distress to a sentiment arising from confidence. This Act inaugurates the spiritual convergence of all determinations into the actuality upon which they confer the benefit of their influence. When philosophy proposes to elicit action through the attraction of the infinite instead of promoting it through the horror of despair, it is at the dawn of inspiration.

But it is impossible to confuse this dawn with inspiration itself. Every philosophy necessarily looks like an aesthetic to the man who is presented with it as a systematic or mobile interplay of determinations. The intimacy of the philosopher, who converts philosophy from the model of life to life itself, reconciles the absolute to himself. But his devotion, by engaging his whole soul in the idea, makes him go beyond cold knowledge. When others, on the contrary, treat his philosophy as an exterior theoretical object, they no longer sympathize with the soul for whom it mediated happiness. That which was real for the philosopher becomes artificial for them. Whether as refuge or as virtuosity, every philosophy, insofar as personal intimacy does not pour out its passion upon it, necessarily seems to be less a method for escaping suffering through salvation than a diversion to evade reality in a dream. Just as the phase of tranquil knowledge from which objectivism proceeds offers a harbor to souls who are victims of a torment they are unable to dominate, so has objectivism often made a contribution by turning a consciousness too acquainted with the depth of evil away from despair toward a beautiful image of order.

It remains to be seen whether experience has anything better to offer man than a guard rail against vertigo. False optimism condemns value to appearing as nothing but a lively illusion. But if an illusion is such that it mediates happiness, the joy of creating, and the love of life, it is a specification of the very idea of God. Through his idea, as through every determination, God offers man salvation. As soon as man recognizes this idea, he will seek, insofar as it depends on him, to join this idea of God to that vital thrust without which the idea would be merely a substitute for an absent God, merely a negation of God's intelligible structure. Obstacle, without which the distinction between God and the idea of God could not have been made, now becomes a condition of discovery, the means whereby the self adapts God to itself in value without thereby being suspected of merely giving in to its own egotism.

Through this intimate revolution, the phase of cold knowledge which a consciousness mired in "bourgeois" laziness could make the mediocre goal of its ambition now picks itself up to become, as it were, the pivot through which the forces born of compulsion, instead of dissipating in negative acts or sterile emotions, converge in a creative inspiration. Through a synthesis which is more existential than ideal, in a process which brings together material energies and more or less voluntary dialectics, inspiration presents itself as the harmonized resultant of two earlier phases, one of which furnishes the power and the other of which furnishes the ideal means for creation. By virtue of theoretical reflection, which supplies the will with whatever intellectual and practical technique is necessary for action if it is at least kind enough to itself not to decree its own sufficiency, the will can collaborate with spontaneity. Spontaneity will then lose the dangerous characteristic, proper to its naivete, of being blind. Value will have been merited. Clear consciousness will have acquitted itself of its mission.

This description is confirmed by *the instability of the phase of cold knowledge.* This phase is the constantly threatened equilibrium between the forces which undermine the self and those which nourish it. The discrimination which descends from existence to determination can be a useful mediation. It is also always both fatigue and flight. The limited self can in no way escape from the degradation of the superior energy, for this is the law of pure materiality. The self must compensate for this degradation by conquering other finite sources of usable energy. Likewise, maintainence which is not used for creation is doomed to destruction. Wherever personal invention does not renew and fertilize the tradition, the tradition is deserted by value, and soon after by existence. The churches byzantinize themselves; teaching conserves ideas which have exhausted their fecundity; art and society are ossified into worn-out and restrictive forms; and the official masks the real until either a trivial, extrinsic accident reveals the fragility of these façades or a moral initiative rediscovers the sources of its life. When it dawdles, existence-which-is-only-existence invisibly becomes debilitated and weakened. And by creating the illusion of a nature whose necessity suffices to give us security and the illusion of a given or proximate order which is preserved for our enjoyment, existence-which-is-only-existence demoralizes men by making them forget the sacrifice, work, and love involved in every creative life.

C

62. *Inspiration*

Morality has its origin in compulsion through the act of the self which prevents compulsion from being prolonged in unreflected impulsiveness, the act which breaks with passivity and distress in order to regain control. Morality is continued in cold knowledge through the discovery of indispensable mediations. Morality finds completion in inspiration, where it terminates by losing itself in value. The will, through which all virtue begins, is still only an action of the self in and on itself, almost an action against itself. It is this limitation which gives the will its worth, since the will, in distinguishing itself from the self and the self's free flight, provides the self with the local and ostensive verification of the power which the self has by reason of pure spontaneity without knowing it. But no partial power has any value unless it mediates the entire free flight of the self. Thus duty's destination is to complete itself in happiness. If happiness does not proceed from duty, then eudaimonism would be merely a happy accident and therefore suspect. If, on the contrary, happiness is the culmination of duty, then it confirms duty's claim that it reunites us with the Absolute.

In the course of these three phases there occurs *the reversal from the extrinsic to the endogenous,* from what imposes itself on us to what radiates from us. Compulsion regrettably excludes us from reality both by making us feel it as hostile and repulsive and by reducing us, or almost reducing us, to the condition of a material object buffeted by incoherent pressures. The self finds itself in the miserable situation of an almost beaten boxer who can no longer do anything but successively move his hand to all the places where he is hit. He is reduced to transitory, passive, sterile actions. Cold knowledge forgets the brutality of the obstacle, but it is still subordinate to the determination of the object. The punch has become a given. But as every given is as such still extrinsic to that which receives it, theoretical knowledge remains faithful to the conception according to which the self is fabricated from outside, and ultimately is nothing but the location of determinations. It is the common postulate of both science and objective history, which today inspire so many of the works on man, that man is nothing more than the intersection of some necessary laws and some contingent causes.

One could not eliminate value in a more subtle and radical manner. But science itself would be condemned to wither if he who should dedicate himself to research is not ready to subordinate all his intellectual prejudices and all his private interests to the love of truth. It is from value that truth derives that sacred characteristic which demands absolute respect from us. But as truth would be identical with falsity if it were not thinkable by us, it must bear the mark of our limitation. This fact establishes the negativity of the determinations which constitute it. Every human truth can then be only an aspect of the absolute truth, and absolute truth must be pure value since it is necessarily free from determination. Each truth separated from others becomes false. The human spirit diffracts absolute truth like a prism which divides light into colors. The love of truth is the impatience to arrange truths in order to obtain an image of reality at once more and more dense and more and more simple. It is therefore the love of God which animates the love of truth. And the disinterestedness without which intellectual effort is destined to dry up is inseparable from the devotion to value through which the self expands by successively surpassing its limits. The recurrent danger of pure intellectualism is that it does not consider men. And without considering them, ideas are either powerless or murderous.

Technique, even coarse technique, that which is appropriate to brute matter, furnishes the tools for the *activity of determination* which is proper to cold knowledge. To the degree that value insinuates itself into this activity, e.g., bringing genius to one's trade, beneficence to one's effort, truth to one's searches, the relation between determinations and existence is turned upside down. The more one gets away from elements and laws to syntheses and highly original operations, the more unlikely these syntheses and operations become, or, more precisely, the more difficult it becomes to define that likelihood. How could one have guessed that matter would not produce carbon anhydride? Who could foresee in 1769 that Napoleon would sign the treaty of Tilsit? From bottom to top, the future, as the path which creation travels to scatter its works, is open. Just as every volition is a cleavage, since there is nothing to will where continuity, necessity, or free flight suffices, so creation, whether theoretical or artistic, practical or affective, manifests the transcendence of value with reference to the given. But this transcendence comes to sanction the originality of a soul who has done everything necessary to render itself worthy of such transcendence. A spiritual psychology is needed to describe the diversity of the relationships which unite the apostle or the artist to his work. But these determined relationships are only the expression of an aim of value which is intermingled with the liberty of a self where value is triumphant. To claim that these determined relationships are the sufficient causes of inspiration would be to mistake a mask for a face.

There is no man who in the mediocrity of existence does not hear the solicitation of value. The solicitation of value can be detected at the origin of corruptions made possible by the will's weakness as well as at the origin of the most noble efforts. Why does the vainglorious man look for a scandal that will make his name known? Why does the old man seek a title which will testify to his importance and allow his name to remain on a list? Why does the artist not enclose his experiences of life and beauty in the secrecy of an unexpressed love? The cloistered monk expects that the spiritual communion of souls in God will universalize the most intimate movements of his heart. The explorer looks for value in the unknown, the historian draws it from the past, the hero finds it in the severest of dangers. The only real contempt is that contempt which condemns the man who betrays value through weakness of soul. Everyone recognizes that if it were even possible for the sufferings, the efforts of men and living things, and their objective and spiritual posterity to be interrupted and blotted out by a sudden nothingness, then value would be impossible. But no one wants this. For everyone searches value trying to find the Absolute. There is no crime which the criminal's dialectic does not color with a reflection of justice. The interests of Durkheimian sociologists involve a remarkable predilection for suicide. One can well understand this, for suicide is the act whereby man makes himself a thing. There could be no experience more favorable for scientific objectivism. Still, suicide would be nothing but an accident unless the perverted will, crushed by its situation, continues, by its longing for deliverance, something like a struggle for value.

Scheler's hierarchy of values would be dangerous if, in elevating the sacred above the spiritual, the vital, and the agreeable, it led one to think that value does not always have the sacred as its essence. A hierarchy of values is close to being reduced to a hierarchy of quantities. It projects value onto the plane of determinations. One should be fearful of defining value, for a definition will always replace value with some specific value, and this would be a denial of value's infinity. One expresses the same truth when one admits that God exists for every spirit and that each spirit must assimilate value to itself in the way which is appropriate for it. One of the most important aspects of every self's limitedness is the diversity of characters. The man who is fit to participate in value through scientific research is hardly familiar with the exigencies of the heart; another, exclusively concerned with intentions, will misunderstand the certainty and efficacy which intellectual knowledge can confer on action. Value requires them to comport themselves toward one another with intelligence and sympathy instead of converting their differences into conflict. Morality has its place above and independent of all natural determinations. But morality cannot suppress determinations and assign one and the same vocation to all men, since their situation and make-up differentiate them from one another. Every man is alone before God. All the mediations which can help him to find his way will promote, not suppress, the indescribable originality of his union with God.

One might be tempted to present the love of value as the consciousness of a debt. In fact, experience confirms that this sentiment can intervene as one of the factors of free flight, for example, a sudden turn orienting the self toward its own best future. The sentiment of indebtedness is a necessary condition if the self is not to conceive of itself as the unique and absolute sovereign of experience. But it is no less true that the juridical image of debt still manifests the plight of a consciousness oppressed by a determination coming from the past. And that which gives a debt its sacred character is not the determination of its matter, which is always to some degree and within certain limits arbitrary, but the fact that a debt results from an agreement whereby two particular wills have encountered each other in love for order and in hope of a beneficent collaboration. When love for order and hope for collaboration are missing, the law, as Pascal has profoundly seen, is nothing but an occasion for quarreling.

Thus it is the love of God or of value which inspires respect for debts. A debt is nothing but a localized specification of this love. The sentiment of debt is nothing but an existential mediation directed toward acceding to the free flight toward the divine. If one reduces morality to the question of debt, one ends up with the conclusion that one has to multiply the obligations which weigh upon the self from the outside. This would be the surest way for the self to lose the power to fulfill any of these obligations. The scoundrel would rejoice to see the honest man reduced to his own weakness. A debt can be fully paid by a man only if he has at his disposal a power considerably in excess of that required for payment. A sure way to propagate contempt for laws is to multiply them. A sure way to discredit faith in treaties is to change or repeat them from one moment to the next. Every determination is established to serve, aid, and direct the free flight toward value. Those determinations which shackle, compromise, or choke it must be corrected. But in no way can a determination substitute itself for value, for it gets its own value from value.

Value would not even have a name if there were not one

or more experiences in which it gives itself and from which it casts sparks of its fire like a torch on those who come near it as well as on those who run from it. We use the word *inspiration* for the common soul which these experiences bear to denote that its essence is to existentially unite God, who inspires, and the self, who is inspired by him. Since value exists and goes beyond every determination, one cannot avoid mysticism. But when there are errors in mysticism, they do not come from its source but from the reduction of mysticism to the determinations which can serve to lead to mysticism but which can also serve to convert it into passion. What is serious about denying that every human life has something of mysticism about it is that one does not suppress it. Instead of purifying the essence of mysticism, one promotes a degradation of mysticism which restricts it to serving some determination or other now taken as absolute.

The love of value, liberty, and God are one and the same reality. In inspiration there is a convergence of the memory of the self's crises, the ideas furnished by history or springing from the intellectualization of perception, the energy which is material inasmuch as it results from the situation of the body and spiritual inasmuch as the infinite adds hope to it, and the existential maturing in which the contributions of the will are condensed. But at the point where every mediation terminates in immediacy, the pure Spirit is revealed as without parts and is known as total free flight, endowed with existential sufficiency having neither regret nor impatience. It is revealed as the union of intimacies and the source of all emanation. When the sovereignty of the pure Spirit manifests itself, no doubt can break in.

Human experience insofar as it is human is tormented by interior contradiction. Human experience insofar as it is divine is animated by the Spirit. The former aspect expresses itself in duty, which commands us to put forth the effort needed to go beyond it. Without duty man would mistake his own spontaneity for divine revelation. By bringing to the fore its severity, by making us feel again that what we must do is something other than what our nature would produce by its acquired dexterity, duty prepares the soul to receive the powers which it still lacks. It makes one worthy of value. Value, in turn, is indispensable for duty lest duty turn into hatred for man and into contempt for the person. For it is definitively necessary that duty be valuable, yet it cannot get this value from any demonstration or any other utility since it would then lose its essence. Unable to be a term of an ideal relation, duty cannot be anything but a term of an ideo-existential relation. Immediately beyond duty is value. Their hyper-relation closes the *I* toward itself and opens it toward infinity.

Every description of inspiration, which is always the same and always new, is the work of reflection occurring when obstacle leads us back to cold knowledge. Excluding every fissure in the course of its reign, engendering the atmosphere of existence through ideas, and verifying the ideas in existence, inspiration excludes all doubt about itself. When obstacle has awakened us, value prolongs the sentiment of inspiration's passage. The recollection of our most spiritual experience, in which we create ourselves, overshadows the prestige of natural spontaneity, in which we wear ourselves out. But this will still be only a memory. Having no further resource for the moment except in reflection and will, the philosopher will be led to seek for and to define the determinations capable of promoting the revivification of these spiritual experiences. His situation, his character, and his limitations will distinguish his philosophy from some other one. But if an intemperate dialectic does not impose itself on him so as to lead his effort astray, his thought will bathe in the same atmosphere of unity and infinity which vivifies all our efforts.

Two modes of description exhibit inspiration more frequently than any others. They are the modes which present it *on the one hand as a contemplation, and on the other as an action.* Since the expressions of value necessarily diffract value, inspiration has to reconcile in value these two aspects, contemplation and action. The convergence of determinations toward intimacy, a convergence of which beauty is the most exalted image, is the precondition for intimate expansion. A conflict between contemplation and action would impede expansion. Contemplation would be merely a "mute painting on a canvas" if, as has been seen, the charm in beauty did not elicit an outpouring of the infinite leading to creation.

This is the aspect of contemplation to which classic intellectualism gives prominence. One of the most beautiful illustrations of this aspect is the Cartesian theory of light. One knows that light, shot forth instantaneously in a straight line like an unbending stick, expresses to everyone's eyes the unity of divine action with reference to which matter must be absolutely passive. This conception remains relatively true insofar as the propagation of the light, even if it takes some time, necessarily shows the identity of the impulsion which has emitted it. And if one recalls that when Cartesianism deals with thought, it is the clear and distinct consciousness which defines the highest degree of our existence, and that perception can lead to identification with the true only through the natural light which dissipates confusion, light will appear at the intersection of the two substances in themselves, as transcending their dualism. After having theoretically distinguished these two terms, Descartes reconciles them in the unity of intelligence. Malebranche, in turn, conceives of Paradise as an inundation of light.

When the terms of the existential unity of the relation-soul converge in it, the relation-soul requires inspiration to present itself in other modes, less as light than as passion. It also requires contemplation not to blot out action. For inspiration not to paralyze itself, for it to conserve its living essence as eruption or divine irruption, and for it to be more than the mere reflection of a nature in a mirror, determinations must, as it were, continuously be thrown into absolute existence and compensate for one another's negativity. Every determination necessarily has an aspect of darkness. Darkness is recognized in all the modes of inspiration. The thought of an idea presupposes the rejection of all the expressions which merely adapt it to a given situation, for an idea is infinite only by reason of such a presupposition. Spinozism ends up in acosmism. The Gospels command one to renounce all specific attachments to attain to the love of God, and the mystics find God in the depths of obscurity. At the highest degree of heroism, moral sacrifice extends to the annihilation of all the determinations to which life attaches us.

We will not try to penetrate with description further into an intimacy which description can only represent *by means of the contradiction between the infinite and the finite*. The upper limit of the description of consciousness is that point where the described and the description are intermingled. Description is enclosed between the lower extremity of experience, which would be the pure *I* and where there would be nothing to describe, and that summit which there would be no purpose to describing because the *I* that the obstacle has opened up is reenclosed within the union of God and self. The ultimate consequence of the theandric relation is that inspiration cannot lead to a confusing of God with the self. At the very core of this union, if it is to be a union of wills, determination must retain something of its influence. It does so in two ways. First of all, it *establishes channels,* not as a rigid direction or a rut leading to self-sustaining necessity but as a controlling direction leading to the self's participation in the theandric relation. It is through some channel that a specific self participates. This canalization permits one to say that all love of God is an intellectual love. But this term underscores the limitation we are burdened with rather than the infinity which is given to the self in this relation. Further, determination intervenes *to diminish* the experience of union. If in inspiration the intellect and will are ennobled but still preserved, inspiration must retain that aspect of time whereby the spirit knows itself superior to the instant. A happy and generous dynamism is still a dynamism. As such it presupposes some slowness.

When one is far from this experience of inspiration, which is as rare as it is precious, if one is unwilling to trivialize value by reducing it to the objectivity of determination, one can have only a presentiment of and a love for the virtues which duty calls for at the limit of an illuminated existence. One triptych involving *admiration,* which allows us to rejoice in the beauty of determinations, *passion,* which thrusts us toward adventure and exploration, and *love,* which invites us to unite ourselves existentially to others, is opposed to another triptych involving devaluation, which delights in negative cricitism of things and deeds, discouragement, through which man kills off self-confidence, and denigration, which turns another's words into nothing but occasions for hating. Every man has to choose between the life of competition, which compares men in terms of the determinations to which they adhere, and the active enjoyment of the Absolute, or the love of God, which necessarily inspires men to unite and collaborate. The *I* is at the center of experience, but it leaves the value of experience undetermined. At every instant value can be reduced. But the value which God offers us will verify its existence in proportion to the quantity and quality of the efforts which we make to impregnate determinations with it and to have determinations emanate from it.

These efforts must not be put forth without anxiety. War would be inconsequential if it were merely an accident. But an accident already presupposes some sentiment of value in one who concretely experiences it. Still he is little more than a witness to it. On the contrary, war always presupposes that the belligerents participate in it with the most intense activity. They would not become capable of the most generous or most absurd sacrifices if war merely involved conflicts of interest. To speak as though war is a matter of calculation or a business is an abstraction which verifies for us once and for all the impossibility of separating determinations from value. Rather, it is necessary to recognize that calculation and business themselves presuppose an intimacy of existence which gives them all their worth. Every war, and the more profoundly so the more serious it is, presupposes a virtue in the belligerents. Each fights for that mode according to which value presents itself to him. Likewise, every war is religious. And we can do nothing unless, with recognition of this fact, we acknowledge that war admits of no solution which excludes metaphysics and religion. The idea of God has at least this meaning for men. It reminds them of the infinity and indivisibility of value. And, further, it makes them understand that, throughout whatever differences determinations can maintain among them, if value presents itself to them in modes which seem to them to be exclusive, the reason for this is not in God but in their limitations. Value does not exist to blend men together in an identity in which all have the same determinations, or to set their aims in opposition, but to permit them to serve, by aiding and loving one another, the development of the consciousness whose infinity animates them.

There is no experience where value has no lesson to teach. The most tragic experience is the most instructive. If war can pit one mode of value against another, it is because every finite participation in value can only amount to a paltry knowledge of value. Beyond every philosophy and every concrete human experience, the principle of value rests in the depths of God-for-himself. Value conceals itself after being given secretly to us, because it would betray the infinity of its origin if every knowledge that it permitted of itself were more than a sample of its inexhaustible fecundity. And the relation-soul, by comparison with which all the antinomies of experience merely set terms in opposition, is in itself existential only by intermingling with the infinite Power which is constantly better known and yet constantly more profoundly unknown, a Power which any finite knowledge, however broad and sincere it is, necessarily confines to its own limits.

8 / Program for the Description of Consciousness

63. *Personality*

WE HAVE JUST IDENTIFIED IN THE *I* the "suspended" existence of personality. Personality is to be found in the wavering of the *I* between two intersecting thrusts, namely, the thrust to consolidate, which, when it prevails, tends to merge God, self, and object into the undividedness of a punctiliar, subpersonal unity, and the thrust to expand, which would mix everything together in the suprapersonal integration of the continuous one or God-without-us if it were not curbed by the inertia of the determination which it more or less gloriously subdues. *Personality exists only on condition of having to make itself without being able to complete itself.* Personality does not appertain exclusively either to us, who without God's immanence would be mere things and who even with him will always remain half-persons, or to God, who apart from us would be lost beyond personality in the fiction of God-without-us. Personality is neither a substance nor a state nor a category. It is existence as lived by the double *cogito*, shackled by obstacles and elevated by and toward value. At each moment it grows either weaker or more lively depending on whether the obstacles mediate its degradation or its ennoblement. But no experience can be degraded without the entirety of experience being proportionately degraded. And the entirety of experience cannot be undervalued without each experience being thereby affected.

The solidarity between obstacle and value places personality *at the intersection of an expansion and a diffraction.* To the degree that value triumphs, Consciousness and consciousnesses personalize themselves. But if an impediment constantly intervenes somewhere or at some time to heighten the distinction between them, this progression will require as a counterweight that they *personify* themselves. That is, they will have to divide themselves into personages among whom the mutual independence will become progressively deeper to the point that they die from it. The artistic consciousness is the model of concrete consciousness. Whereas science only gives us laws about things, art provides us with the image of the spirit. Just as an actor develops his talent by successively undertaking roles which come to an end with the last scene of each play, so the continuous penetration of universal consciousness into value can only take place through the histories of subordinate consciousnesses.

A twofold consequence, which falls outside of our present study, necessarily follows from this. On the one hand, each self must participate in the absolute existence of God and be eternal with him if it is to exist at all. And by reason of the connection between existence and determination each self must develop itself, under the restrictiveness of crises and reversions which allow it to be limited or immoral, in an existential maturation which converts its original dynamism into the most exalted symbol of the divine dynamism. On the other hand, insofar as the encounter between a heredity having many sources and a complex situation forces it to incarnate itself in a certain body, the self must embark on one history after another. But the wear and tear on the sensitive body condemns this sequence to come to an end. Each life should be for the self what every intention is for the goal of value. It is currency for it and serves it as a kind of mediation. This conception is compatible with widely divergent interpretations of death and human destiny. From one life to another, as from one role to another, the memory preserves deep traces or documents capable of being historically rediscovered, and recollection preserves spiritual continuity. How could value not be absolute? If it is absolute, then death, which reduces existence to determination, cannot be absolute. This is what the Kantian postulate of practical reason expresses concerning immortality. But if scientific invention is also of the order of value, this postulate of practical reason is likewise the postulate of theoretical research. One fails to appreciate this only if he lets himself be frozen in the partialness of cold knowledge.

64. *Program for the description of consciousness*

The description of all the aspects of personality is the principal object of the description of consciousness. Up to this point we have merely taken cognizance of the universal traits which condition the possibility of such a description. To bring this work to a close we have to foster the hope which should be placed in this program by giving a foretaste of its fruitfulness.

A

The functions of the object. The first task of description is to study the ideo-existential relations between the object and the self. This study has been started inasmuch as we have considered in passing the allegation of transcendence, the distinction between obstacle and object, and the modes according to which determination presents itself. But these indications are not enough. For example, the allegation of transcendence, which is meaningless *relative to experience*, since no one can prevent transcendence as well as everything related to it from being within experience, has a whole variety of meanings *relative to the self*, since it is the inverse of the self's limitation. In what situations does this dialectic appear? What processes does this dialectic inaugurate? Why is existence fictively separated from determination in order to make the transcendent something incomprehensible in itself? What influence does this dialectic exercise on the self? What is the worth of this dialectic and of the mixture of this dialectic with others? All these questions can be pursued only through a history less concerned with coming into contact with documents taken as objects to be discriminated than with availing itself of them as mediations to rediscover the spirit which is expressed through them. Physiology can investigate the muscles and the relations of innervation intensities which come together in a smile. But it ends up by making one forget that the smile is the indefinitely varied expression of a soul. In any study, an idolatry of determinations suppresses the spirit.

Likewise, the abridged summary account which we have

given of the spiritualization of obstacle—first as objection, then as object, idea, relation, and finally as action grounded in the free flight of the self—far from constitutes a sufficient study of the relations between the self and determination. Depending on its position with reference to the processes and dialectics suffered by and performed by the self, any given can be an occasion, a signal, an instrument, a model, an aspect, an emblem, a currency, a sacrament, etc. A table of categories is nothing but the ideal projection and reduction of the limitless multiplicity of attitudes and movements of which the spirit is capable. Such a table indicates how determinations can be reunited with one another, but by stereotyping the fundamental relations between determinations and the self it makes these relations uniform. The single fact of replacing the word *determination* with *object* presupposes that one has taken an intimate stance whereby one turns away from all the other possibilities. The description of consciousness has to recognize these other possibilities.

B

The ideo-existential relations among subordinated consciousnesses. In addition to the study of the ideo-existential relations between the self and the object as existent or as determination, there is the immense domain of ideo-existential relations between one self and every other self. One of the traits which recurs both in cold knowledge and in pure mysticism and thus indicates that they are correlated is that both of them describe a confrontation in which the self stands alone. The scientist is alone before nature, as the mystic is alone with God. This shows that the relation between man and determination or value constantly involves the self's responsibility. But without undertaking here the description of the processes whereby the self transforms the given from being impersonal to being personal, one can observe that at the moment when obstacle diffracts the self and brings to light the duality between the limited self and the infinite God it likewise reveals the definitive inadequation of the self to God. The sentiment of this inadequation opens a gap from which there emerges the imagining of numerically and qualitatively different possibilities of existence than one's own. Consequently the affirmation of the other, and the sympathy necessary so that this affirmation will do more than merely posit a determination, must coincide with the emergence of the *I* from the solitude of the self. It is true that these are still only possibilities. But value confers real existence on them in proportion to what we allot them and to what they are suited to, if God consents. Just as the indefinite series of determinations, whose temporal succession manifests both that determinations repel one another and that there is an endless succession of them, ideally spreads out divine infinity, so the innumerable people with their limited existences refract the spirituality of value.

By positing the reality of the *us*, which is composed of souls which are both distinct and united, one opens up another perspective for description. Durkheimian sociology lifts physics out of the domain where it can be successful. It encloses physics in itself by replacing the protean life of the interpersonal relation, which produces all the mixtures of friendship and enmity in the course of oscillating between war and love, with the identity of a collective representation. In such a representation men are merely ciphers.

This sociology cannot yield the laws it promises. It hides under a theoretical façade a normative claim the essence of which is that the State is to replace God. The transcendental myth of a perfect and sufficient order recurs here in the ideal of the universal State. But like every ideal, this ideal is partial. Order, like the determinations which it harmonizes, is not self-maintaining. It presupposes existence and value. At each instant it is transcended by actions which manifest the irreducibility of the real to the juridical. The State is never anything other than a form. The forces which it tries to organize, and which it all too often does disservice to, do not come from it. When this form solidifies into a structure it is necessarily limited in such a way that the exclusive aspiration toward the constitution of the universal State ends up—with the complicity of science, which puts matter at the service of any government—by rigidifying a plurality of States. When these States clash there is war. How can a sociology which comes from postulates of cold knowledge understand anything about war, when nothing is explained about war unless one takes account of affectivity, urgency, and the search for value which transcends every actual or possible society?

The first obligation which is aimed toward an understanding of the *us* directs one to return to the lived experience of the ideo-existential relations among men. This experience presents description with the buyer's bargaining, the seller's advertising, the military commander's strategy, the diplomat's ingenuity, the swindler's wickedness, and the democratic politician's technique. The scientist, for whom determination is an object, goes astray if he applies to determination postulates which deny communication. In the course of life, which is serious by reason of the threats and hopes which inspire it and which is irreducible to pure necessity by reason of the uncertainty which indeterminateness brings into it, the idea is only the means of a mutual strategy whereby one self enters into competition with another if one does not succeed in uniting oneself with the other through some kind of communion. Two limits are presented to the *us* in experience: (1) disarray, which occurs when individual competition deepens and generalizes anarchy and when dishonesty encourages everybody to distrust everybody else; and (2) military integration, which generalizes scientific and juridical statism, inasmuch as the State is the physical power of sanction and science arms the State. In the space between these limits and in the course of the oscillations which make up the intrinsically indifferent matter of history, value inspires us to love the spiritual convergence within which each man yields to value in ways and modes which are appropriate to his own situation and structure.

C

Transcendental description. Like every relation, the *us* supposes the identity and the distinction of the limited existences which it unites ideally through communication and intimately in communion. If by abstraction one isolates the ideal and more or less impoverished identities which allow one to place the subjects back in the extension of a relatively universal class, one gets the ordinary definition of the "transcendental" subject. The psychological subject is opposed to the transcendental subject both by reason of the determinations which distinguish it from other things and other subjects and by reason of existence.

But it is evident that in either case neither an ideal nor a nominal definition can express anything other than determination. What one calls the transcendental subject is either a structure or some givens which one tears off from undivided experience to make them independent of the psychological subject. If one does not want to sacrifice value to determination or spirit to thing, here any more than anywhere else, there are operations and processes which he must describe so as to give some content to the experience of the transcendental subject. By reason of their value these operations and processes cannot fail to refer to the Absolute, or God. By reason of their determination, they express the limitation of the self, which must rediscover itself in the transcendental self that has been abstracted from it by induction. When the pattern of these operations is simple, they are categories, which are precious modes of intellectual mediations between *the ego quatenus Deus* (the ego as God) and *the ego quatenus homo* (the ego as man). These categories are necessarily either truths or prejudices. They are truths when they serve thought, and prejudices when they hamper it. But still they are real only by reason of the intimacy of the spirit, whose dialectics and processes can utilize them but still surpass them.

Therefore one should distinguish within the description of consciousness *a transcendental description* whose end is to recognize the universal modes of bifurcation through which experience is more and more spiritualized by moving away from the quasi indifference in which the *I* casts only an errant and feeble glance on the given. This development takes place because of an ever more creative demand which brings about the divinization of the *I* and of the content of experience with it. It is clear that what holds for this segment of description holds for description in its totality; it must remain open. Subsequent experience will not be limited by actualized experience. But, after having refused to sacrifice contingency to necessity, if philosophy wants to avoid sacrificing value to chance it must admit that the future will preserve in its movement not the works of the past but the best of their spirit. And we must henceforth recognize in this movement the elements of eternal knowledge which eternal knowledge preserves in it. The value of transcendental description lies in the help it gives in discerning the cost or the dangers of each of the operations which regulate the spirit.

We must limit ourselves here to merely setting the stage for, initiating, this description. Inasmuch as obstacle does impose and will always impose itself on personality insofar as personality is individual, and inasmuch as the essence of obstacle is that it cannot be immediately removed by a spontaneous process of attack, obstacle will always condemn the self to mediation. When faced with the impervious, one has no other recourse, at least if one does not want to leave it alone, than to go through some other thing on which obstacle depends. Science, which is born of human infirmity, is a double mediation. It is ideal when it proceeds by way of law. It is existential when it proceeds by way of cause. Science is a technique of thought prior to being a technique of action. Seeking at one and the same time both to make means available to us and to guarantee that we may conserve and use them, science has to preoccupy itself with alternately opening and closing intellectual knowledge. By means of a systematization, which is better called a *schematization* because of its necessary solidarity with perceptual space and time, science organizes, or tends to organize, a totality of truths which is doomed to incompleteness because the influx of new truths issuing from contact with new experiences necessarily always breaks the unity of old truths. Science disembarks only in order to embark anew.

Transcendental description is engaged in both to ascertain and to evaluate. Thus it must show the scope and the limits of the schematization whose efficiency and terrible insufficiency are both concretely experienced by contemporary man. In fact, if there is any principle which rules over the description of consciousness, it is that description may not reject any given of experience. By admitting the idea that the critical spirit does not know limits, philosophy forbids itself to stop at the transcendental postulates of either science or the critical spirit itself. If one begins with judgment, one cannot withhold anything from judgment. Consciousness is the undetermined power to apprehend determinations. It is the mistress of its own destiny.

Schematization, then, must embrace that domain which it helped to bring about. But this domain cannot be circumscribed within experience, even if the domain were indefinitely deepened and expanded, without being surpassed by experience. Positivism is partial in claiming to confine the spirit within the domain of schematization, which is the domain of rigidity. The domain of rigidity is displayed in the most profound parts of conceptual metaphysics, mathematics, and physics, as in the higher reaches of the law. At its lower level, the relation of necessity and will has necessity prevailing. But still science involves postulates, conventions, and unities which presuppose the consent of the scientists. At its upper level, necessity disappears behind the will, for if any constitution whatsoever could be established in France in 1875, there had to be a vote to institute it. Somewhere in biology one would find the pivot point at which the prevalence is reversed from necessity to will.

Since determination is positive and exists only by reason of value, and scientific research itself presupposes this, other transcendental processes should be set in opposition to schematization in order to balance it, to prevent it from degenerating into passion, and to subordinate it to the goal of the spirit. When science sacrifices value to a standard of measurement which turns out to mediate everything through the objective one,[1] then science expresses its defects through its own negations. Springing from a movement of extraversion, science knows nothing of intimacy, tyrannizes liberty, and recognizes persons only to make things of them. But how can the self be reduced to an object? If this reduction were accomplished it would entail an indifference on the part of the self to truth as well as to all value. Such an indifference would retard scientific development. Thus the preconceived view of theoreticians, far removed from compulsion as they are, who take the postulates of their professional attitude to be the laws of reality and who take consciousness to be a mere spectator, is of little consequence. Before and after having been thought of as object, the object has been and, in a new form, will again become obstacle, and it will restore the self to itself. Compulsion will over and over again refuse to grant the self, whose limits can be stretched but which cannot disappear, the pause needed for theoretical analysis. And theoretical analysis will always be inadequate to the uniqueness of events.

It is at this point that the other transcendental processes, which are expressed in ethics, art, and religion, necessarily offer themselves to the self. Imitating science has led to treating all three of these as objects susceptible to determination. But this attitude is a misinterpretation of their value. First of all, at this point the uniqueness of facts resists schematization. After announcing that one will create the science of these three

1. The "objective one" is the static formal unity which serves as the keystone for objectivist metaphysics. Its content, of course, can vary from one objectivist philosophy to another.—Trans.

processes, one simply begins to give a history of them. Further, objectifying these processes evaporates the existential intimacy without which these functions are soulless. By what right does one take some feature of mores in order to look there for an indication of morality? The same act, the same rule, depending on the situation and the goal by which it is defined, is either moral or immoral. Where is art—in the objects of perception or in the beauty which the intimate sentiment brings to them? Finally, how can pure religion, which is the effort to deliver the spirit from all determination, the effort to experience the spirit concretely in its own existence, be encountered in the expressions in which one seeks it? What history can establish the divinity of Christ in some document or other? If a history is inspired by the mechanistic postulates of science, it excludes his divinity a priori. To be preoccupied with oneself is, for the spirit, exactly the contrary of loving. The fact that life counterbalances love and self-reflection does not remove the fact that partiality for one of them brings about a suppression of the other.

Thus description must progressively be turned from discrimination toward concrete experience if it is to reach the other processes of the spirit. The operation whereby every self, regardless of which self it is, of whether it is alone or with others, and of whether the technique it uses is more or less vigorously pursued, starts to tend beyond obstacle is the *operation of commanding*. Whether the activity of the self is coerced or merely inconvenienced by determination, it is no longer the free flight of spontaneity and is not yet the free flight of inspiration. Obstacle is no less presupposed for the activity of commanding than it is for schematization. Where reason or logical continuity would either theoretically or practically suffice, authority would be superfluous. However, we have seen that liberty is brought to completion in authority, for authority is, or should be, nothing but the creative power of the self. But this power is still yoked to a distinct determination by reason of some resistance. Thus, wherever authority has to intervene, whether to act on ourselves or on another, it is because the will, which is the relation of the self to a determination, has been distinguished from both self and determination. Psychological theories alternately assimilate the will to the appeal of determinations or to a sovereign decree because the scientific schematization which levels all the rough spots of experience can do nothing but separate life into matter and illusion, into the body-without-the-self and the self-without-the-body, into the spirit's dissolution in things and the spirit's reign over phantoms. Experience cruelly belies both pure objectivism, which makes man nothing but a well-oiled machine, and pure subjectivism, which offers us the ease of a dream with no awakening.

Like all operations, the activity of commanding is delimited by a relation. It extends from actions which the will does not have to command, because spontaneity suffices, to actions which the will should not command, because the self does not have either the energy or the instrumental means to execute them. It is important to note that if the activity of commanding dominates technique insofar as it expects technique to provide intellectual and practical means for conferring existence on determinations, which it treats as ideals, nevertheless its objective efficacy must not make one fail to see its subjective efficacy. *On the side of the object, the activity of commanding is an effectuating; on the side of the subject, the activity of commanding is a kindling.* The activity of commanding in fact has at its disposal only minimal resources of energy. It has to enkindle a sudden combustion of more powerful reserves, either interior or exterior to the organism, in order to convert the dialectics of dynamic intelligence into emotional movements. Description should recognize all the manifestations of the activity of commanding, its field of application, its scope, its limits, its dangers, either in the individual life when the *I* is turned into a self to be controlled, or in the collective life when one self puts pressure on another self by means of an order, or when a group of men, in a military fashion, use publicity or propaganda to try to enkindle the affectivity of a social unity.

The solidarity between the activity of commanding and the self as self is enough to give one a presentiment of the insufficiency of this activity. It is clear that the self, which can have only a perfunctory knowledge of situations where it is under pressure to act, cannot be reduced to clear and distinct determinations. Likewise it is clear that a will which is merely will is deficient. The discrediting of a universal mathematics has destroyed the sufficiency of deduction in all domains. When one wants to serve value, he must surely begin by celebrating duty. Effort is one of the modes of existential mediation between our weakness and our power. But still duty aims higher than duty, and what is important about duty is not only that it is a source of determinations but that it is also a stimulating influence.

Thus we are here thrust back by the insufficiency of will to the mystery and inexhaustible profundity of personal existence. Nothing is more terrifying than a mysticism which rejects the lights of intelligence. By suppressing determinations and the reflections of light whose existence determinations color, mysticism would simultaneously reduce value to absolute nothingness. On the other hand, nothing is more treacherous than an intellectualism which forgets the disproportion between the determinations we recognize and the infinity of experience, whether actualized or still to come. Such an intellectualism deifies the human will. The intimate progress of the self, which acts can merely symbolize and tone down, presupposes that the will is helped by the possession of schemes useful for converting obstacles into instruments. But disinterestedness will not elevate the self above utility unless the spiritual energy, of which the natural energies are merely inferior and subjugated species, grants the soul that participation without which our ideas, sentiments, and acts are merely psychological phosphenes in which the absolute posits only the evanescent value of a mirage.

Since God, the source of value, is both transcendent to the self in proportion to the self's limitation and immanent in the self in proportion to the self's degree of morality, value necessarily presents itself to the self through the mediation of two operations, discovery and creation. Sometimes value illumines the finite in order to make it testify to the glory of consciousness. Sometimes value inspires in the self the sentiment of the infinite in order to hurl the self beyond determinations. Art is only one form of this function of *transfiguration* whereby the self makes beauty the means for a creative participation. When a subjectivity, which is oppressed by the obstacles of life, looks for its glory, it finds its glory by softening determinations into images which the will either stabilizes or renders mobile so as to satisfy the artist's tendencies. Suffering is both deprived of its danger and made noble. Harmony takes on the charming form of beauty. Suffering and harmony cooperate for the happiness of the artistic consciousness, which now becomes the model for all consciousness. Like every model, it is both an ideal and a fiction.

Someone other than the artist might see here only a diversion. But that would be precisely because art remains almost entirely foreign to him. Where the creator finds a mode of participation, the amateur makes an object for enjoyment. Luxury is ordinarily the social degradation of beauty. But the value of a work comes to it from truth, as the value of the artist comes from his sincerity. The artist suggests a sentiment which is true of consciousness with its distress and glory, as the scientist suggests a scheme true of the order among perceptions. The artist would not unreservedly devote his life to art, with all the sacrifices which art has always demanded from those who consecrate themselves to it, unless value gave itself to him in art in such a way as to make art a mode of participation. This is why the highest art, by virtue of its own thrust, tends toward the universal soul of things, whether it depicts the sentiments of the man who feels himself separated from the universal soul or whether it sings of the joy of the man who has rediscovered this soul in himself. Where value is missing, everything is diversion. Where value inspires, everything is participation.

The artistic *cogito,* which is turned toward perception, spiritualizes the obstacle into an image of the obstacle. Thus it is opposed to the religious *cogito,* which makes determination an occasion for canceling determination in order to participate in the creative infinite by virtue of a soaring of the heart. There is no religion without dogmas and rituals. But the believer as believer does not expect these to suggest further determinations. If he did, then dogma would be nothing but a metaphysical principle, and ritual nothing but a technique. But if spirit consists in canceling matter, the formula of the dogma and the action of the ritual must refer to existence and must thrust this existence toward value. In scientific discovery, existence remains for the sake of emanation. At the core of religion, whatever matter remains in the self remains for the sake of the influence it will have, and that influence aims at the infinite. Objectivism, which art elevates to its highest degree of intimacy, leads to an ideal of beauty. It subordinates God's infinity to his perfection. But if perfection is superior because it actualizes infinity, it is still merely the negative shadow of infinity. There is nothing for God to receive from the outside. But if this perfection were to exist by itself, then God would become the world, a given. It is not enough that the source of value be self-sufficient. Such a source would still be isolated in indifference. Description protests against this extremity, which is mixed with the lower extremity of the "objective one," because description is just as respectful of becoming as it is of being. God exists both to love and to be loved. And if he animates subordinate existences, it is because he possesses superabundance. He has no need to receive in order to be always capable of giving.

In fact, the verification of the existence of God is nowhere found in a more striking fashion than in the acts in which love reveals that the self participates in a value which transcends it. At its closest point to matter, in contact with the most organic life, it is God, it is value and not the "instinct for self-preservation" which sustains the basic acts of the individual. As long as the infant is in the mother's womb one can reduce what the mother does for it to the effort for self-preservation. But inasmuch as, after birth, lactation reveals the very orientation of her body to a good which is not for her, the egoism of the instinct for self-preservation is belied and surpassed. What an absurdity, from the viewpoint of psychological individualism, is this ordinarily indefatigable and often heroic attachment of the mother for her child! Nowhere does utilitarianism, which is the ethics of cold knowledge, more blatantly show its insufficiency. Nowhere is the reduction of love to exchange more shocking. Not only is the utility that a mother can receive from her child almost nothing compared to what he receives from her, but this calculation is false to the more profound fact that the sacrifices which she makes for the baby are, for her, actually reasons for loving him more. If one follows Schopenhauer and makes the individual the servant of "the species," one would be giving merely a verbal answer to this problem. For "species" is merely an abstraction unless behind that term the exigency of value, taken as a revelation of an eternal inspiration, is recognized as the source of the indefinitely renewed effort of the living not only toward *their own* lives but to the expansion of life and consciousness themselves.

One is being arbitrary if one reduces the call to love to its most restricted scope by considering it only when it moves bodies. It often seems that moral grandeur strikes fear in a man and that to protect himself from its radiance he has no rest until he reduces himself to matter, foolishly pretending that he would not have to have gone beyond matter in order to be able to recognize it. Beyond sexual and maternal love, all love is recognized insofar as the negative characteristics of self-love are converted into disinterestedness in the intermingling of love of oneself, love of others, and love of God. He who loves life gives it. To love, to live, to risk is always a sublime adventure for the self, an adventure whose orientation reason expresses but cannot predetermine. A humanity which would no longer want to pursue this adventure would simultaneously lose both life and the right to live. And there is no one but God to thank that no organization, whether natural or social, can ever substitute itself for the free love of value.

Thus a love which is restricted to maternal love is insufficient for the expansion of the spirit. To reduce love to an instinct which merely supplies love with organic factors is to calumniate it. To claim that this "instinct" is sufficient is to compromise the future of consciousness. Love can be distorted and robbed of its efficacy in numerous ways. Love should impregnate the entire life of humanity like an atmosphere if one does not want those very children who are alive only by reason of the generosity of maternal love to betray the precedent of love in their actions. Beyond the transcendental functions of schematizing, of commanding, and of transfiguring, whose value the scientist, the hero, and the artist receive in the mode appropriate to them, there must be a function, namely, religion, which presents itself as an *animation* in which determination intervenes simply to stimulate limited existence to go beyond its current limits.

When society breaks away from religion's impregnation, it is undoubtedly both because those who devote themselves to religion's maintenance and propagation have used determinations clumsily and because the other members of society lacked that emotional sympathy which adds the intelligence of the heart to that of theoretical thought. By reason of this more or less profound rupture, determinations become causes of separation and desiccation instead of serving as means of communion and expansion. Their influence now has a minus rather than a plus sign. But when the evils which science, when separated from morality and love, sheds so profusely around itself lead back to the sentiment of the existential indispensability of religion, one will have to hope that without violence and through the radiation of love the most religious souls will turn determinations back toward value.

Philosophy can cooperate in this redirection of determinations only through making the broadest and most precise description. Philosophy has its own proper duty, which is to serve value by preserving and propagating the idea of value. *All dia-*

lectics and processes are in experience, but they are not all equivalent. Against the dialectics of dissension, dissolution, and disarray, against partiality, philosophy must always restore to honor the dialectics of creation, union, and convergence. The *I*, the principle of all divisions, is at the core of experience. The *I* is consciousness creating itself. Still, consciousness must acknowledge the *I*. The *I* can preside with almost equal indifference over either destruction and war or cooperation and love. God offers us value. Thus it depends on subordinate consciousnesses whether experience will be good or bad, and it depends on them alone whether God, who is just and good, is ready to reply to their activity of determination with grace.

D

Adhesion. The transcendental subject is merely an abstraction from the existent self. It has no will. Description therefore must progressively extend to the self, which is the psychological self when considered by itself and the metaphysical self when it lives in quest of value.

The structure whereby the self is relatively determined in nature, and which is the system of the disponabilities [2] whereby it can act on experience, is at one and the same time, but unequally, both submitted to and willed by itself. Insofar as the self submits to the structure, we have said that it is *affected* by the structure. Insofar as the self wills the structure, it *adheres* to the structure. Since affectedness represents that which is in the self but is independent of it, it is the study of adhesion which is particularly precious. By adhesion we fashion the various layers of our nature either spontaneously or deliberately. It is adhesion which lays down the more or less fundamental postulates of our action. Most of the time our action will simply apply principles whose appropriateness is no longer questioned.

Since this is not the place to describe adhesion, we will present only its common pattern. We feel adhesion introducing itself when in the course of subordinate existence an intention sharply encounters a line of flight arising from compulsion. A

2. "Disponability" is a neologism often used in translating Marcel's works. It connotes open possibilities for an active responsiveness. "Disposition" is too close to "acquired habit," with connotations of prestructure.—Trans.

man is crossing a street and an automobile surprises him. If he can save himself from the danger which suddenly appeared by jumping onto the running board of another automobile, he immediately becomes united with what he has embraced for safety's sake, and thereafter, with the protection he has, he resists actions which try to break that solidarity. The self is enriched by what it has. As a consequence of these more or less cohesive embracings and joinings, which persist beyond the circumstances in which they have been both submitted to and willed, the self modifies and adapts its structure to the situations which provoke its investigations and, within the limits of its power, it orients its structure in accordance with its goal of value. This structure is a solidarity of either chaotic or organized functions which make up one's body, one's character, inveterate and recent habits, one's profession, and many other more or less durable determinations.

A concrete description must move from the general definition of the dialectics and processes which follow, for the self in general, from the encounter between a structure as little determined as possible and a nonspecified situation to the inventory of the mixed dialectics and processes by which a specific man has procured or failed to procure value in reacting to certain givens. Of all the services which can be rendered by philosophy, understood as a spiritual psychology which does not intend to objectivize man by reducing him to determination but which studies him in his struggles with the obstacles which separate him from value, there would be no service more precious than a *characterological noology* which would discover the special dialectics by which men of diverse characters are capable of increasing their passivity or activity.

E

Idiological [3] *description.* There is no chasm between the character and the person. The self is always the connection of a structure with the *I*. Further, the structure, whose character defines the most intimate traits according to which the self and God are separated or are joined together, is either like matter and thus restricts the self's expansion or is like a beloved rule and thus fosters expansion. Thus character presents

3. See Translator's Introduction, p. xxlii.

itself alternately as a measure of weakness or of power. Not the least advantage of the determined limitation of the self is that this limitation reminds the self that it can do nothing without first joyfully accepting the situation and the structure, which intersect at the point where the self is incarnated. But it does not follow from this that the self should attribute more than a local and relative objectivity to its situation and structure.

The most intimate liberty consists in a man's conduct with respect to his character. If he twists the determinations which constitute his character into reasons for giving up, he materializes himself. But neither passion, which submits the self to a character trait insofar as this trait channels a movement, nor inertia, which subjects it to immobility, has any meaning for us except by reason of the value it prevents us from attaining. The art of living or, to stress its essence as obligation, morality requires each man to seek through renewed efforts and continuous experimentation to make his character the instrument of his spiritual progress and not of his enslavement. The most profound opposition among men separates those who subordinate value to interest and those who, by reason of respect for the absolute source of value, do not preoccupy themselves with questions of utility except when value requires them to do so. The soul of the soul is the delicacy with which it refines in its own inmost depths its sentiment of value. The rest of the self is simply the expression of this sentiment.

Thus character is a negative reality only in the first phases of human experience, that is, in compulsion where its rigidity complicates a hostile situation, and in the tarrying of existence-which-is-only-existence where it ostensively offers itself to discovery and analysis. As soon as the self enters into the phase of value, the phase of inspiration, character no longer imposes itself as a determination on the sensitive consciousness of the self. It mingles itself into existence at the same time as the other determinations do. And if it contributes to a person's happiness, it does so, like every object, insofar as it slows down the enjoyment of happiness and insofar as it specifies the mode according to which value is given to the self. Through the effect of grace, there is no more character. It will only be rediscovered on account of a retrospective analysis. Naive spontaneity subordinates metaphysics to biology. Participation reverses the relation. Or, better, participation allows the *I* to rise at a certain time above the opposition between the body, or the structures which determine the self, and the value whereby God gives himself metaphysically to the self.

The characterological analysis must always stop while still incomplete. The determined character is never real except in a most complex, uniquely possessed, singular [*idiotique*] character, a character special to Peter and distinguishing him from Paul. It immediately follows that the searching, which is our very life when it is oriented toward value and of which every intentional act is simply an expression and a restriction, must be pursued by each person in the course of an original history. Each person goes toward himself—if one understands "himself" to mean that beyondness which characterizes every ideal self, that infinitely singular self which at its limit would be merely a facet of God-without-us, a soul of the "celestial Rose."

The description of consciousness will furnish the content for this idiology which investigates the choice of the dialectics and processes whereby every person sometimes yields to and sometimes controls situations, sometimes suffers a deforming influence from them and sometimes exploits their favorableness, provided that this study goes beyond a psychology exclusively inspired by a claim to copy physics. One knows the paucity of the results thus far obtained in this psychology. One can wish such a psychology a happier future. But that wish does not in any way suppress the fact that the essence of science is to sacrifice value to measurement. Science is the theory of our impotence. And as every theory naturally transforms itself from a speculative construct into a group of pragmatic rules, science would become the cause of pragmatic rules while waiting to fall victim to them. From a passive man, the scientist can construct only a puppet. But when this man comes alive, he develops all his awareness, all his strengths, and eventually virtues, with which the scientist is not familiar, to attain value.

The idiology, which stands between concrete psychology and personal morality, never overlooks the differences among characters, differences which become more pronounced as one knows the characters better. The significance of this idiology lies in its reminding each self that other selves are different from it. The other-self is similar to the self; otherwise communication and communion would be impossible for us. But if the other-self were completely identical with the self, it could not be the other-self. At the most profound depths of love, the mutual participation of souls in each other must not amount to their fusion. Further, it is always tyrannical for a group of men, uniting less for the sake of value than on the basis of some definition of value, to claim to impose on others the proper way to attain value. Determinations can only be auxiliaries. Idolatry consists in viewing determinations as more than relative ends, as if there could be some other end for a spirit than the absolute Spirit. When the temporal and human desire for gain or domination compromises the spiritual mission of religion, a reform provoked from outside but inspired from within rectifies religion's course. It is the destiny of all institutions that they must be constantly renewed and restored through disinterestedness and love of value. And it is no more legitimate for scientists than for anyone else to convert a competence of which they are the sole judges into the source of a despotic prestige which will assure a State-sanctioned power, which regiments souls and bodies for a minority of specialists who are frequently seduced by the postulates of their specialty and closed to other modes of value.

Characterology is designed to acquaint us with the diversity of souls. It is also designed to help them have sympathy with one another. The virtue of intellectualism resides in the necessity which submits the communication between initially heterogeneous and hostile men to the discipline of the knowledge of ideas. The vocation of intelligence is to serve love. But love goes beyond theoretical intelligence, inasmuch as intelligence can become, as in the case of a scoundrel, the means for subjecting and tricking others. Thus religion, which stands over against science as the process of the existential stands over against the function of the ideal, is needed to counterbalance the force of the temptation which so readily makes man fall into idolizing determination. Religion should counterbalance this temptation by supporting man's free flight toward the infinite, by making love beloved, and by fostering the conversion of communication into communion. Over and above the laws indicated by ethology, sympathy with the intimacy of the other permits one to embrace the emotional processes which combine with situations to engender sentiments and acts. Once again, the description of these elements should not be discredited beforehand by a conception of psychology which condemns it inevitably to drag the study of man back to that which is most elementary and mechanical about him.

F

Axiological description. If the being of determinations and the existence of the knower are simply localizations and concrete experiences of value, *ontology and the theory of knowledge are simply aspects of axiology.* The most exalted part of the description of consciousness is thus the description of value, not of course in its source, but in its modes. Value must be both one and infinite. An absolute contradiction within value would annihilate it. Further, contradiction presupposes in the contradictories an inflexibility which is characteristic of determinations. An external constraint would either suppress value or transfer it to that to which value would be subject. But as value is the existential relation between God and the self, the self must determine for itself a mode of infinity. Through this appropriation finite value is born.

We have seen that from this restriction of value to finite value there results the possibility of the most intimate and most tragic conflicts, conflicts in which human weakness pits the highest revelations of the spirit against one another. For example, truth is pitted against holiness when science and religion do not appreciate each other. Or courage is pitted against love when patriots and sincere conscientious objectors detest each other. One should also immediately stress that a mode of value remains faithful to value only if it is the movement of existence by which the soul turns to the unique and undefined source of all possible value. The order of determinations and the expansion of souls are simply the back and the front sides of this unique source. What distinguishes the greatest works of art, Handel's *Messiah,* or the Sistine ceiling, from a hymn to God? All the technical ingenuity and all the intimate suppleness of the great artist are brought together in triumphant heroism. Some of the greatest mystics have been the most practical administrators. Scientific genius stimulates artistic admiration and reveals the order in experience. The point where a mode of value reaches such a purity that it no longer distinguishes itself from other modes, so that any particularizing name is false to its richness, is the point where the Spirit both exists and creates.

We call this convergence *love of God.* But this phrase does not indicate that we are setting a new mode of value in opposition to other modes. Love of God is the very soul that the Infinite, which is indivisible in its source and inexhaustible in its manifestations, infuses into the love of life and into courage, into the contemplation of beauty and into intelligence, into the concern with interior perfection and into charity, into the fear of doing evil as into the ambition to do good, into the investigation which intelligibility has just satisfied as well as into remorse which terminates in purification and generosity. In brief, the Infinite infuses this soul into the indefinite number of modes in which men concretely experience the presence and efficacy of God in a way that is always personal. By trying to make one love the images of God's presence and efficacy which these modes can catch hold of, axiological description serves to spread this presence and efficacy.

The description-of-consciousness finds its justification in its most exalted moments, that is, when it is dealing with humanity's most precious experiences. It is a justification which can only come from on high. The description-of-consciousness is neither a pointless curiosity nor a spiteful diversion. Born of suffering, awakened and honed by all the difficulties in the face of which it conducted itself with a boldness proportionate to its generosity, consciousness finds in the description of itself the mediations, either reflective or ideal, determined or emotional, named or felt, which are indispensable for its expansion. But no mediation can find its end in itself. At the lower terminus of existence, description is abandoned in the intolerable compulsion which hurls one from suffering into death. Value cannot be found in such compulsion. Each time that some torment lacerates consciousness, it does so to revive horror in it. When one can no longer hope that a man will subordinate interest to value, nothing but fear can lead him back to the spirit. But it would be the collapse of all human effort if this monstrous mediation were the final resource of consciousness.

It is possible for the last word to testify to confidence, to that faith which is not a surrogate for an impossible possession but that is the progressively developing appropriation of the Spirit by us. It all depends on us. To the degree that motions of attraction, which descend from God, predominate over the motions of impulsion, which push us from the rear, Consciousness deepens and enlarges itself. Value imprints itself on experience. At the upper terminus of existence, description comes to a culmination in the absolute. As the inverse of death, the absolute assures the future, and in one and the same act the self gives to God the confirmation of experience as it is offered to him, and God gives to the self the concrete experience of his own Liberty.